POSTCARD HISTORY SERIES

Around Utica

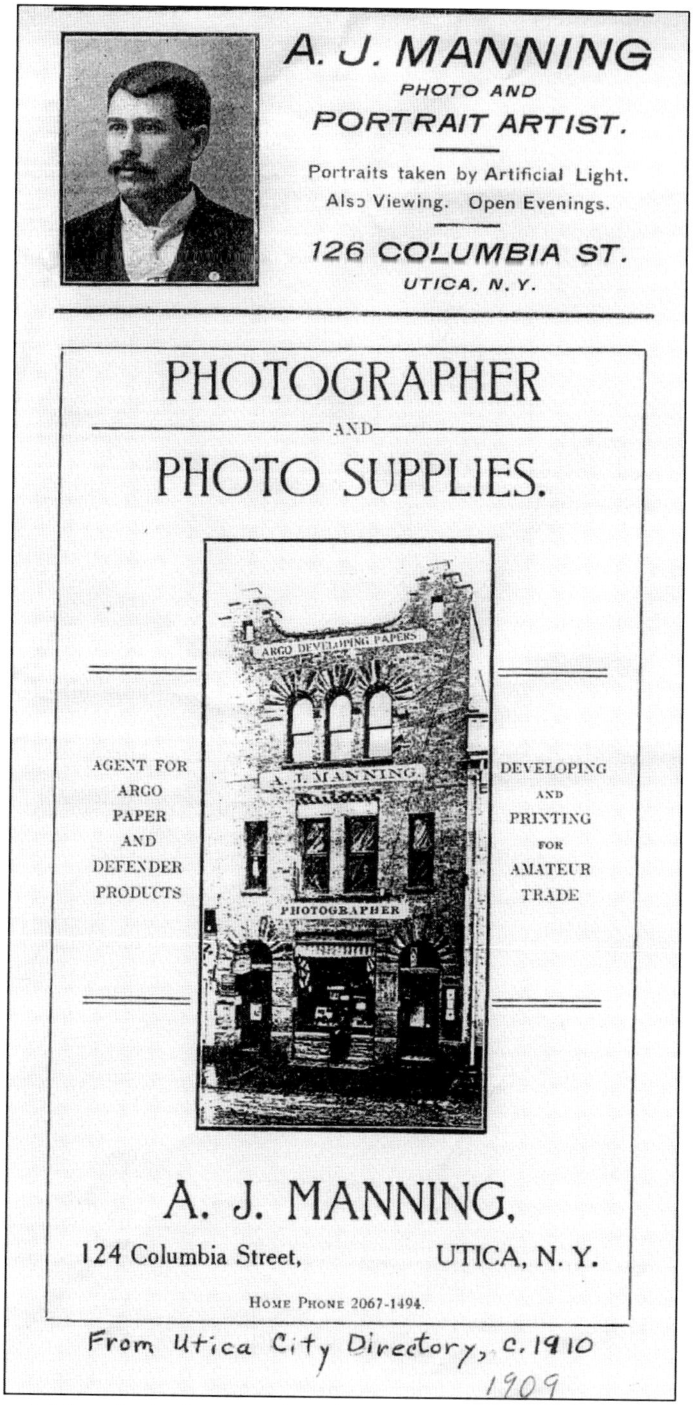

Pictured are Allen J. Manning's photograph and an advertisement for his photography business.

On the front cover: Please see page 52. (Courtesy of Oneida County Historical Society.)

On the back cover: Please see page 49. (Courtesy of Oneida County Historical Society.)

POSTCARD HISTORY SERIES

Around Utica

Evelyn R. Edwards

ARCADIA PUBLISHING

ISBN 978-0-7385-4938-5

Published by Arcadia Publishing
Charleston, South Carolina

Printed in the United States of America

Library of Congress Catalog Card Number: 2006931605

For all general information contact Arcadia Publishing at:
Telephone 843-853-2070
Fax 843-853-0044
E-mail sales@arcadiapublishing.com
For customer service and orders:
Toll-Free 1-888-313-2665

Visit us on the Internet at www.arcadiapublishing.com

This book is dedicated to the memory of Grace Ellen Heustis Hughes, my great-aunt, whose postcard collection provided the inspiration.

Contents

Acknowledgments

Many people gave of their time, loaned postcards, provided information, and otherwise contributed to this book. First and foremost is my husband, Melville Edwards, whose help with research, transportation, and moral support was invaluable to this project. My thanks also goes to all the individuals and organizations that generously provided information and assistance: Earl Allen, Bridgewater Historical Society; Dorothy Ames; Mary Andrecheck of South Columbia; Betty Barron and Theresa McFadden, Westmoreland Historical Society; Joe Bottini; Bernice Coston and Rosalie Orr, Madison County Historical Society; Craig Crowell, Sherrill City Historian; Archibald and Zelma Davies, Limestone Ridge Historical Society; Scott Dillenback; Ray and Sandy Drake, Central New York Postcard Club; Don Foley; Tom Gates; Sue Perkins and staff, Herkimer County Historical Society; Ken Hartzell; Jack Henke; Jack Kelly; Henrietta Kuhn; Esther McCarthy; Milford Morris, Clark Mills Historical Society; Jim and Marge Mortis and Bonny Niles, Town of Paris Historical Society; Barbara Munde, New Hartford Historical Society; Jim Norton; Douglas Preston, Forest Park information; Richfield Springs Library staff; Connie Roberts, Holland Patent Historical Group; Rome Historical Society staff; Jerry Schafer; Sherrill Library staff; Joyce Shephard; Noel Strobino; John Taibi; Frank Tomaino, *Observer Dispatch* columnist; Don White, Judy Wisnoski, and Carl Saporito, Oneida County Historical Society; and the Utica Public Library staff.

Acronyms included in picture credit lines are as follows: New Hartford Historical Society (NHHS), Oneida County Historical Society (OCHS), Limestone Ridge Historical Society, Oriskany Falls (LRHS), and Town of Paris Historical Society (TPHS).

Additions or corrections to this book are welcome and can be e-mailed to eveygram@adelphia.net.

INTRODUCTION

Allen J. Manning was a Utica photographer with a studio and store downtown at 126 Columbia Street. He produced all the real-photo postcards that appear in this book. He traveled to many towns and cities, snapping photographs of various people, events, and buildings, creating a valuable historical record for later generations. Some of these photographs were used (either sold or appropriated) by commercial publishing companies and also appear in colorized versions.

Manning's time in Utica can be traced in Utica city directories. In 1892, 1899, and 1900, he is listed as a clerk at National Express Company on Genesee Street and a resident in 1895 on Taylor Avenue. In 1901, he appears under "Photo Supplies, Weaver Building." The 1902, 1903, and 1904 directories list his business at 126 Columbia Street, with his residence at 172 South Street. By 1910, his residence is 25 Taylor Avenue. After 1910, he is no longer listed. From a friend with a cousin who had Manning relatives, it is learned that he left the area and never returned. A wife and son remained in Utica and are listed in city directories until the 1970s. Why he left and where he went is a mystery. Did he continue with his passion for photography? Did he continue to make real-photo postcards? In any case, it is fortunate that so many historic postcards of the Utica area survived.

Manning also took photographs of various groups of people in the surrounding area. One in the New Hartford Historical Society's collection shows some people on the stage at Butler Hall who appear to have given a dramatic performance. Also in their collection is a 7-by-14-inch photograph of some 100 employees in front of the Willowvale Bleaching Company, taken around the early 1900s.

When looking at the many dirt roads on the Manning postcards, one might wonder how the photographer traveled. Private automobiles were rare in the first decade of the 1900s, and camera equipment was heavy and bulky. How did he get to Pine Camp 70 miles north of Utica? It is likely that he traveled by train; he did take many photographs of trains and depots.

The locations in the Oneida County chapter have been arranged alphabetically with the exception of Sherrill (Kenwood). This smallest city in New York State is located partially in both Oneida and Madison Counties. The Oneida Community Mansion House is in the city of Oneida in Madison County, but many of the Oneida community's other buildings are in Sherrill in Oneida County.

Although it is a bit of a stretch to include Pine Camp (now Fort Drum) in a volume titled *Around Utica,* the Pine Camp postcards do illustrate the enthusiasm early photographers had for their work, and to what lengths they would go to get memorable photographs.

A book of this nature can only touch the surface of these interesting places. There are many excellent books on the Oneida community by various authors. John Taibe's railroad books and Jack Henke's books on Oneida Lake and Sylvan Beach are recommended reading for anyone wanting to learn more about these fascinating places.

One

Town of Paris

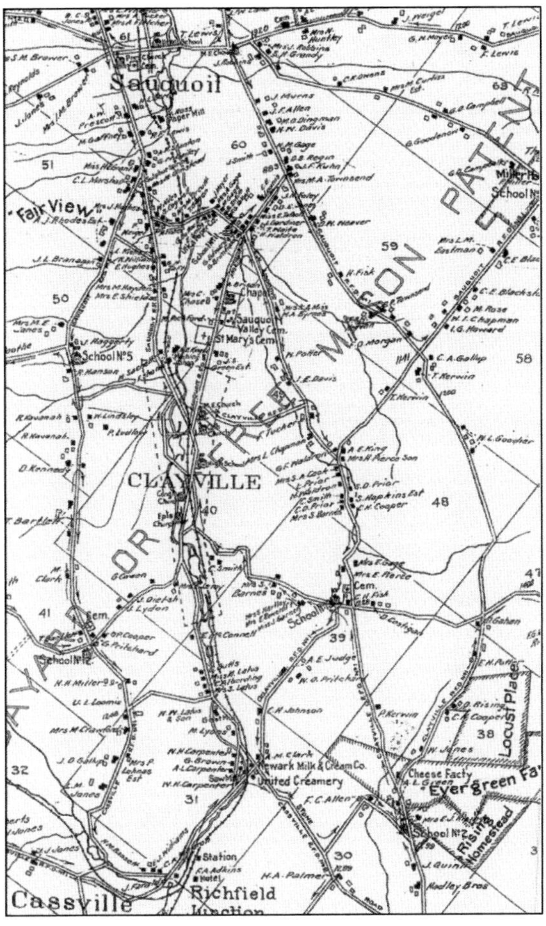

Shown is a 1907 map of the town of Paris.

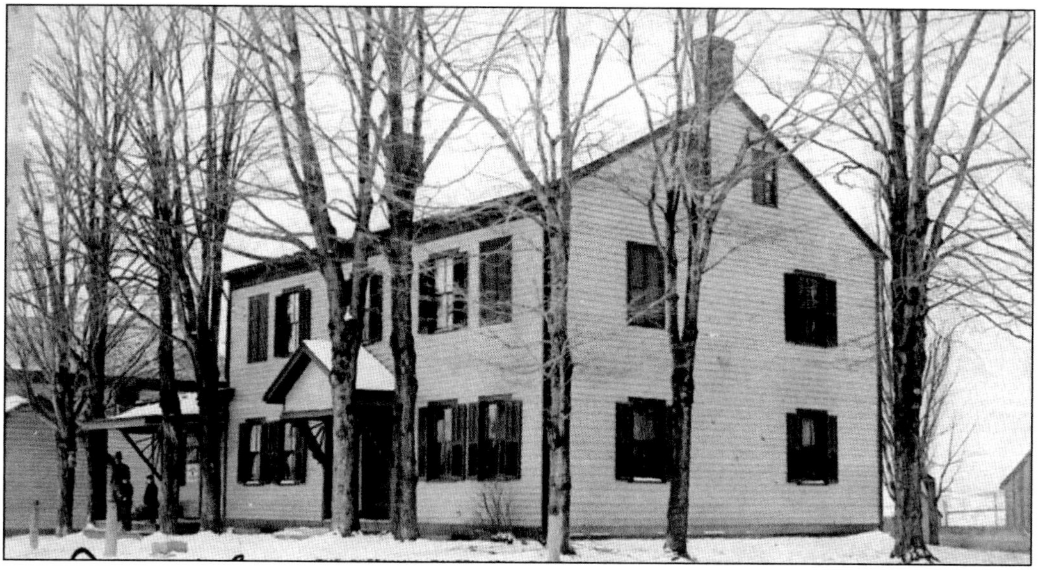

The Greenhill Tavern, established in 1799, is pictured around 1905. William Greenhill, a teacher in the Paris Hill School, volunteered for the Civil War in 1862 and served with the 8th Cavalry. Another Paris Hill teacher, a Mr. Denison from Syracuse, boarded at the hotel of Joseph Greenhill, who "kept the tavern on the corner." The relationship of the Greenhills is unknown, but the old red schoolhouse reunion booklet, which mentions both William and George, likely brothers, stated, "From the families of Joseph Greenfield came boys and girls that gave great credit to the school." (Courtesy TPHS.)

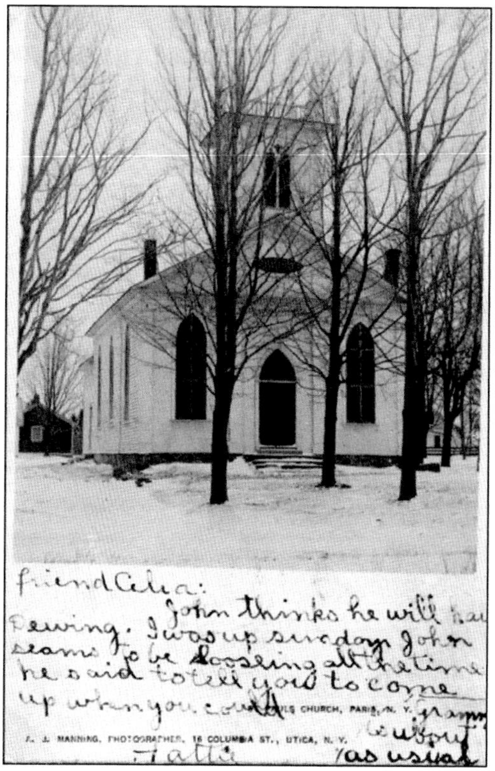

At the north end of Paris Green behind St. Paul's Episcopal Church is a cemetery where Col. Isaac Paris, the hamlet's namesake, is buried. In 1789, Colonel Paris aided early settlers by providing flour and meal during the harsh winter. An 1880 celebration of his re-interment from a Fort Plain cemetery was held in this church. One hundred years later, 2,000 people attended memorial ceremonies to mark the anniversary. St. Paul's Episcopal Church, completed in 1819 by a pioneer church group that began meeting in 1797, is the oldest church in the Episcopal Diocese of Central New York. (Courtesy TPHS.)

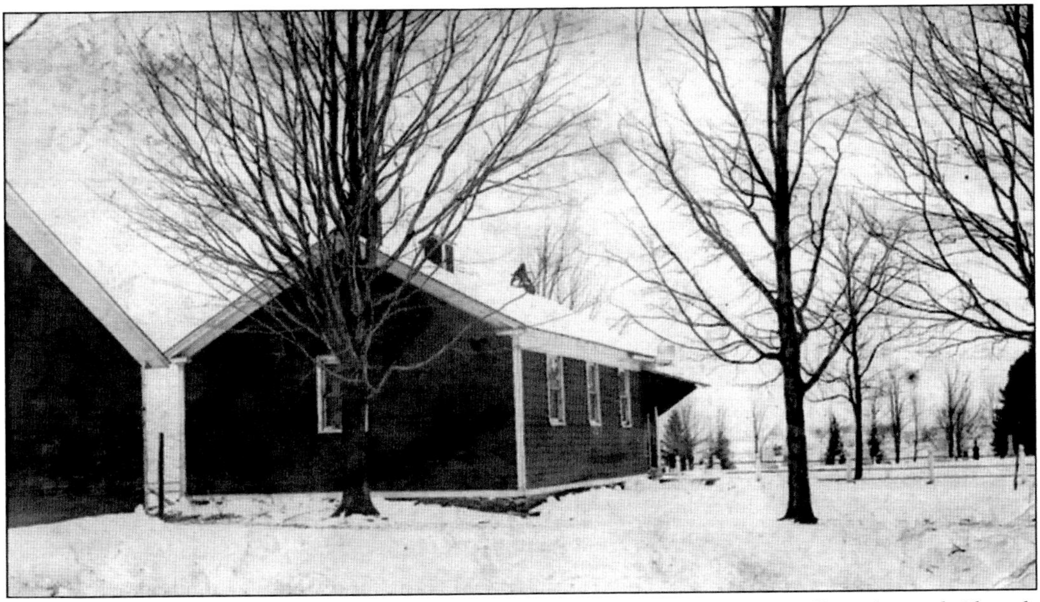

The old red schoolhouse, erected about 1813, was located behind St. Paul's Episcopal Church just south of the cemetery on Snowden Hill Road. At a school reunion on June 30, 1896, letters from several of the old teachers and pupils were read. A poem was read and a hymn written for the occasion was sung with music furnished by members of the choirs of St. Paul's Episcopal Church and the Paris Hill Congregational Church. Stories of old school days were enjoyed by all. (Courtesy TPHS.)

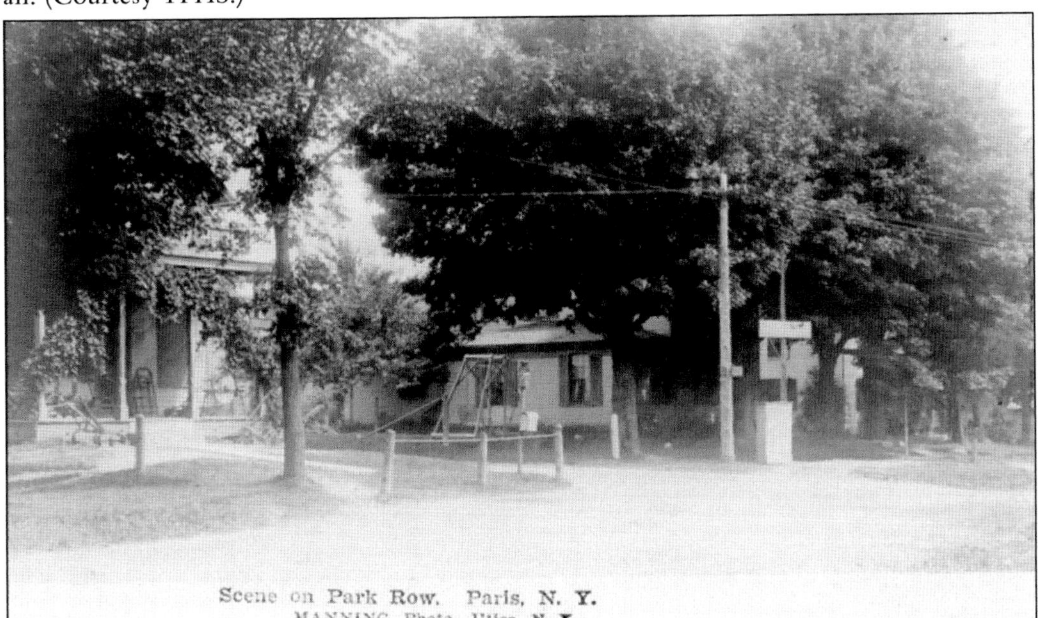

Tree-lined streets edge the park at Paris Hill Green. The green constitutes the center of the village through which, until recent years, passed the main road through the village. State Route 12 now bypasses the green and leads south to Waterville and Route 20, and north to New Hartford and Utica. The large building at left was probably a store, as there appears to be merchandise on the porch and a garden cultivator at left.

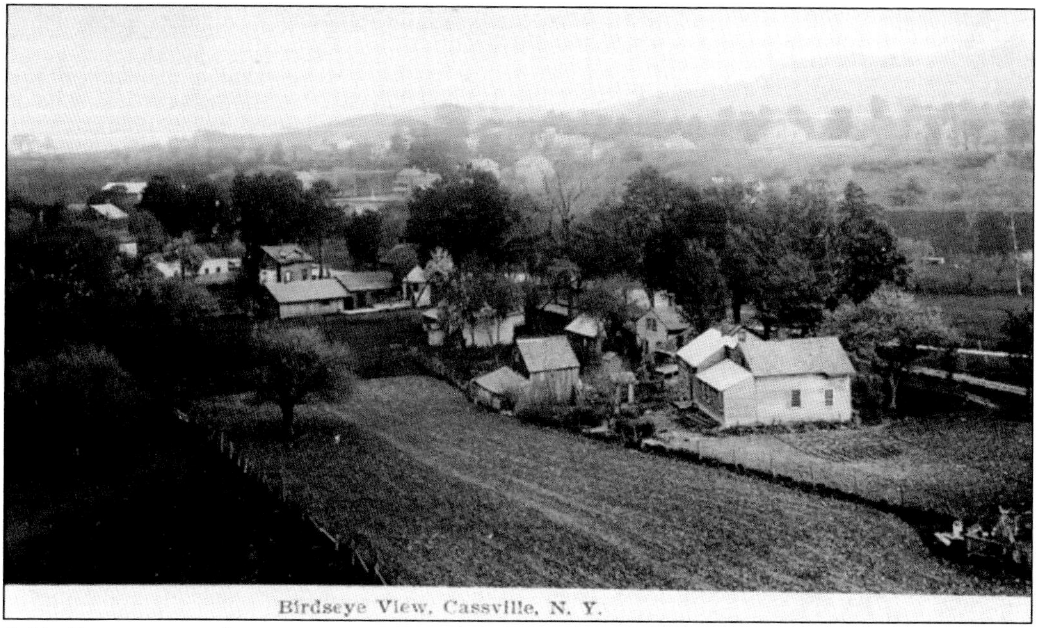

A bird's-eye view of Cassville reveals a small pastoral village with numerous trees and green spaces. In *A History of the Village of Cassville*, by Henry G. Williams (1951), the author states that settlement of the village began in the latter years of the 1790s with more permanent settlers arriving in 1801 when two distilleries were established. A gristmill followed, located on a branch of the Sauquoit Creek that provided the waterpower for various mills.

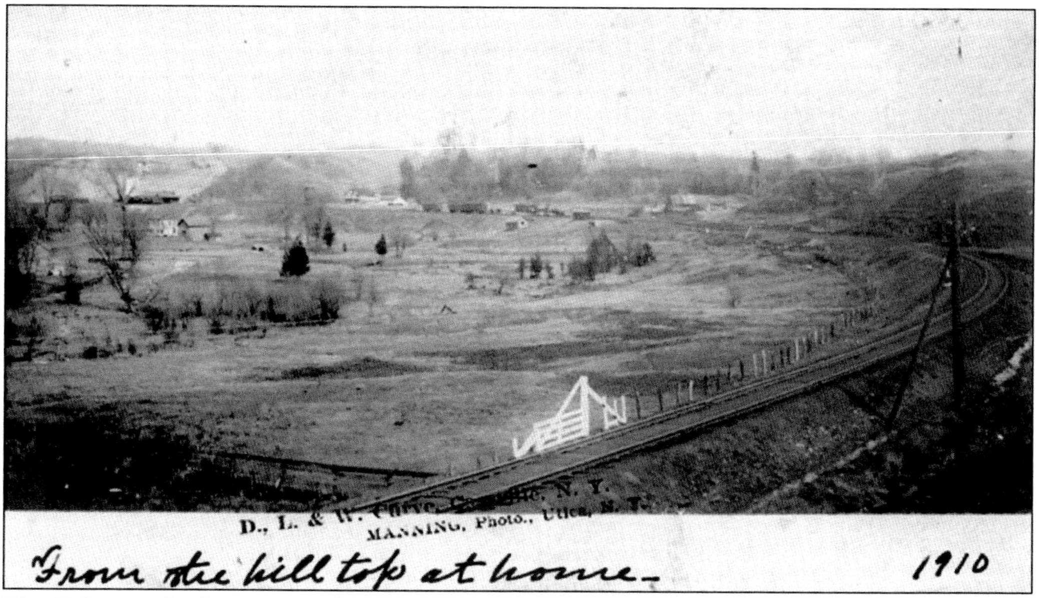

The Delaware, Lackawanna and Western Railroad was a mixed blessing for Cassville. According to Henry G. Williams, the expansion of the village ended when the railroad began operations because of "the competition with local industry from outside producers." It did, however, gain temporary importance because it was a junction with a branch to Richfield Springs, a popular recreation area at the time. When the resort became less popular, a decline in passengers resulted in the station being reduced to a freight stop. It closed entirely in 1953.

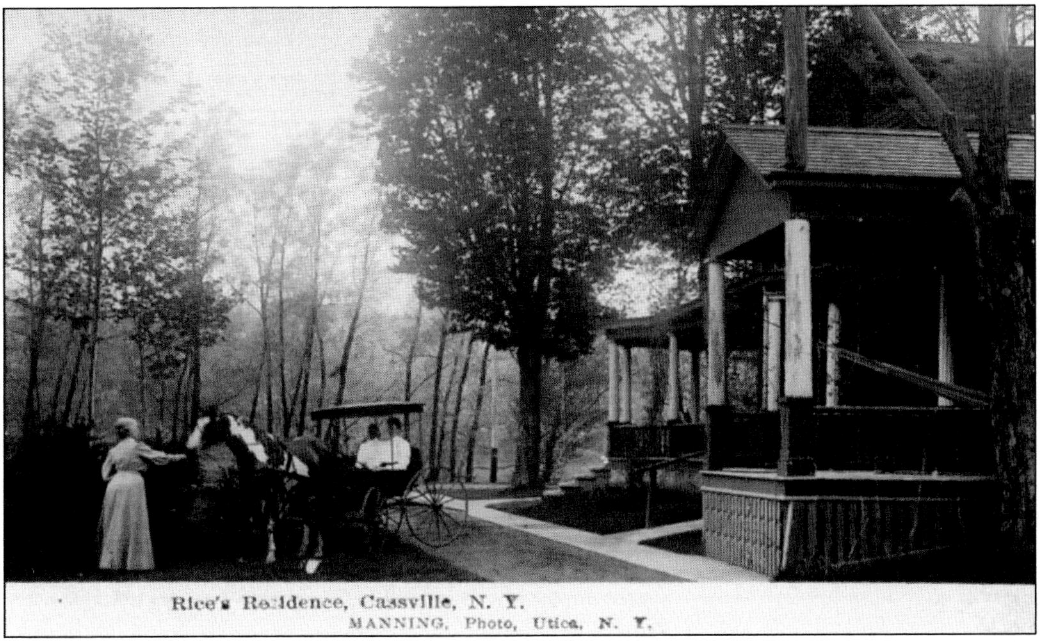

In the early 1900s, horse-drawn buggies were the preferred method of transportation, such as the rig shown here. The woman at the left is likely Gratia Rice, who purchased the home in March 1899. Only a portion of the long porch that once covered two sides of the house remains today.

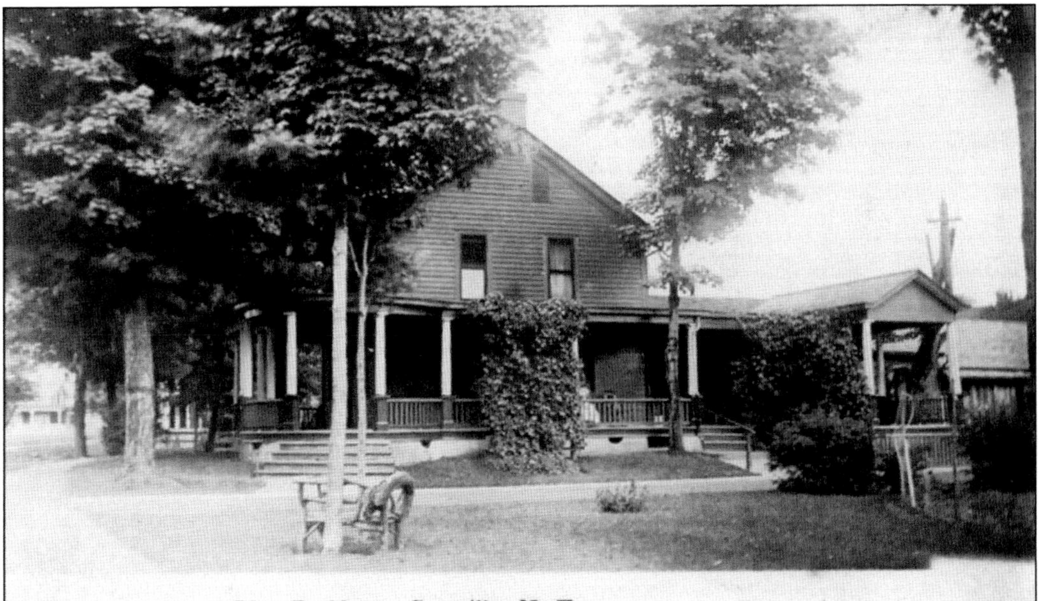

Still a private home, this house was once owned by Gratia Rice from Buffalo. Deed transactions also indicate other land nearby was conveyed to Rice from Charity R. Whitaker or Utica and Amos Anderson. In 1884, Edwin and G. Alecia Loomis conveyed additional property to Rice. A 1907 atlas shows a large parcel occupied by Miss G. Rice and Miss S. Flint. (Courtesy TPHS.)

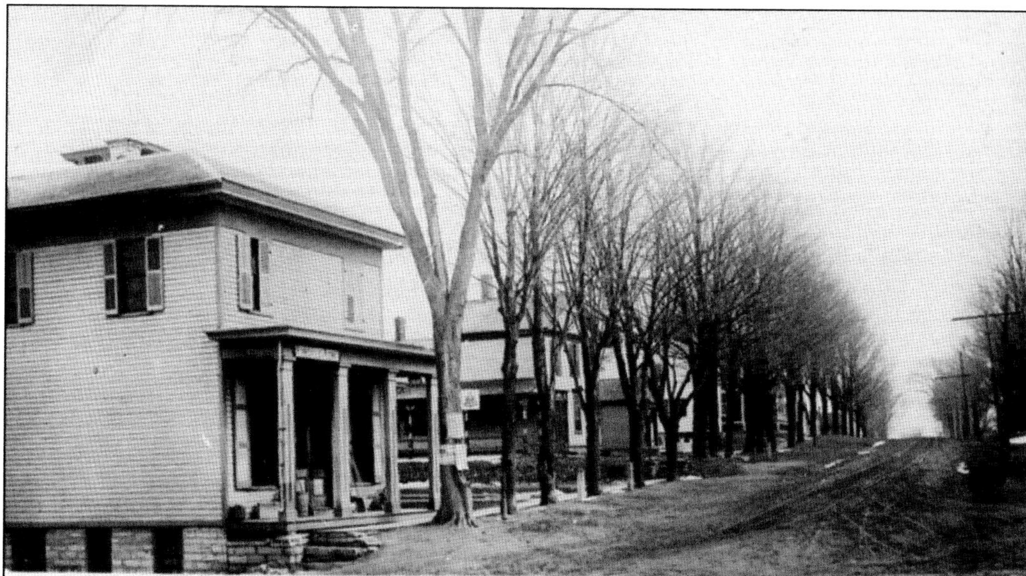

Street Scene, Cassville, N. Y. MANNING, Photo., Utica, N. Y.

Rutted dirt roads such as these in front of the Roberts Store in Cassville were the norm in the early 1900s. As automobiles became more common, there was a demand for better roads. A New York Roads Improvement Association that organized at Bagg's Hotel in Utica was concerned with area road conditions. They worked to procure solid roads for the countryside to get the farmers out of the mud and make it easier to bring their produce to market.

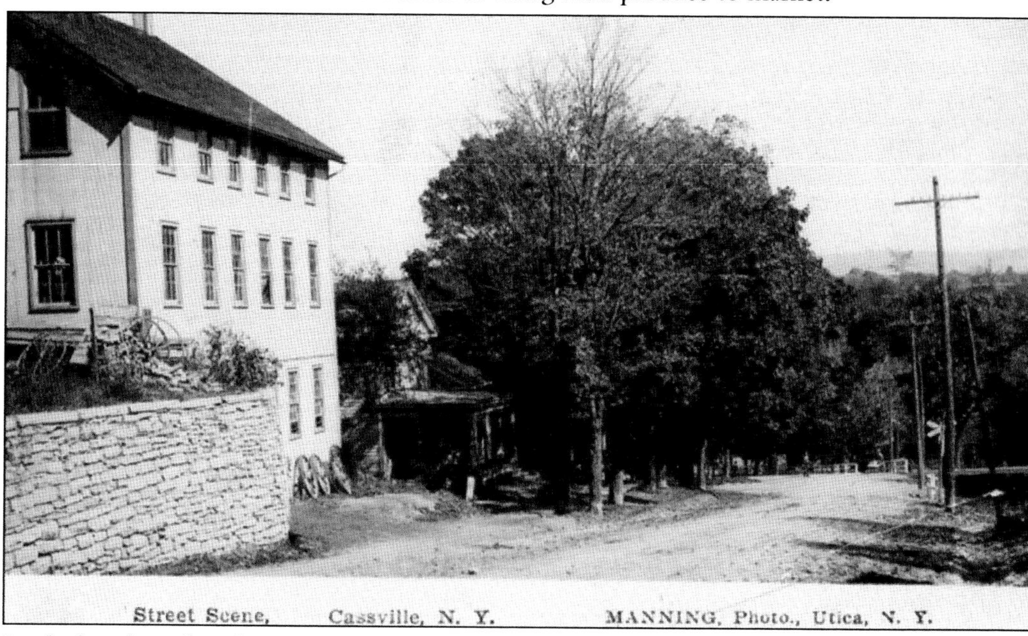

Street Scene, Cassville, N. Y. MANNING, Photo., Utica, N. Y.

Just before the railroad crossing (right) was a picturesque limestone wall next to the Barnum and Davis Wagon Shop, now converted to a private residence. Sections of the wall are visible today. The house to the right of the shop was the summer retreat of Frederick Proctor, half-brother of Thomas Proctor. A prominent Utica family, the Proctors donated extensive land for local parks. In 1891, Frederick married Rachel Munson Williams. He died in 1915, leaving no direct descendants.

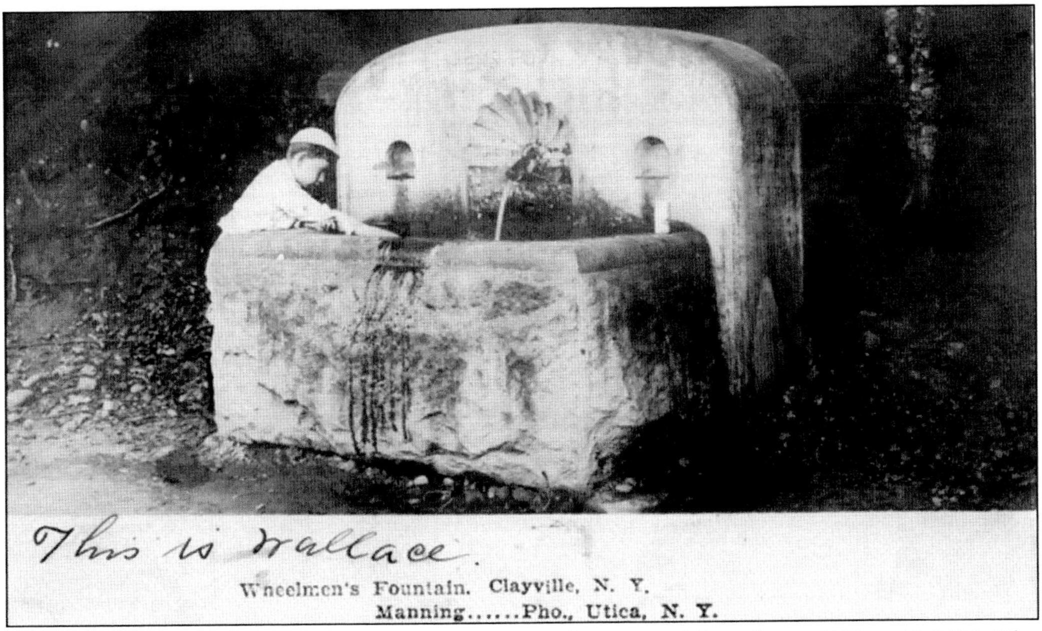

Wheelman's Fountain was a favorite watering spot for area residents from 1897 until 1988. The fountain closed due to concerns of high bacteria levels that posed liability problems for the state, the town, and nearby landowners. Local historical records indicated the fountain was built by bicyclists to provide a refreshing stop. Despite pleas from local people, the fountain was closed in 1988. Wallace, pictured, was A. J. Manning's son. The card was written by his mother, Emma (see page 124). (Courtesy TPHS.)

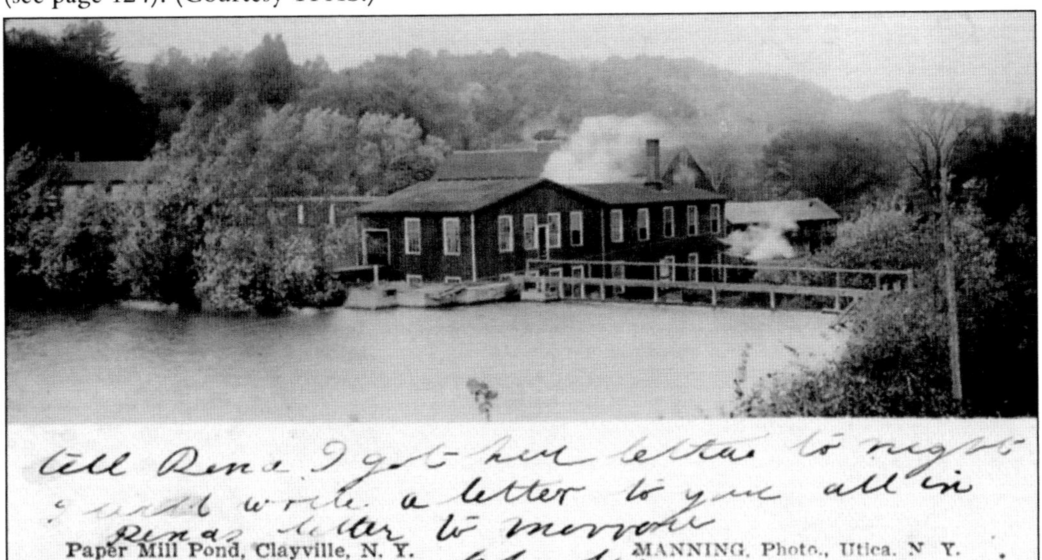

In 1840, David Millard came to Clayville with his father, Charles, and an uncle, Sterling A. Millard. They began manufacturing scythes and hay forks at a mill on the southern end of the pond. During the Civil War, the company manufactured sabers for the Union Cavalry, one of which is in the Town of Paris Historical Society's collection. The Millard works were sold in 1896. Sterling A. Millard established the Clayville Paper Mill at the northern end of the pond. Pollution concerns caused owners to close the mill in 1972.

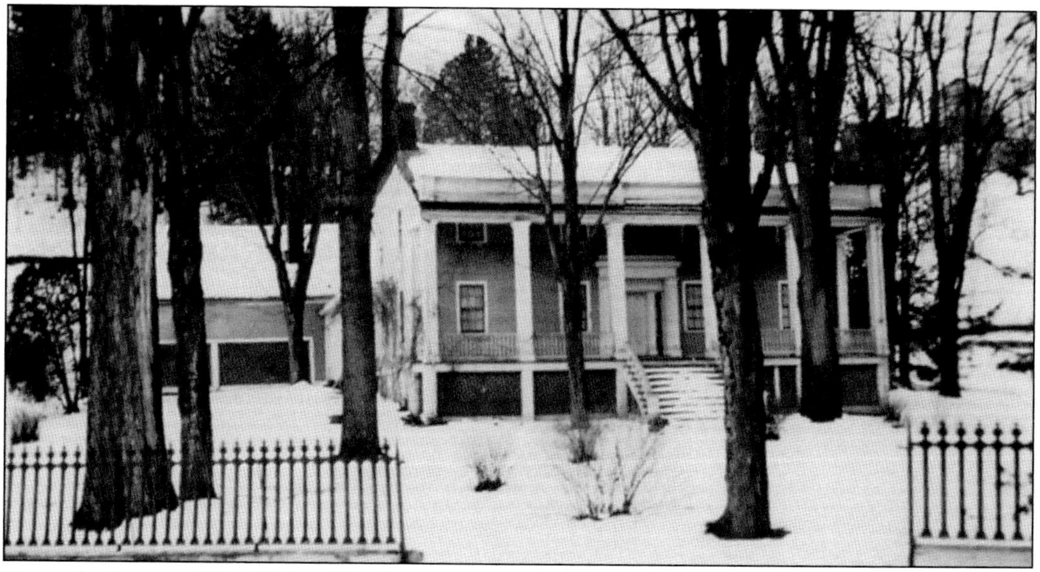

Once the home of David J. Millard, a prominent Clayville resident who operated the Millard Manufacturing Company, the residence still stands on Oneida Street. Clayville was named for Henry Clay, an American statesman and three-time candidate for United States president. He visited the village in 1849 and spoke to a large crowd from the front porch of the Millard Mansion. Other famous visitors to the Millard residence were Pres. Millard Fillmore, a Millard cousin, and Roscoe Conkling of Utica, a prominent congressman and United States senator from Utica. (Courtesy TPHS.)

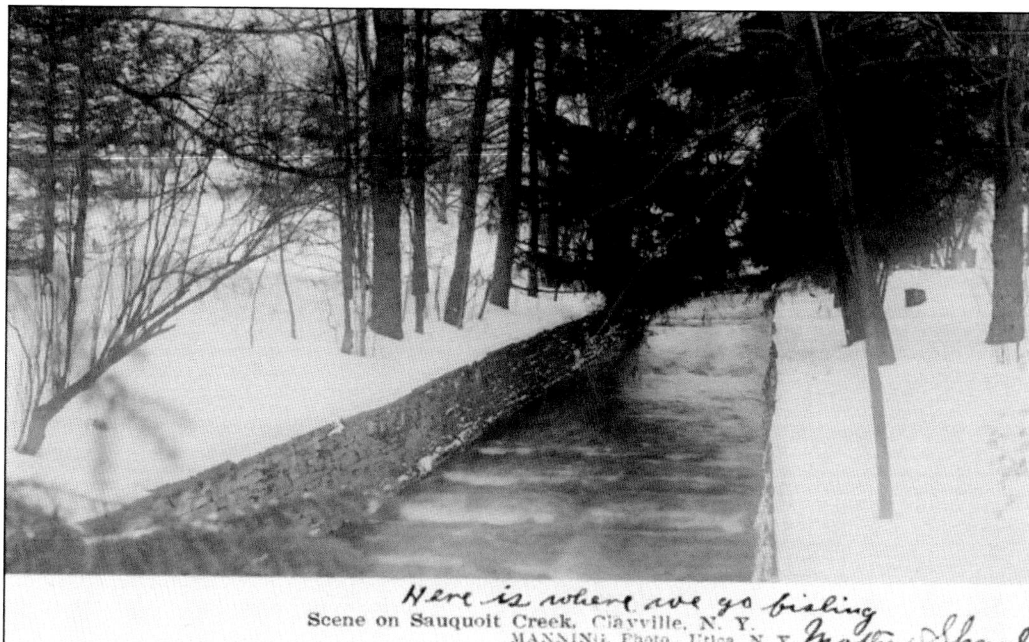

It is said that neither rain nor sleet nor snow can keep a postman from his rounds. Apparently this applies to photographers too, as Manning braved the wintry weather to snap this picture of the snow-covered banks of the Sauquoit Creek. It flows here under old Route 8 just beyond the Millard Mansion.

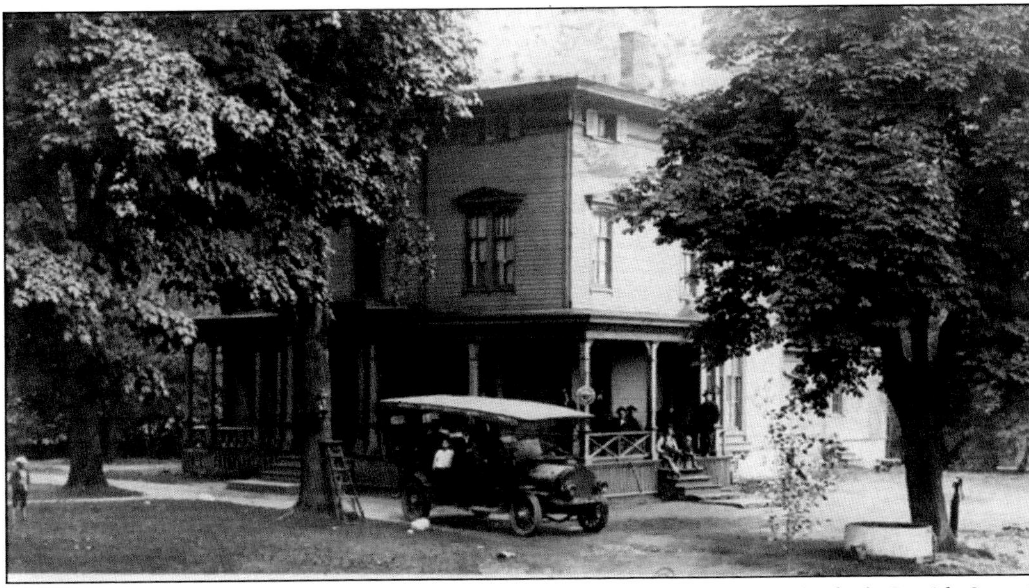

The Cottage Hotel, later called Hardy's Hotel, was located on Main Street (today's Oneida Street) next to the former Episcopal church, now the Town of Paris Historical Society. Jim Mortis, a longtime Sauquoit Valley resident, has fond memories of going there with his father and brother and enjoying their huge pretzels and the Hardy's pet parrot. He recalls the large geese running loose in the yard that chased passing youngsters and the watering trough for customers to water their horses. The hotel burned down in the 1970s.

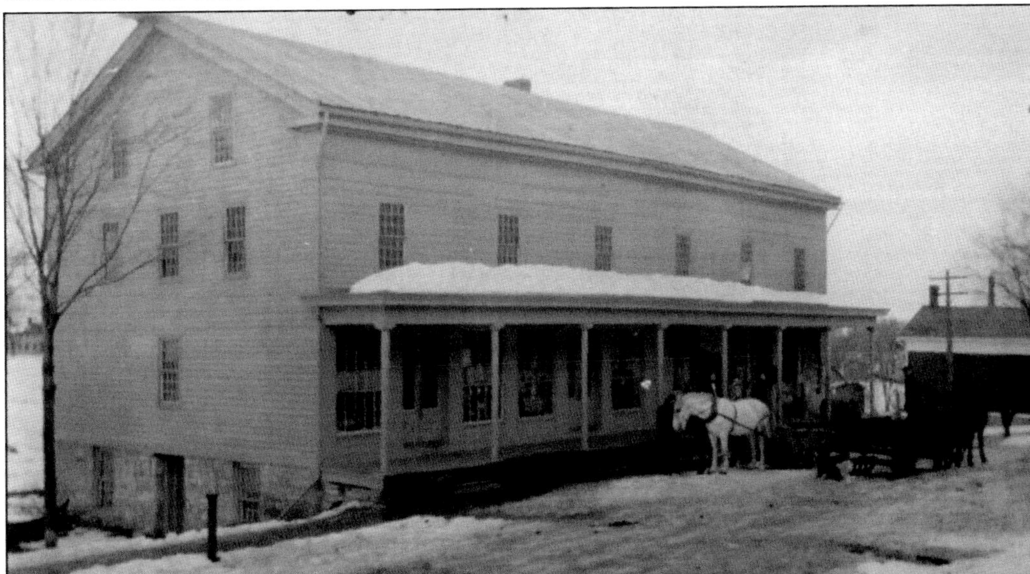

This building was located on the site of the present American Legion Post 231. The post office occupied the first floor, and apartments were on the second story. It also housed the Blue Bird Ice Cream Parlor, a tinsmith, and a barbershop in the early 1900s. The building burned in the mid-1940s and was torn down. The post office relocated across the street temporarily, but moved back to this site after Bob Harjung purchased the property, rebuilt on the site, and operated a restaurant there.

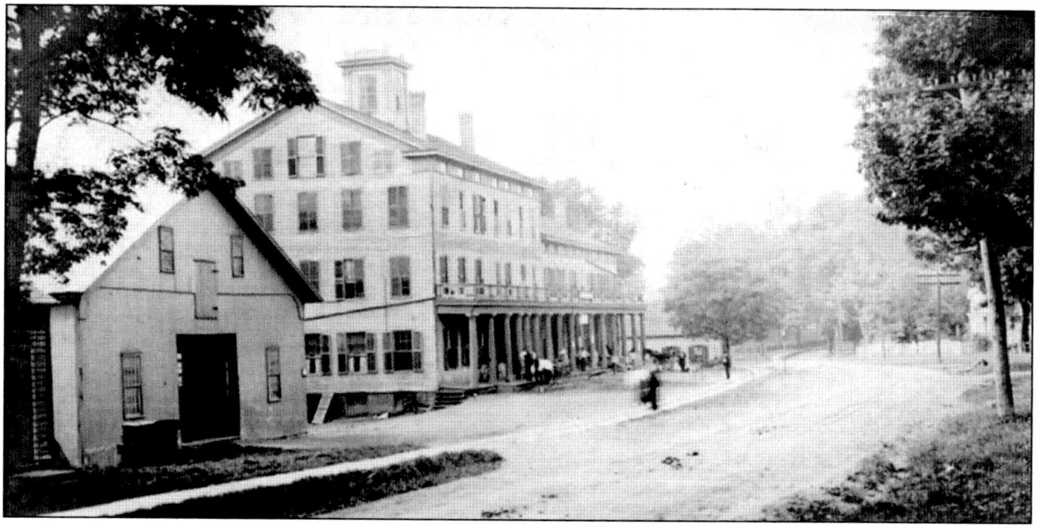

Frederick Hollister, a local businessman and mill owner, built the Hollister House to house his employees. He also constructed tenement houses for mill workers. The hotel served as a gathering place for the community. Hollister, along with David J. Millard, is credited with building Clayville up from a small hamlet to the largest village in the Paris Township, and one of the most important manufacturing centers in the state. Hollister met with financial difficulties in 1850, ending the "boom years."

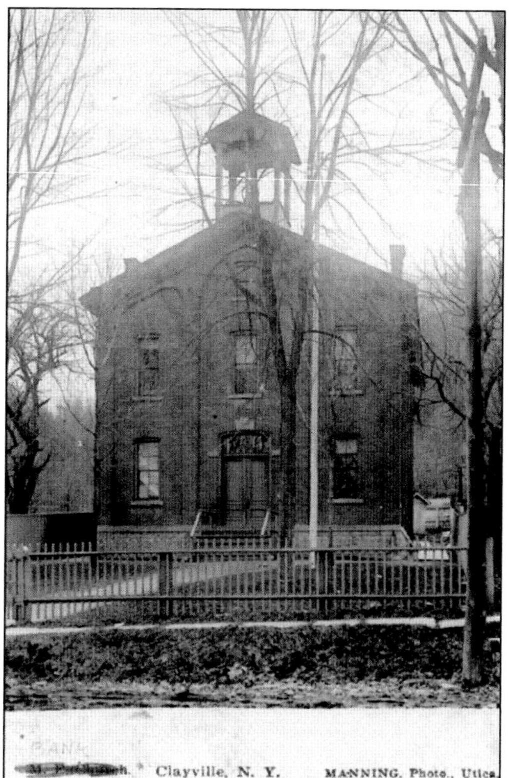

Once the Clayville High School (around 1876), this building later became the Clayville National Bank. A bank failure during the 1929 Depression resulted in the bank's closing. In later years, this was home to the Town of Paris Historical Society; Friends and Neighbors, a charitable organization; and the Clayville Fire Department. The historical society has now moved to the former village library, which had earlier housed the Clayville Episcopal Church.

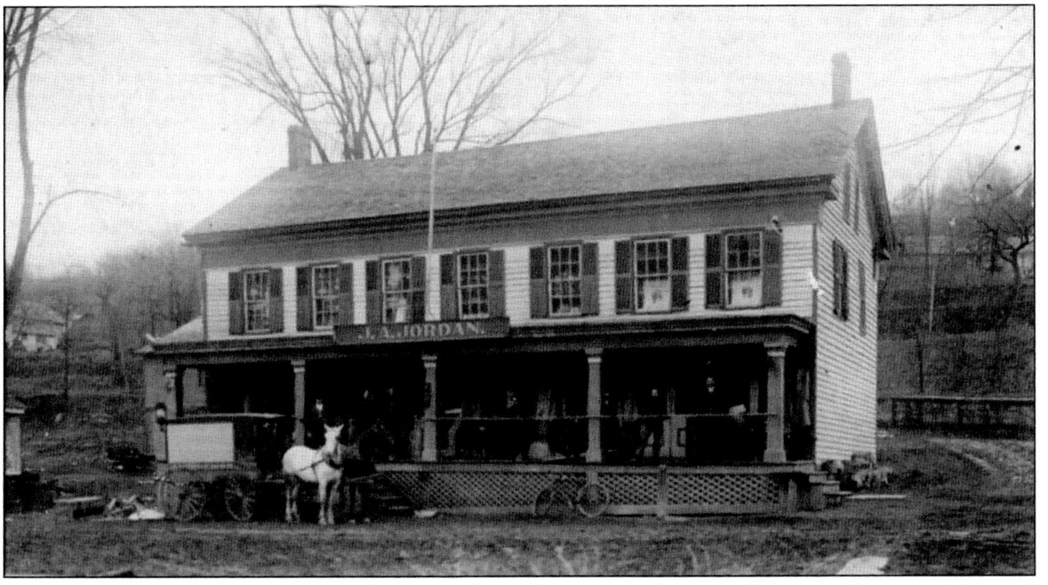

Jordan's Store was located across the street from the present historical society (former Episcopal church and library) on Oneida Street. It was a general store that sold "everything from soup to nuts." When Leslie Jordan died, the store became a Victory chain grocery store. The last owner was George Ludlow, who lived upstairs. After a fire the building was sold to Wayne Ingalls, who ripped the old store down and built a garage. A private residence currently occupies the site. (Courtesy TPHS.)

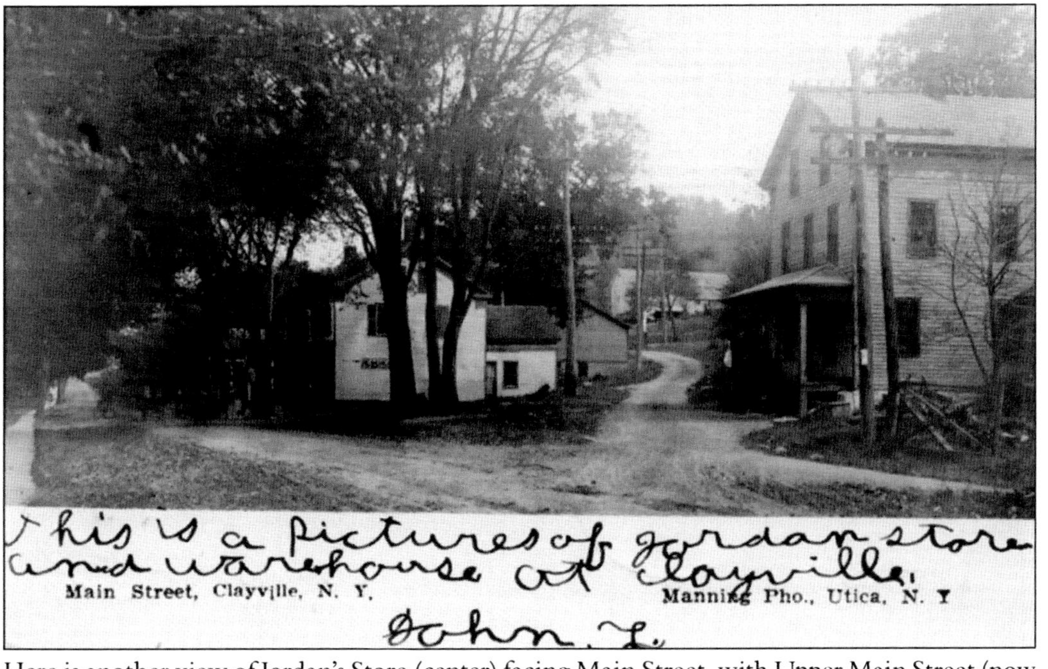

Here is another view of Jordan's Store (center) facing Main Street, with Upper Main Street (now Dewing Avenue) behind it. The building at right is Jordan's warehouse. This building still stands and is a private residence. The house and large barn in the background no longer exist. Running in front of these structures is the Delaware, Lackawanna and Western railroad tracks.

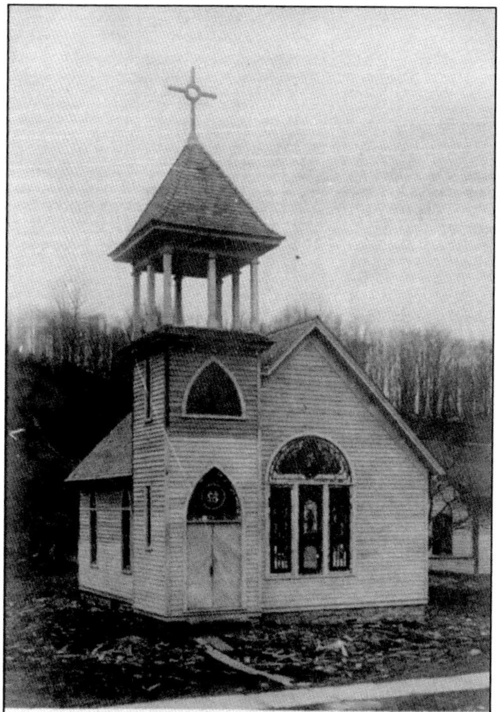

Episcopal Church, Clayville, N. Y.
MANNING, Photo., Utica, N. Y.

This Episcopal church replaced a brick structure built in 1848–1849. The earlier church, farther north on Main Street, had been damaged by a fire. When this second church closed, the building became the Clayville Library. The nearby Congregational church closed in 1999 and donated its church building to Clayville for a new library. The historical society moved into the former library. In this photograph the church appears to be newly constructed.

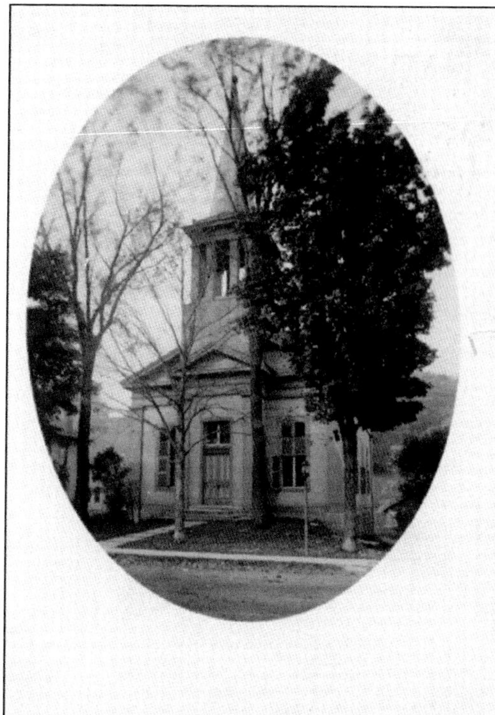

Congregational Church, Clayville, N. Y.
MANNING, Photo., Utica, N. Y.

On April 26, 1999, an *Observer Dispatch* news article heading read, "Clayville Church Says Final Amen." A part of Clayville since 1856, its attendance had dipped to about 12, creating economic hardships that forced the closing. At the final service, Rev. Walter Hillis, pastor there for 30 years, commented on the beauty of the eight stained-glass windows in the sanctuary. The building, with windows intact, is now the Clayville Library.

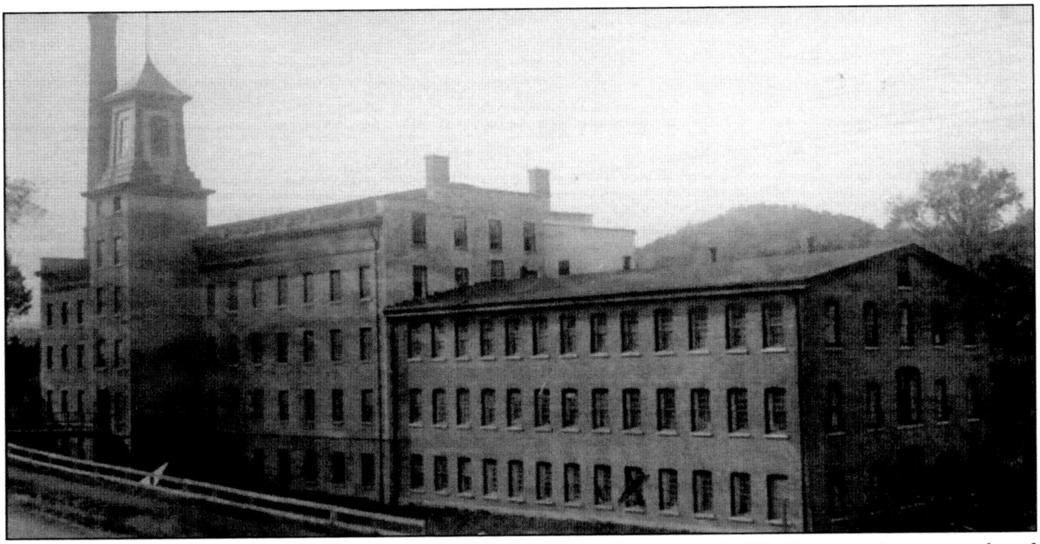

Frederick Hollister purchased the unfinished Clayville and Empire Mills Corporation, completed the mills, and commenced manufacturing about 1843 or 1844. Several additions nearly doubled the size. At one time, the mill employed about 230 people. In 1861, James J. Murray purchased the woolen factory plant and the Hollister House, renaming it the Murray House. The Clayville Knitting Mill closed in 1946. Various businesses followed: Kelsey-Hayes Company, closed in 1959; Central Casting Foundry, closed in 1965; and Concel Inc. (a paper company), closed in 1972. Homogeneous Metals Inc. has been in operation there since 1980 and is still active.

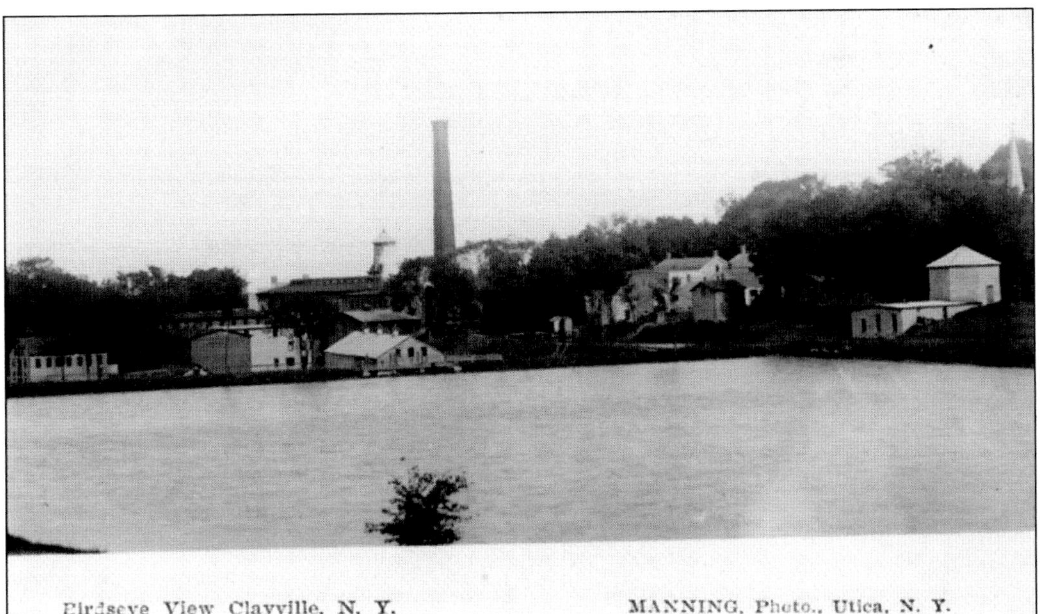

On Main Street in the east and the Canada Street side in the west of the knitting mill pond resided many of the Clayville Knitting Company employees in tenement houses built by mill owner Frederick Hollister. The pond was the water supply for the mill. Canada Street intersected Main Street at both ends of the pond. Building homes for employees is a benefit rarely offered by modern companies.

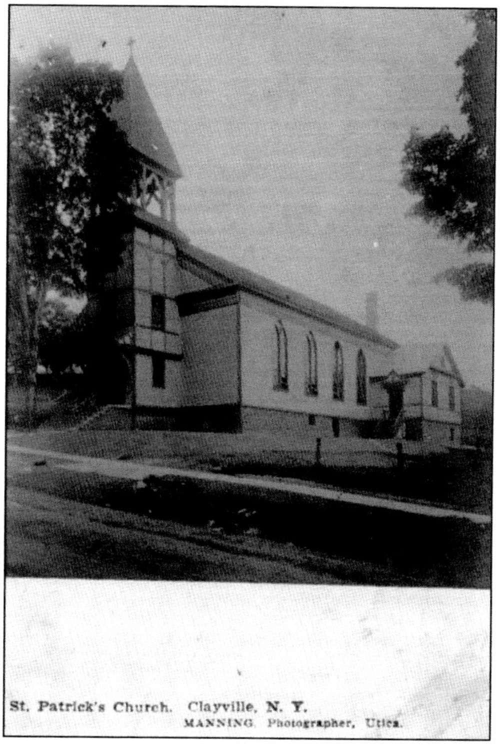

St. Patrick's Catholic Church, the only surviving church in Clayville, sits on a slope on Church Street next to an empty lot where the Methodist church once stood. The Reverend Father O'Reilly supervised the building of the Catholic church about 1864. In 1868, Fr. Philip Smith was appointed to the church. In 1881, the parish family numbered about 700 people. Two Sunday schools were held—one at the Clayville Church and another in the schoolhouse at Chadwicks.

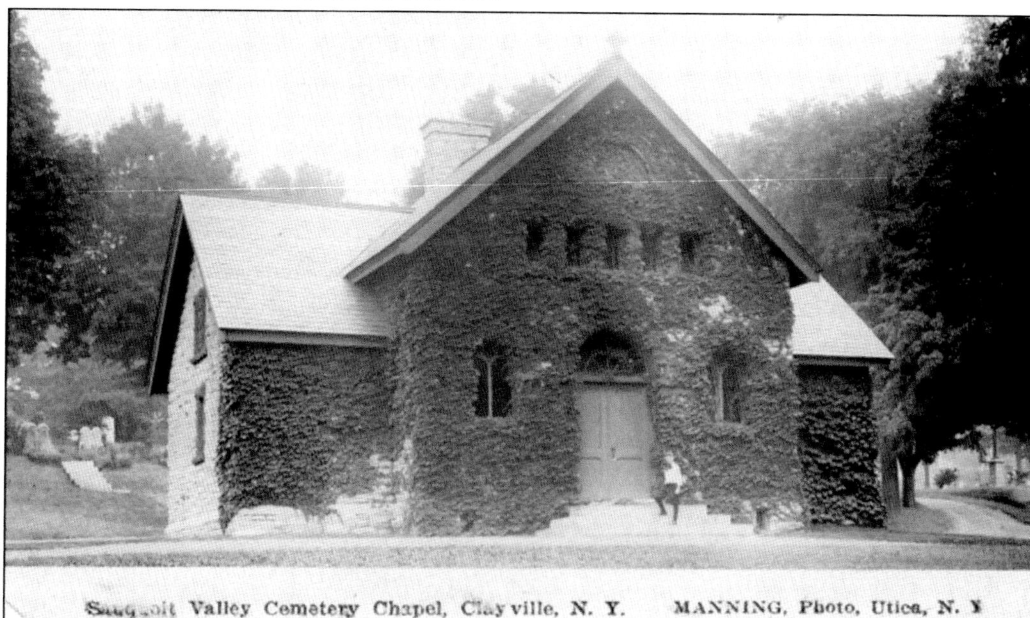

The Sauquoit Valley Cemetery was organized at a Hollister House meeting in 1851. The site selected on Church Street was the property of pioneer Theodore Gilbert. At the formal consecration of the cemetery, the Reverend Spencer M. Rice, rector of a Clayville Church, described the spot as "the very bosom of a . . . most lovely valley, with the waters of the beautiful Sauquoit sweeping by . . . while . . . a more gentle stream pours its bright fountain at our . . . feet." (Courtesy TPHS.)

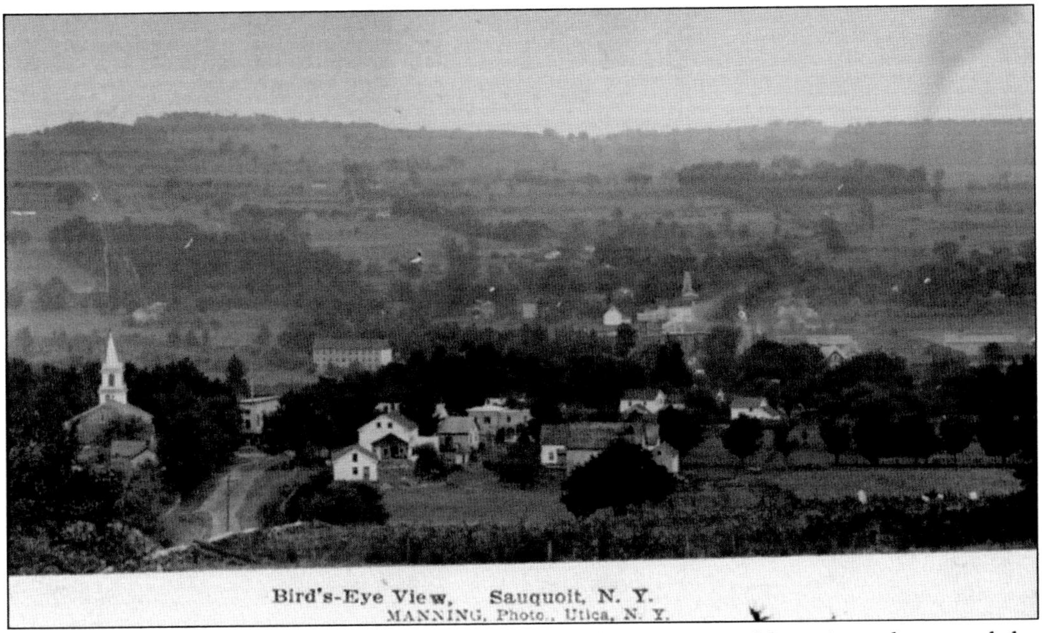

A tree-lined village in the heart of the Sauquoit Valley is captured here in a photograph by Manning. At the lower left is the Methodist church with Norwich Street to its right. The steeple at center right is on the Presbyterian church on the corner of Main and present-day Oneida Streets. (Both Norwich Street and Main Street are now known as Pinnacle Road.) The large house seen below the Presbyterian church is the home of Ladd J. Lewis Jr., who served in the New York State Assembly after his 1906 election.

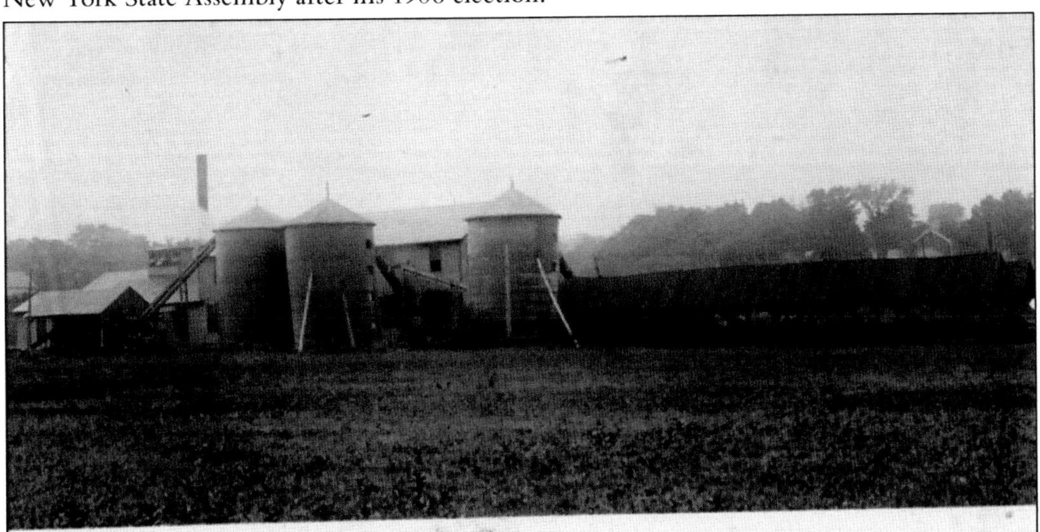

The Sauquoit Canning Factory was located on Mill Street adjacent to the Delaware, Lackawanna and Western Railroad tracks, just south of the Lewis Knitting Company. Alfred Lane, born in the town of Vienna, undertook and completed the building of a canning factory in Sauquoit in the late 1800s, becoming the manager. He successfully operated the facility for about four years. Lane was president and general manager of three factories, "the success of these industries being largely due to his able management and experience." (Courtesy TPHS.)

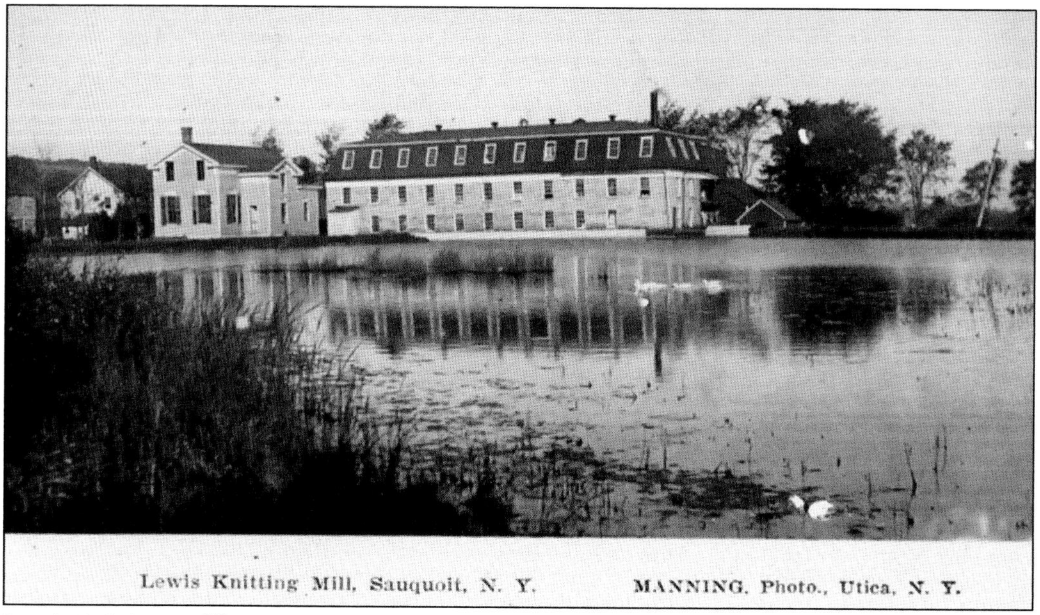

Lewis Knitting Mill's owner, Ladd J. Lewis Jr., operated the mill on Mill Street (north of today's Pinnacle Road) just past the Sauquoit Canning Company. A mill pond and the Sauquoit Creek provided an ample water supply. In a 1907 Oneida County atlas, an advertisement reads, "The Lewis Knitting Company, Ladd J. Lewis Jr., William J. Harris, Manufacturers of Children's Ribbed Underwear, Sauquoit, NY."

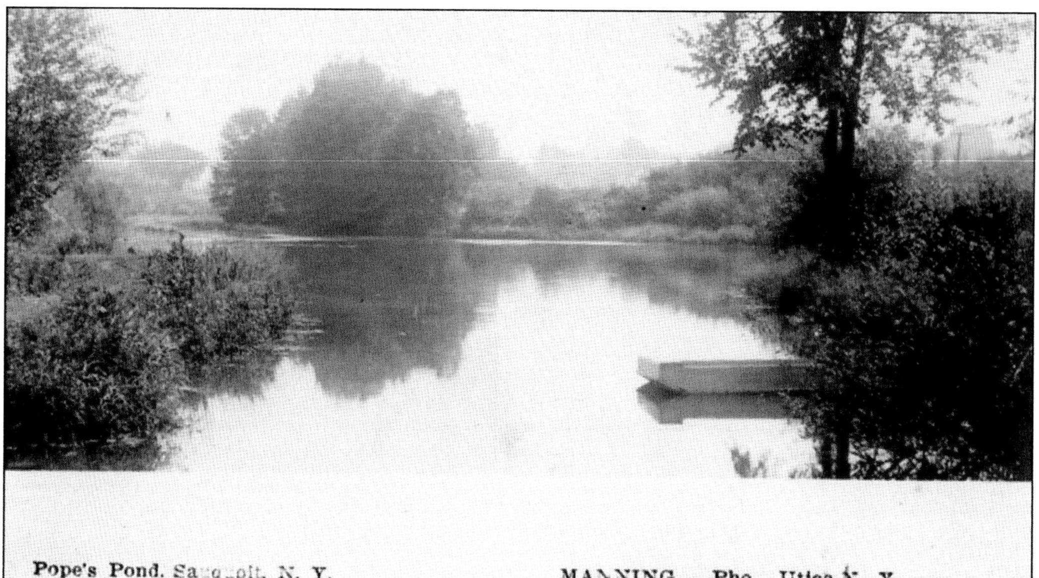

The Horseshoe Knife Factory of T. J. Pope was located at the end of Griffith Lane (south off of Pinnacle Road) where two large ponds supplied the water fed from the Sauquoit Creek. An advertisement in the *New Century Atlas of 1907* stated that Pope's firm manufactured farrier knives and sugar beet trimmers. The three-story stone structure measured 100 feet by 32 feet and was capable of producing 800 dozen tools per day. The advertisement stated, "Entire Output of Plant Disposed of to Welbersch & Hilger."

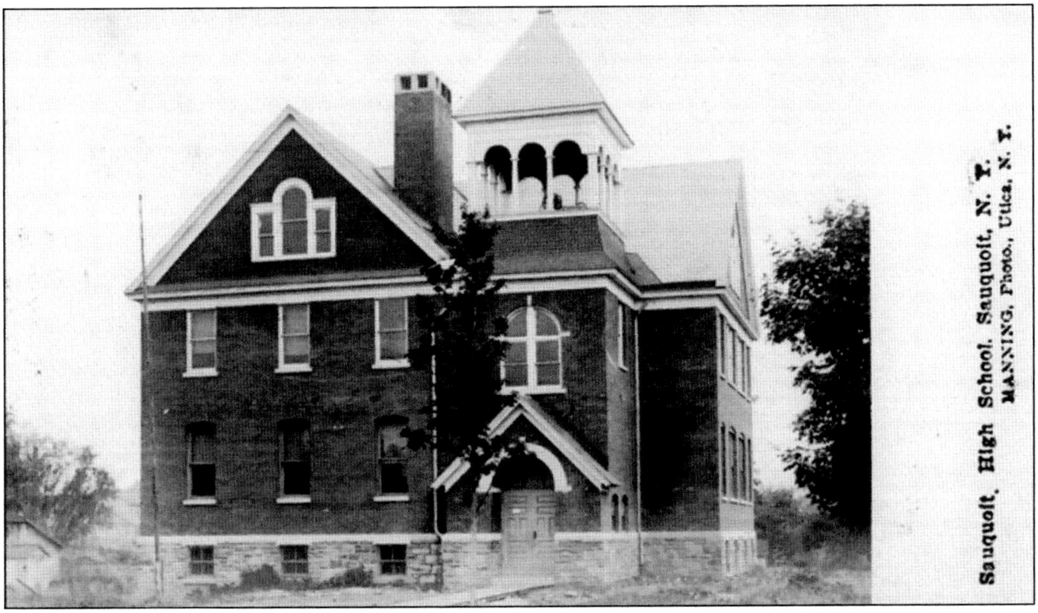

This building no longer exists. It was demolished to make way for the Sauquoit Valley Arterial in 1968–1969. The school pictured was used for a time as a grade school until a new elementary facility was built on Sulphur Springs Road. The Sauquoit Valley Central School on Oneida Street was built in 1932. When Chadwicks High School closed in 1984, these students also attended Sauquoit Valley Central School.

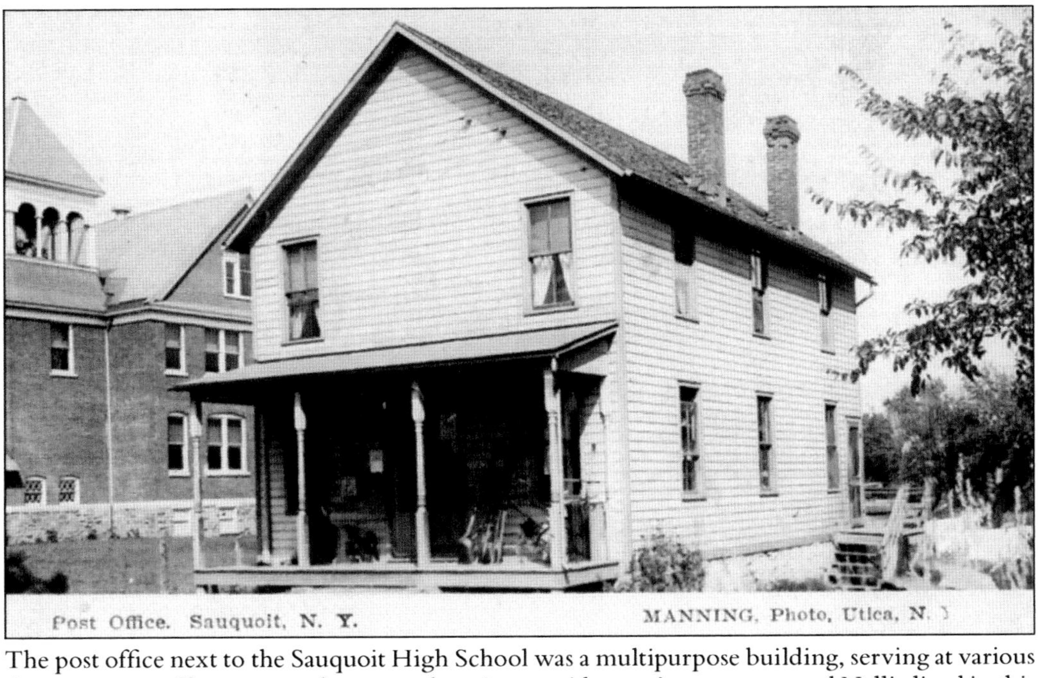

The post office next to the Sauquoit High School was a multipurpose building, serving at various times as a post office, a general store, and a private residence. A woman named Nellie lived in this house in 1909 and sent this postcard to her sister, Mrs. George Green of Utica. She asked her to visit and told her of the funeral of Mrs. J. E. Davis that "was very largely attended, very sad."

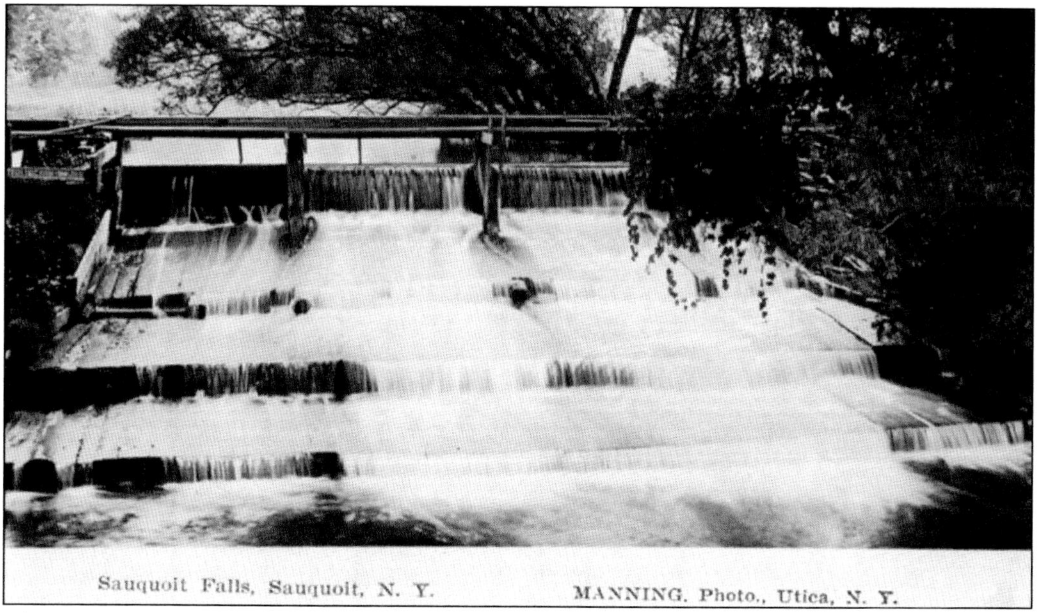

The Sauquoit Falls just beyond the bridge no longer flow there. Many dams were built along the Sauquoit Creek to supply waterpower for various mills and factories. Most of these dams no longer exist, and many of the businesses have left the area, some leaving behind a polluted stream. A Utica *Observer Dispatch* article from June 1998 by John Pitarresi warns that a history of abuses has left the waters contaminated with polychlorinated biphenyls (PCBs). The Department of Environmental Conservation has worked to improve the stream.

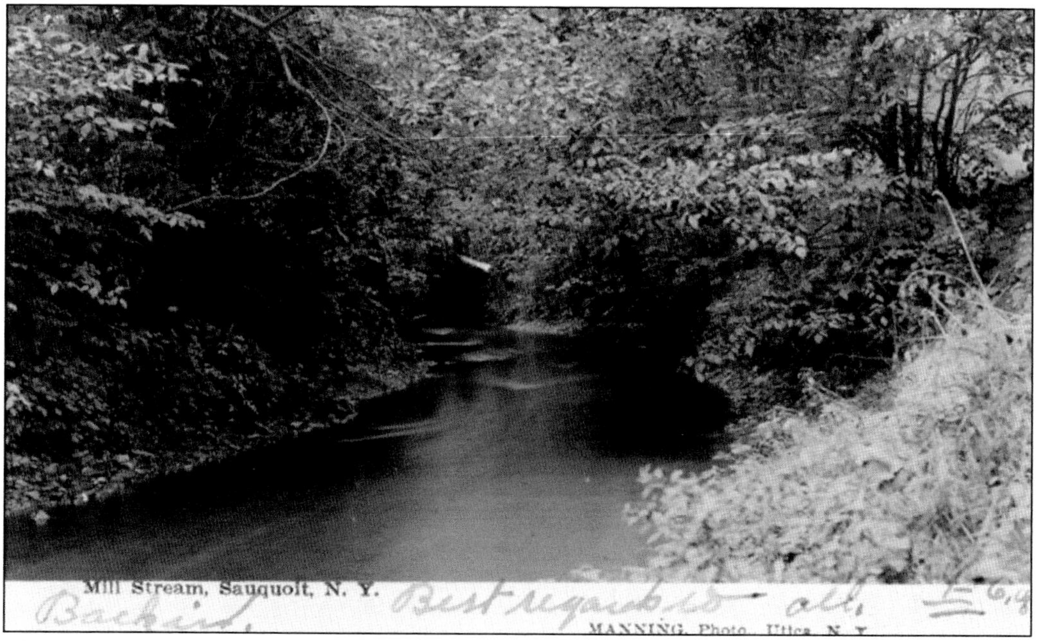

The Sauquoit Creek, rising from its summit at Tassel Hill near Paris Station, flows for 17 miles, descending 1,014 feet. About 50 brooks spill into the creek. Over the years, many mills and factories of all descriptions have operated along its banks and tributaries. Ruins of factories still dot the area, attesting to once bountiful industries that stood on the creek banks.

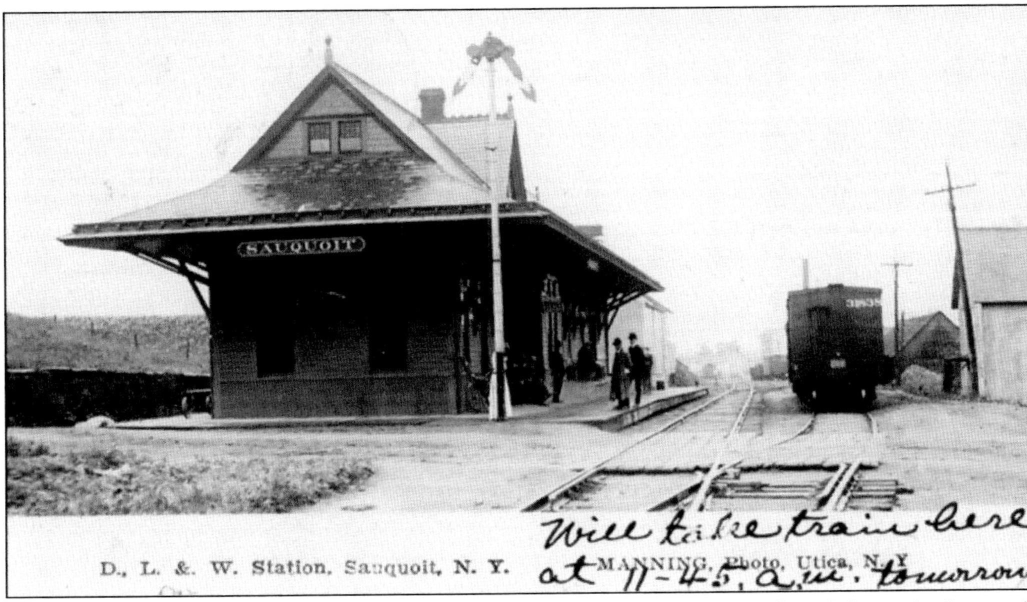

No longer in existence, the Delaware, Lackawanna and Western Railroad depot in Sauquoit once stood on Pinnacle Road, next to the spot where Grande's Pizza Shop is today. In the days before thruways and interstate highways, railroads were a boon to industries for shipping their products. As a supplier of coal for the area, the Delaware, Lackawanna and Western Railroad traveled from Utica to Binghamton with branches to Buffalo, Ithaca, Syracuse and north, and to Scranton, Pennsylvania.

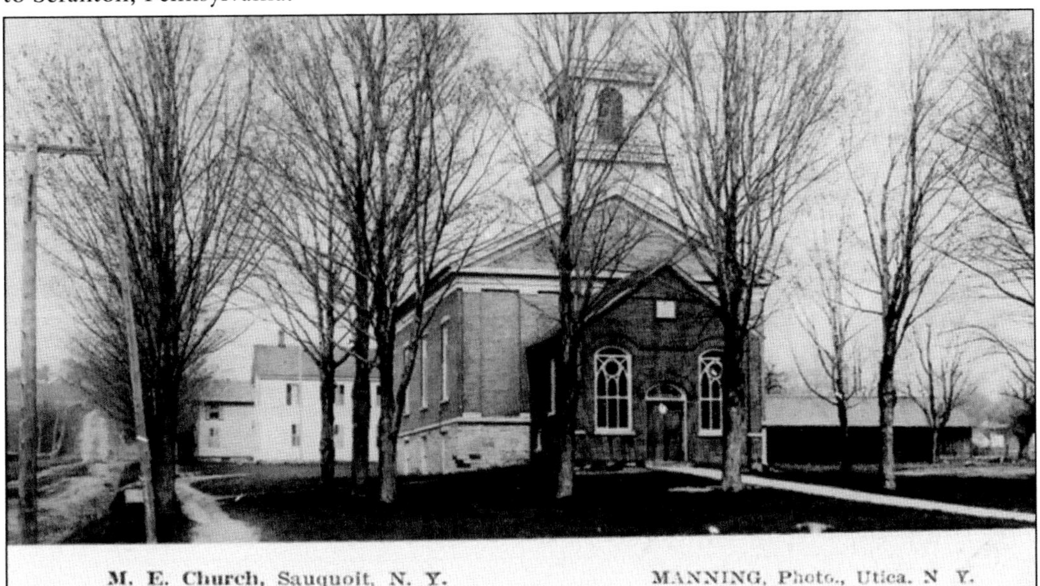

The eastern section of present-day Sauquoit was originally called "Methodist Corners" after the church at the intersection of Pinnacle Road and Mohawk Street (known as Norwich Street and Academy Street in 1907). Replacing an earlier structure that was moved south to an adjoining lot, the brick church was erected in 1816. The old wood church became the high school and academy and was razed in 1906. The former church parsonage now stands on the old school grounds. A new parsonage on Oneida Street was purchased in 1997.

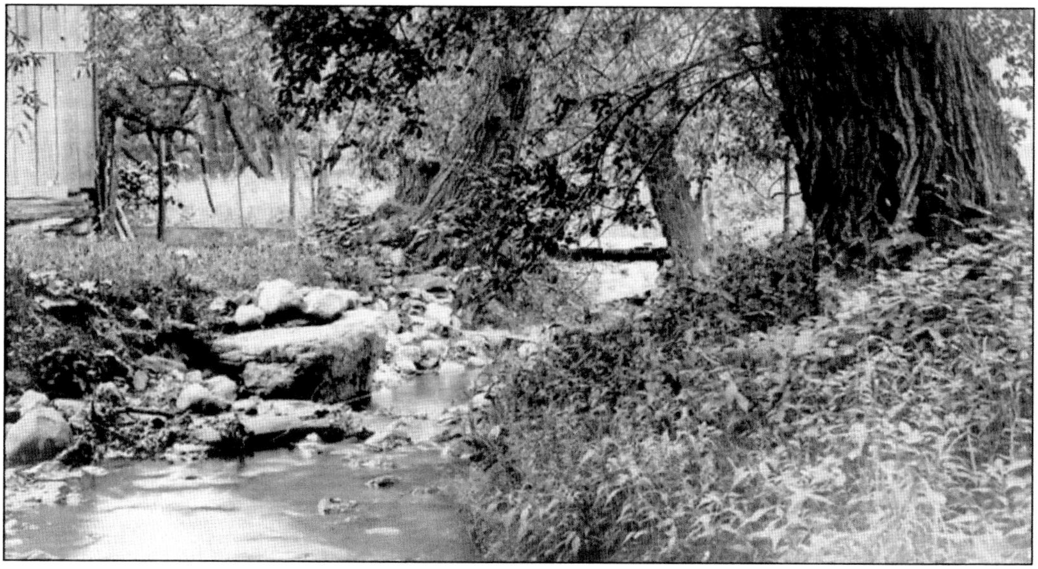

A rock-strewn branch of the Sauquoit Creek meanders under Campbell Road (named for the family who once lived there) about a quarter mile from Pinnacle Road in Sauquoit. A barnlike structure and a chicken wire fence appear in the upper left. A crude bridge seen at center provides a path across the creek. This *c.* 1907 postcard identifies the stream as Fingers Creek. On a Sauquoit Valley Fish and Game Club map from the 1970s, this creek was named Gage Brook.

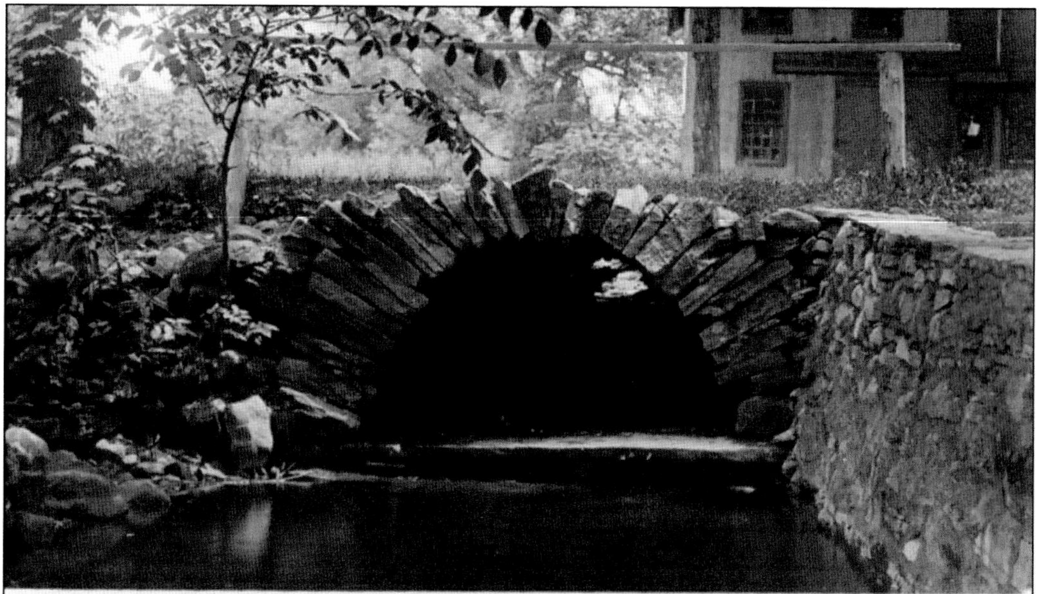

The culvert appears to be near a shop of some type, perhaps a wagon shop, on Fingers Creek. A 1907 atlas shows a shop on Mrs. S. H. Grande's property next to the creek. This building may have been in the same area shown in the postcard above. The name for the creek may have come from a family who lived in the town of Paris. Henry C. Rogers's history lists a Pvt. Martin Finger, 18, serving in the 14th Infantry on April 22, 1861. Over the years, the road has been built up, and today it is higher than it appears on this 1907 postcard. Remains of the stone arch are still visible.

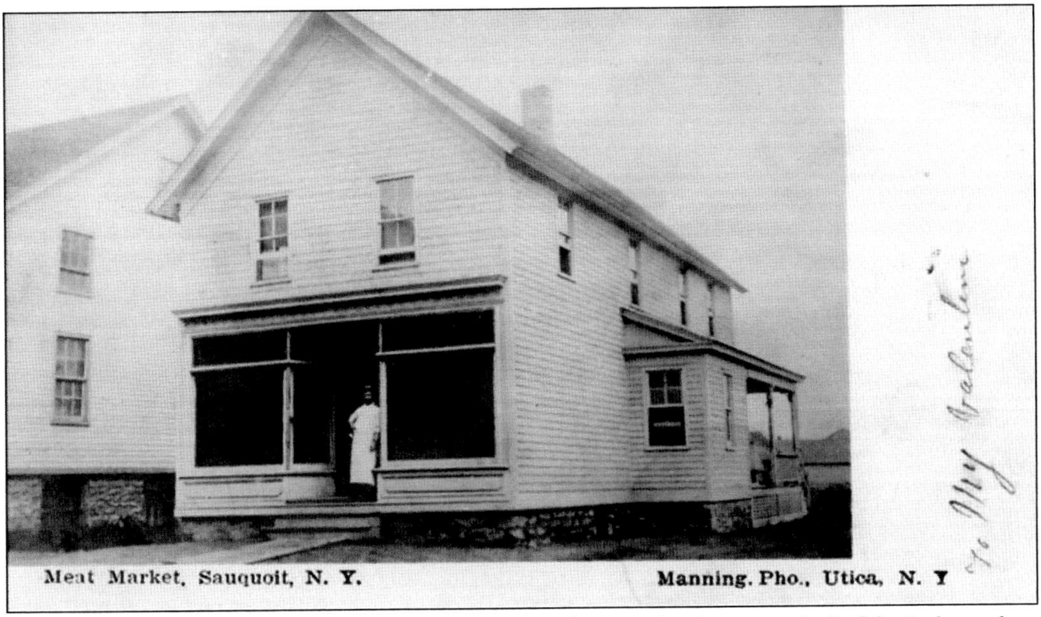

The exact location of the meat market pictured is not known, but it was typical of the independent specialty meat markets of the early 1900s before the advent of supermarkets. An advertisement in the *Sauquoit Valley News* of 1933 advertises "Choice Western Beef, Home Cured Hams and Bacon." Owner August Bozzoni's advertisement also states, "Call and I Will Deliver," a service that is not common today.

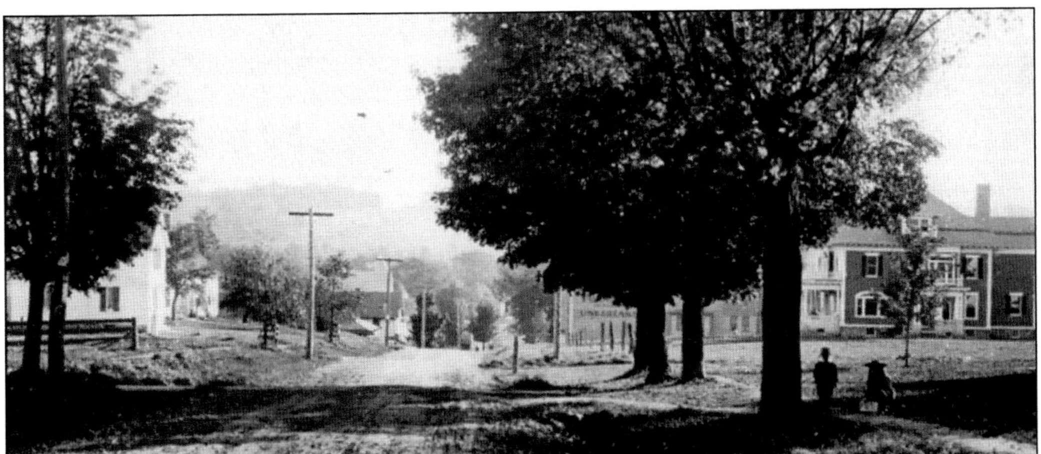

On West Main Street, now Pinnacle Road, was the home of Ladd J. Lewis Jr. (shown at right). At age 13, his family moved to New Hartford, and in 1886, Ladd graduated from New Hartford High School. He spent two years at Vanderbilt University in Tennessee, then returned to New Hartford and began a career in business. After moving to Sauquoit, he started the Lewis Knitting Company. Active in Republican party politics, he was elected to the New York State Assembly in 1906, where he served on numerous committees until about 1910. (Courtesy TPHS.)

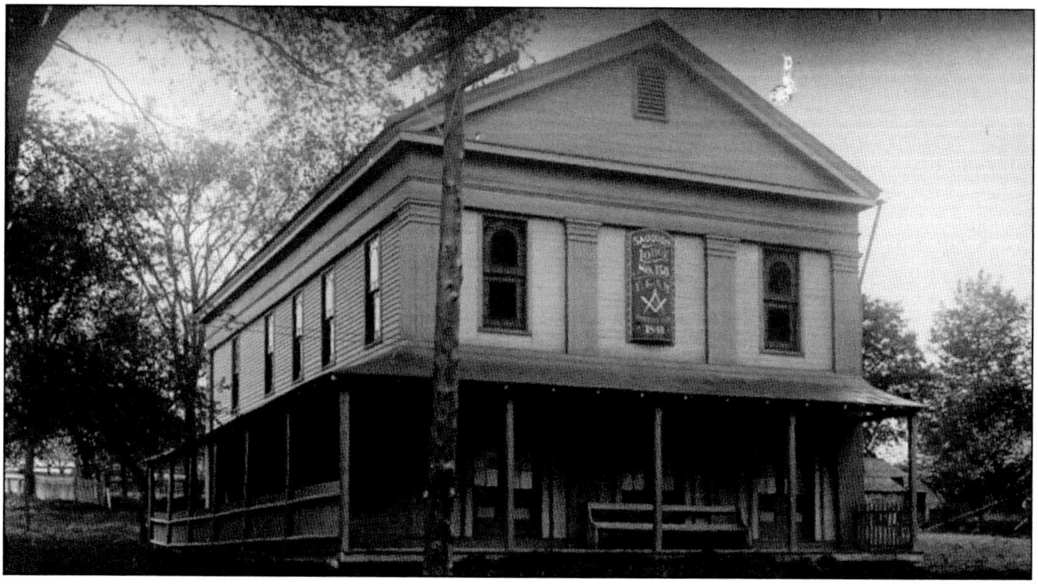

On January 19, 2000, the Sauquoit Masons celebrated their 150th anniversary. The Masonic lodge was organized in 1840 with 11 charter members. In 1873, this building was purchased for $1,750 and remodeled for a Masonic temple. The building had originally been erected by the Union Hall Association in 1849. They leased it to the Odd Fellows, who sublet it to the Masons. There are millions of Masons worldwide whose ideals include fellowship, religious tolerance, and political compromise.

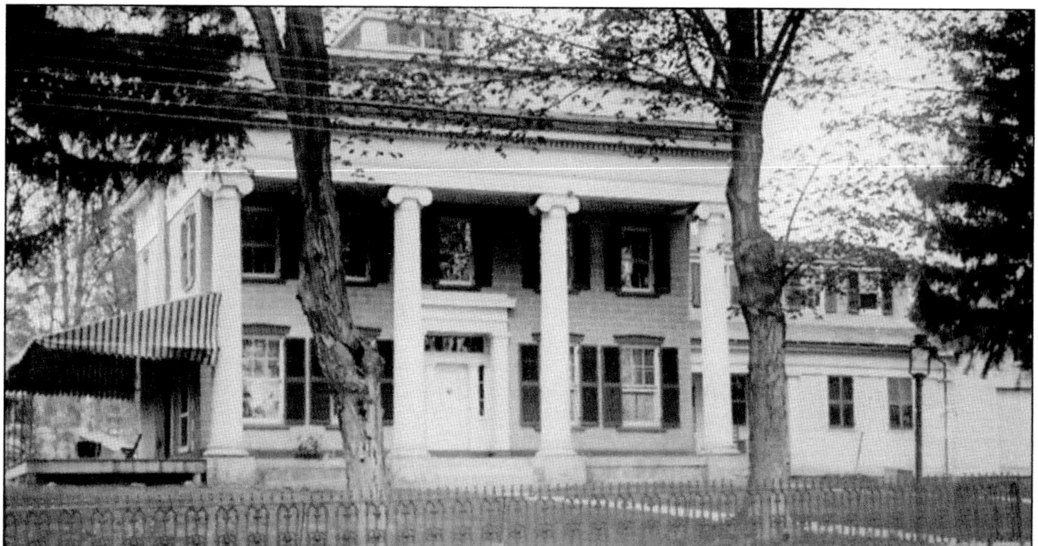

For his bravery during the Revolutionary War, Capt. Abner Bacon of Massachusetts was granted 410 acres by Gen. George Washington. He arrived in 1787 and with his sons built saw- and gristmills. In 1802, he erected a two-story frame house on this site. The first floor was used as a tavern with beverages from John Butler's distillery. In 1840, John's son Chauncey moved the two-story home across the road and constructed Butler Hall on the site. The old two-story frame home on Oneida Street is now a private residence.In 1920, John Whipple of Old Orchard, Maine, purchased the property and renamed it Orchard Hall. Today the building houses a restaurant, bar, and bowling alley.

Two

Town of New Hartford

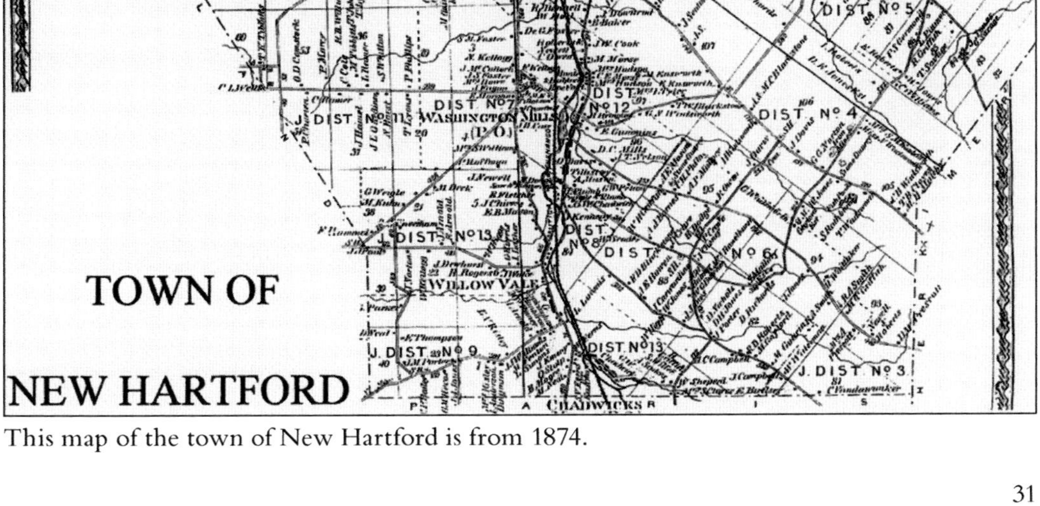

This map of the town of New Hartford is from 1874.

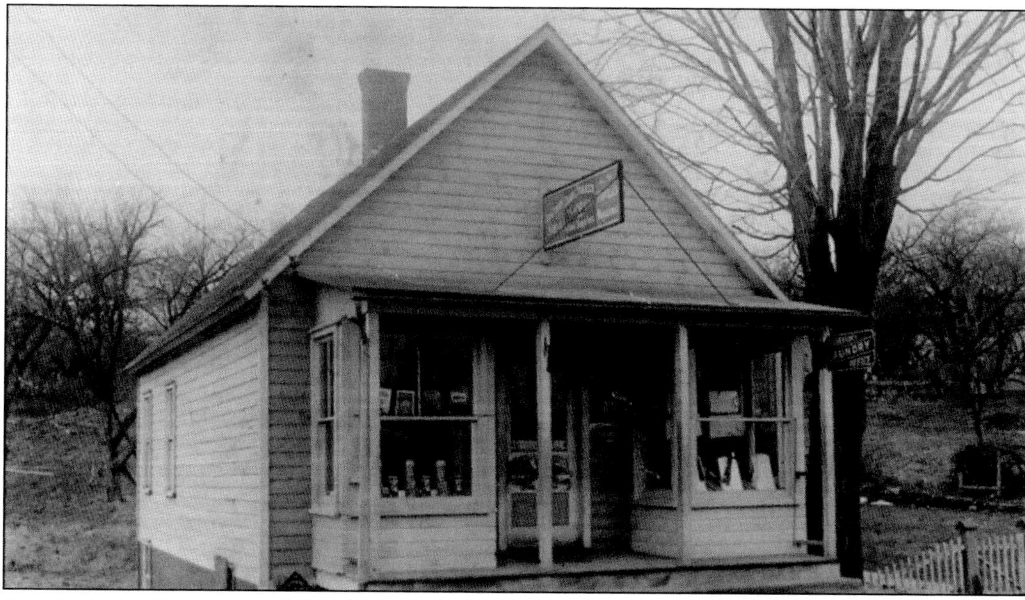

Candy, soda, drugs, gents' furnishings, and school supplies were all offered by Johnson's Busy Store. On the banks of the Sauquoit Creek on Elm Street in Chadwicks, this building was doubled in size to provide room for a post office. The drugstore later was operated by James Reagan and still later by Maurice and Anna Kelly, who sold jumbo ice-cream cones for 5¢. Anna was a descendant of the Chadwick family for whom the village was named. Adelbert Stauring purchased the store in 1946. Later the Porter family operated the store, took over the former post office, and added booths and a jukebox. It was razed for a parking lot for Williams Tool Company.

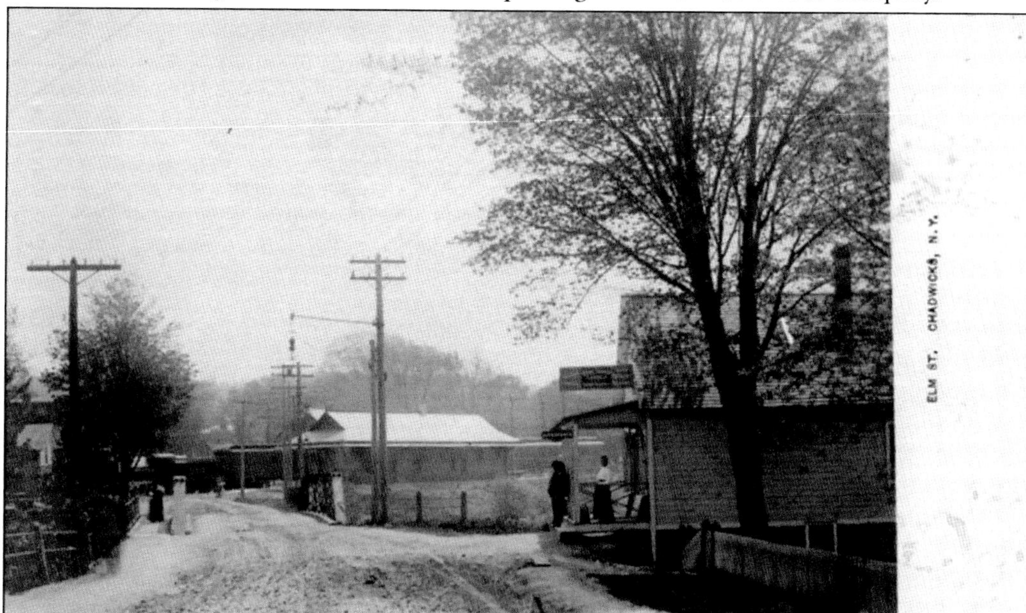

An iron bridge provided vehicle and pedestrian traffic a passage over the Sauquoit Creek in Chadwicks. In 1958, a new bridge replaced the original structure. In the center is the Delaware, Lackawanna and Western Railroad depot, and at the right is Johnson's Busy Store. Like many roads of the early 1900s, this one on Elm Street was unpaved.

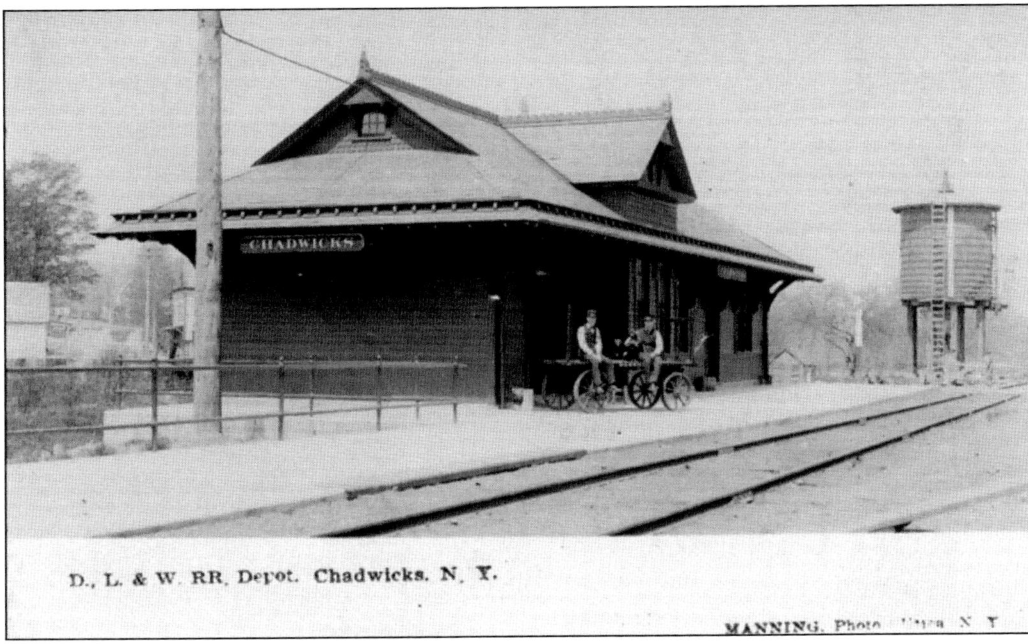

At the Delaware, Lackawanna and Western Railroad depot in Chadwicks, two employees await the arrival of the train (sometimes referred to by locals as the Delay, Linger, and Wait Railroad). The old depot, built in 1910, was restored in 1990. In 1991, it was renamed the James H. Donovan Community Center to honor the longtime state senator James Donovan of Chadwicks.

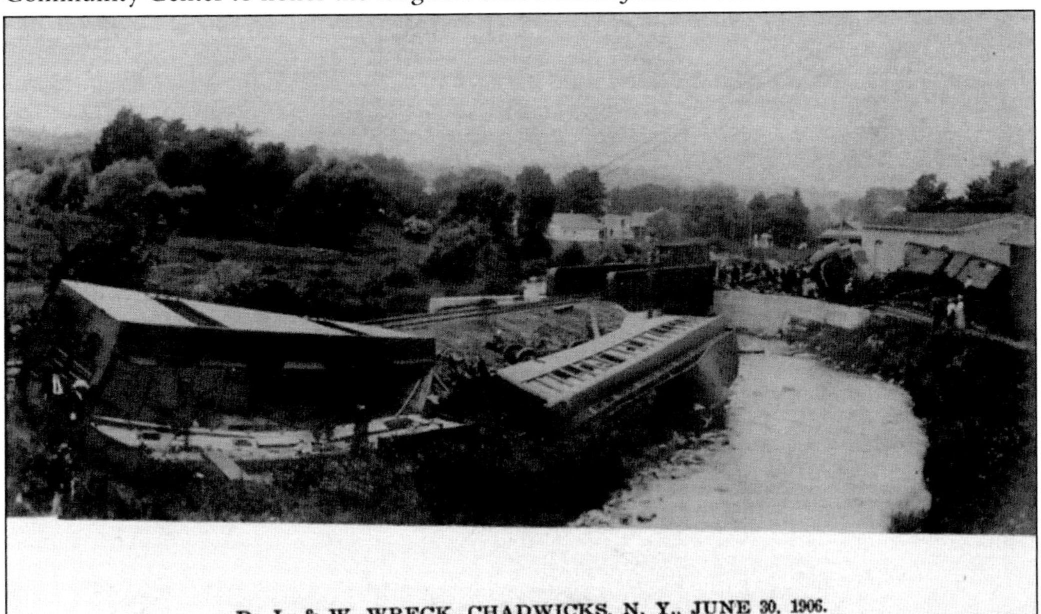

On June 30, 1906, a devastating train wreck occurred near the Chadwicks depot. A group of men were at work building a new bridge when the accident took place. Bridge workmen had removed a switch to facilitate their work, and it was not replaced, resulting in the mishap. The cars left the tracks and shot across the Sauquoit Creek. There were no fatalities, but 25 people were injured. Dr. Edwin M. Griffith attended to the injured.

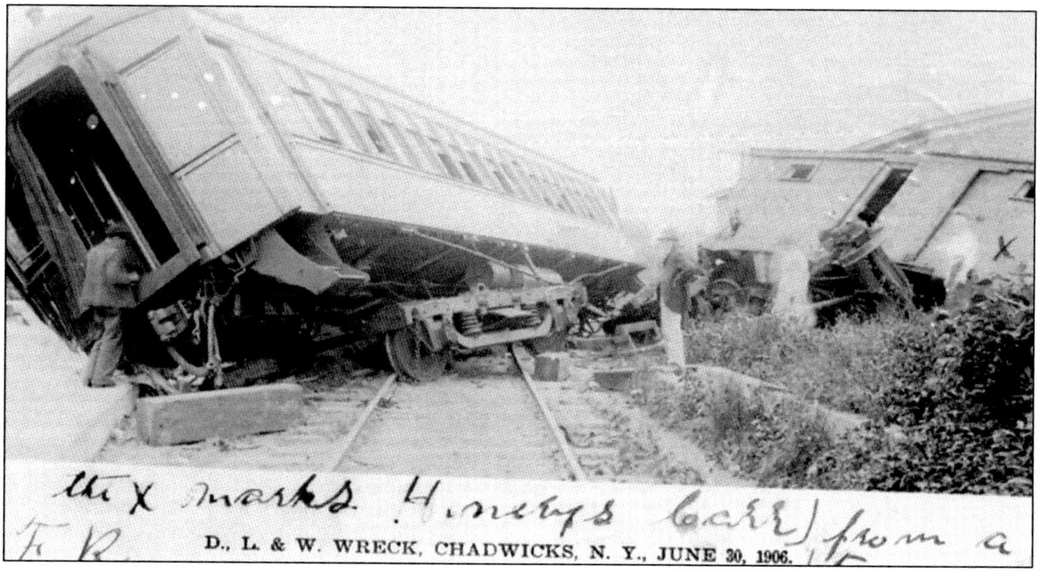

Although not scheduled to stop in Chadwicks, the Delaware, Lackawanna and Western train heading to Binghamton came to an unplanned, abrupt stop. The train consisted of a locomotive and three cars, a combination baggage and express, a smoker, and an ordinary day coach. As reported in the Utica newspaper, just after passing the station, observers on the platform saw the rear car madly swerve from the main track, come to a sudden and crashing halt, and strike and splinter a freight car standing on the siding. It came to a standstill resting on the bridge over the Sauquoit Creek.

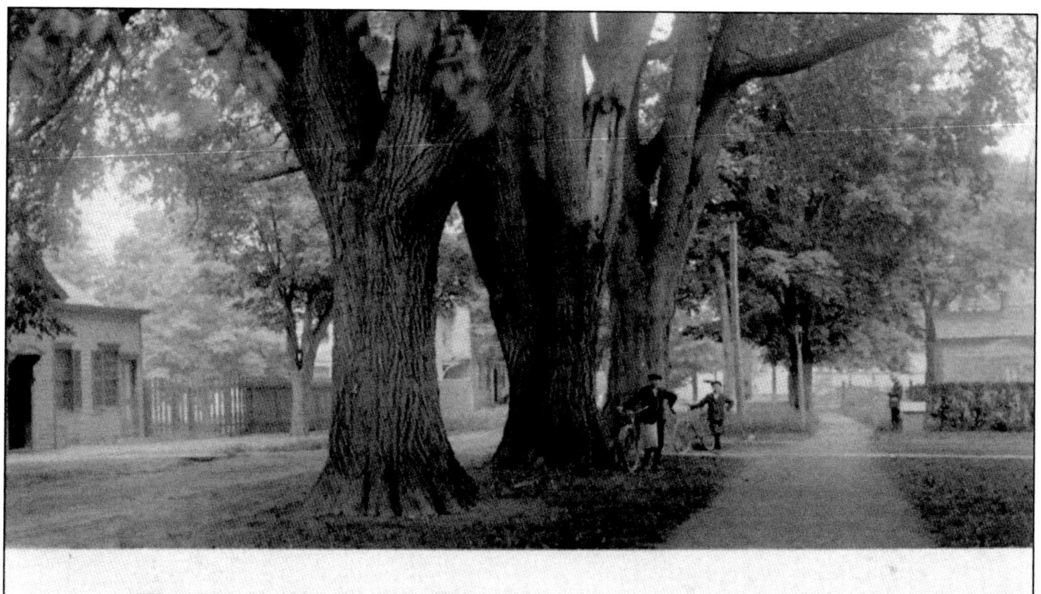

On this postcard, two paperboys are dwarfed by the huge old elm trees. These old elms no longer line Elm Street in Chadwicks, having succumbed to Dutch elm disease, a fungus infection blight in the 1950s. One such tree in the area that was 22 feet in diameter was designated by the Elm Research Institute as an historic landmark. Its plaque read "Planted in the 1700s, this tree is hereby designated a historic landmark to be honored and preserved for future generations."

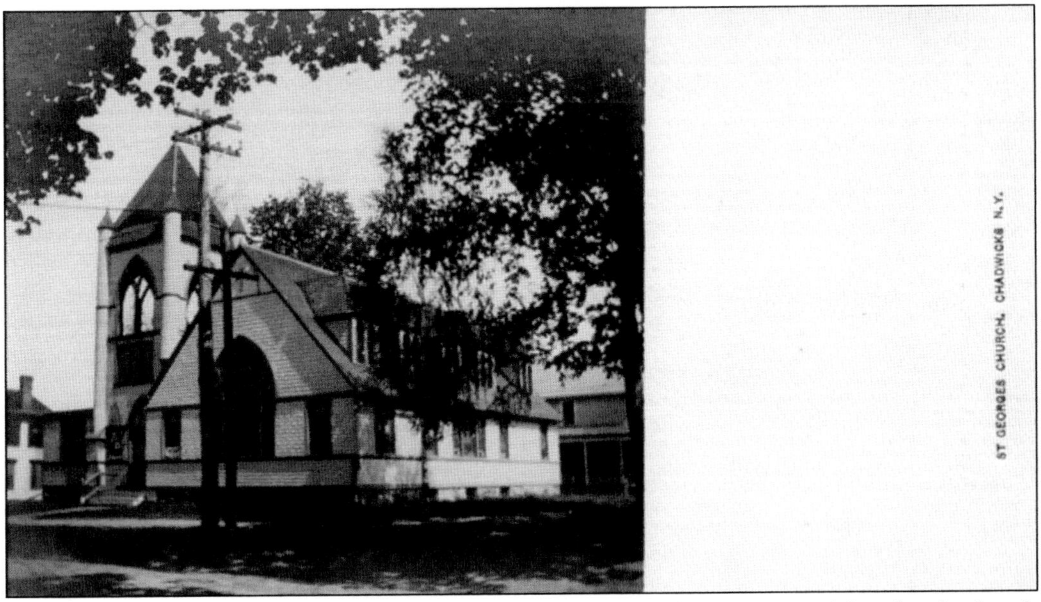

In 1890, Mary Ann Wrigley Chadwick had this church built as a memorial to her husband, George W. Chadwick Sr., a prominent citizen and son of John Chadwick, for whom the village was named. The cost was over $11,000. Under the large stained-glass window is this inscription: "To the glory of God and in beloved memory of George M. Chadwick, born June 16, 1825, died December 4, 1885." The original steeple has been removed, changing the appearance of the original Gothic Revival structure. The church is still active today.

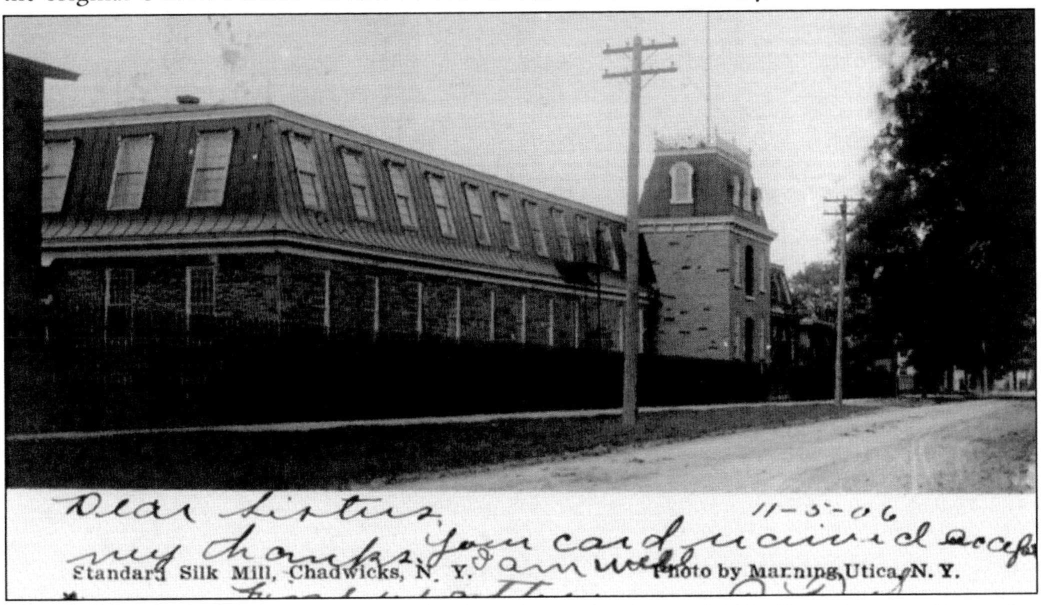

John Chadwick came here from England in the early 1800s. With Abner Brownell and Ira Todd, he established Eagle Mills, a cotton factory in present-day Chadwicks. His partners left the business, and he became sole owner. In 1844, shortly after extensive additions, the mill was struck by lightning and burned to the ground. Chadwick rebuilt a substantial stone mill on the site. In later years, the mill became Standard Silk Mill until it closed its doors about 1952. The building was razed in 1964 and is now the site of Chadwicks Park.

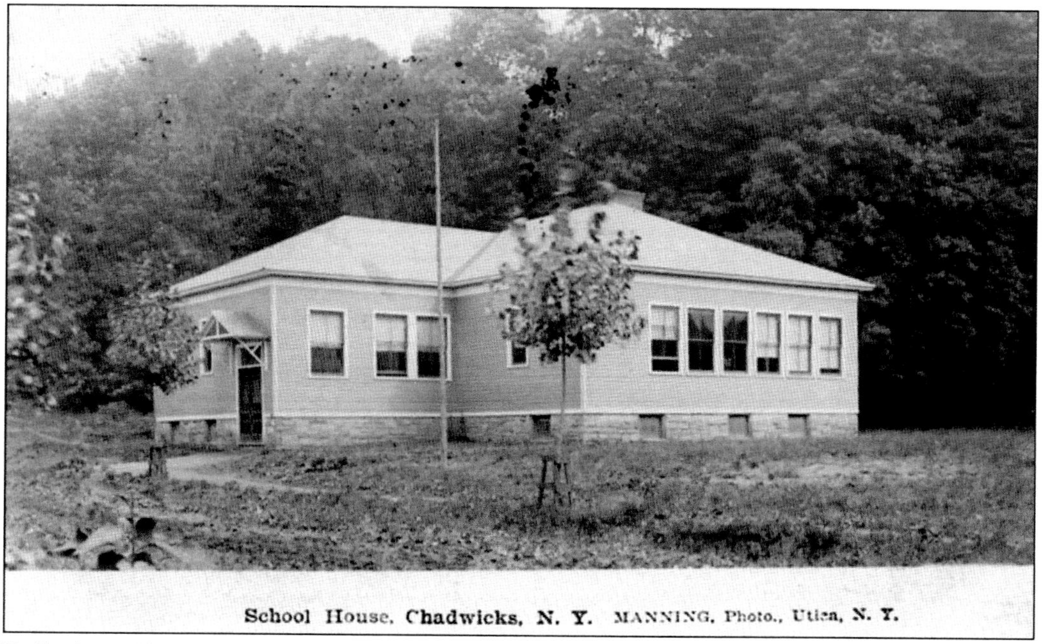

Built about 1906 on Standard Silk Mill property, this school replaced a smaller one used in the late 1800s and early 1900s that stood next to the silk mill and was razed in 1964 after the silk mill ceased operations. The school pictured was replaced by a large brick school built on Main Street (now Oneida Street). The School Street School was used for a time to show old-time movies and today is an apartment house.

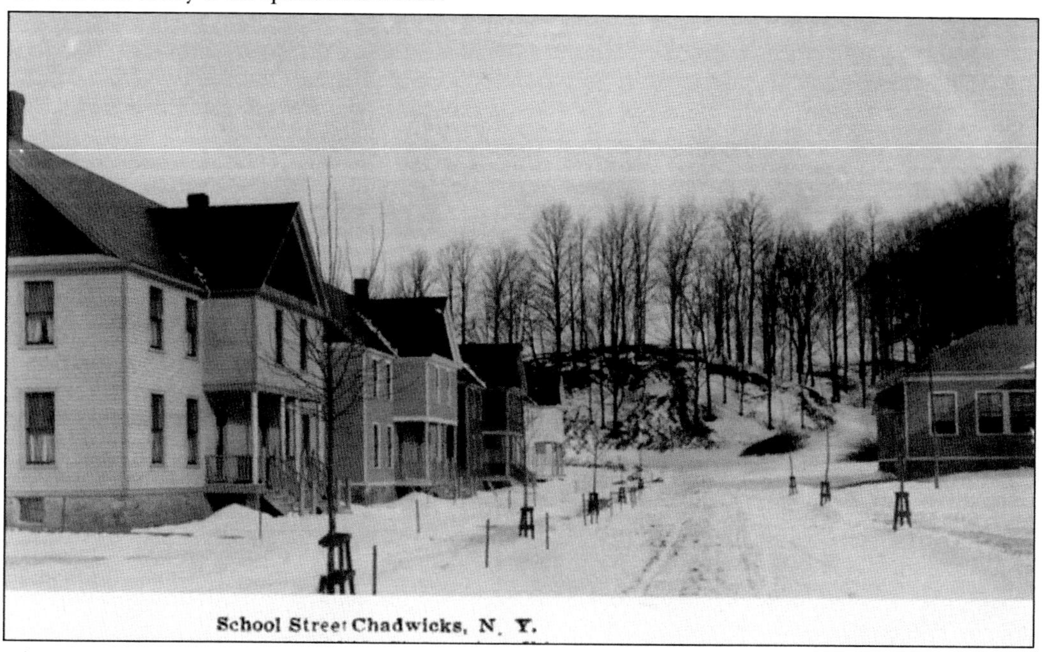

This winter scene of School Street in Chadwicks is lined on the west side by Standard Silk Mill homes provided for employees. At the center is a hill that provided recreation for the neighborhood children. In winter it was used for sledding and in the summer for exploring. At right is the School Street School.

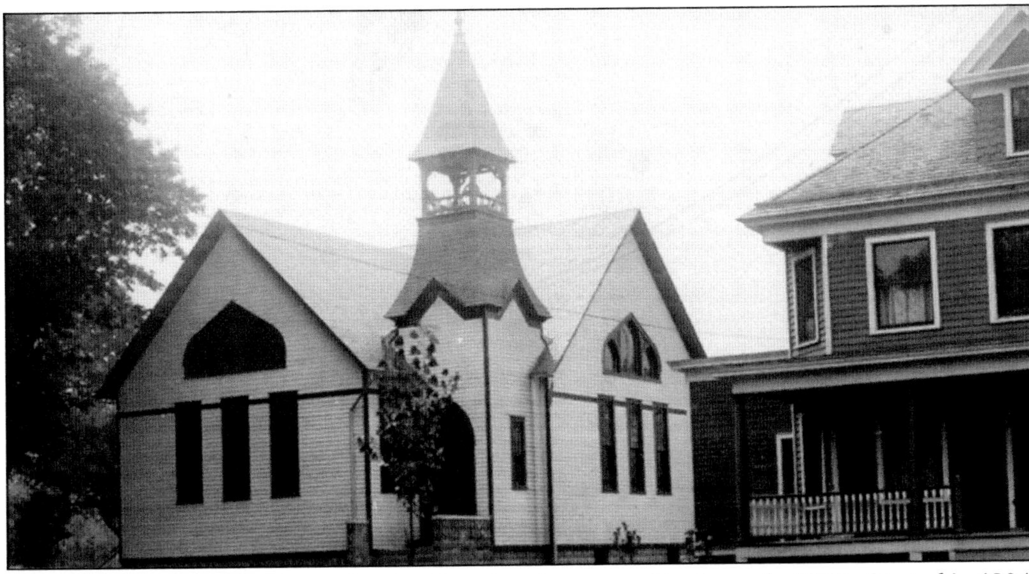

Pictured is the Willowvale Methodist Church as it appeared in the early 1900s. Started in 1904, the church was completed and dedicated in December 1907. In 1919, the building was raised, enlarging the Sunday school rooms and adding a small kitchen. The church merged with the Sauquoit Methodist Church in 1995, and the Willowvale church was sold. The building to the right of the church was the home and office of Dr. Edwin M. Griffith. Griffith was an old-fashioned country doctor who practiced in Willowvale for 40 years. Anna Griffith served the church as organist and Sunday school teacher.

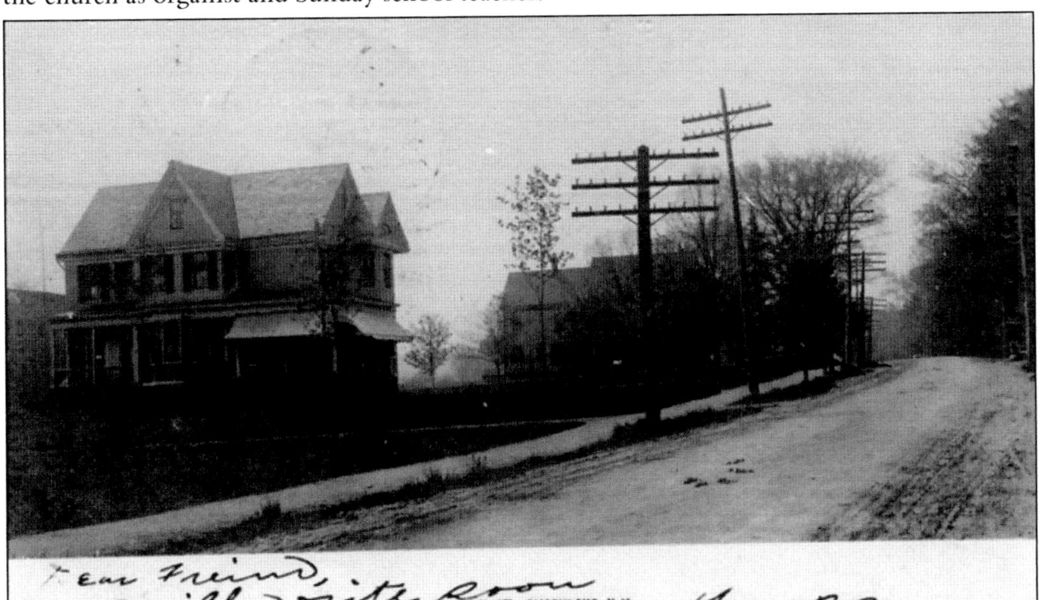

On the northeast corner of Main Street (now Oneida Street) and Bleachery Avenue is a residence provided for one of the department heads of the Willowvale Bleachery. When the business closed in the early 1950s and moved south, many bleachery residences were sold at nominal fees to former employees. The house pictured was later purchased by a local automobile dealer. The building in the center is the Ononda Club.

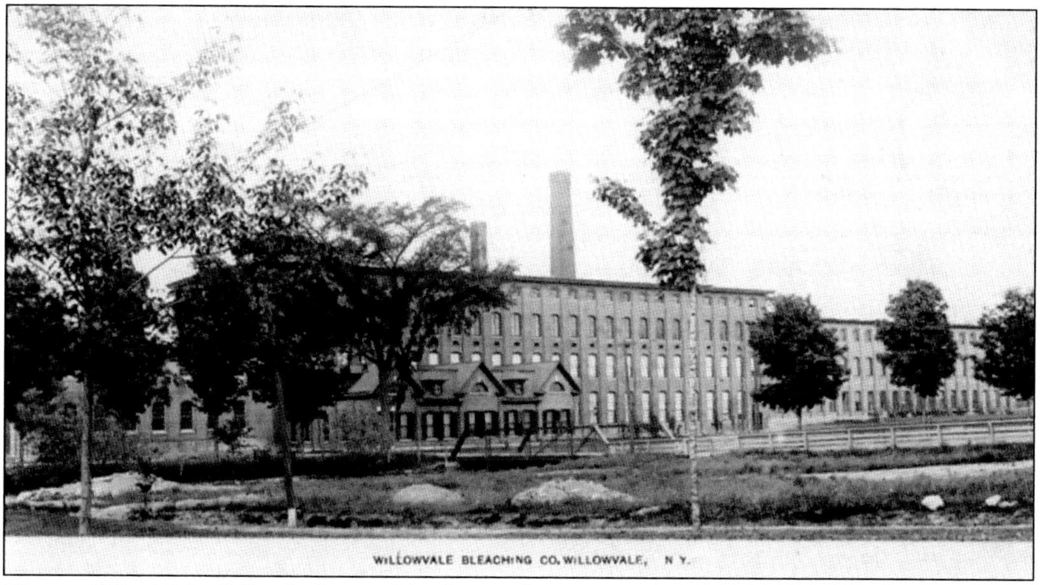

The small double building in front of the factory housed the offices for the Willowvale Bleaching Company. George W. Chadwick Sr. was one of the founders of the plant, serving as president and general manager until his death in 1885. He was one of the organizers and a member of the board of directors of Oneida National Bank of Utica; a promoter and director of the Utica, Chenango and Susquehanna Railroad; and one of the incorporators of the Sauquoit Valley Cemetery Association.

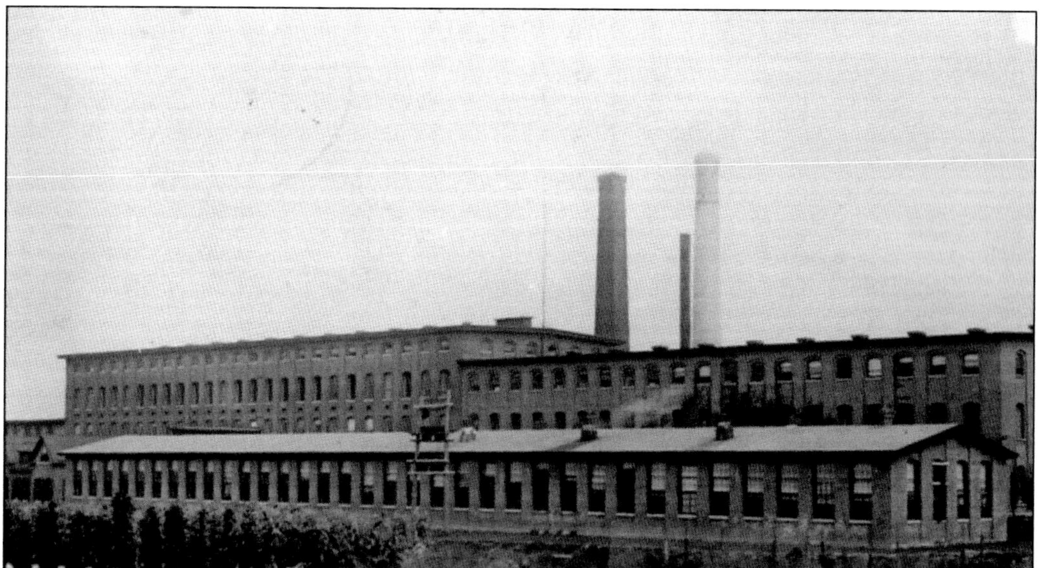

In 1937, a Utica newspaper article reported a strike called by union leaders resulting in nearly all nearby textile mills in Utica and vicinity being closed. Plants were closed by the forced action of strikers, or by company officials voluntarily closing to prevent disorder. A small force of Willowvale Bleachery employees were permitted to finish the wet goods in process to prevent any financial loss from mildew or other chemical action. However, the strike committee objected when they learned some shipments had been sent out. The matter was eventually resolved peacefully, ending the demonstrations.

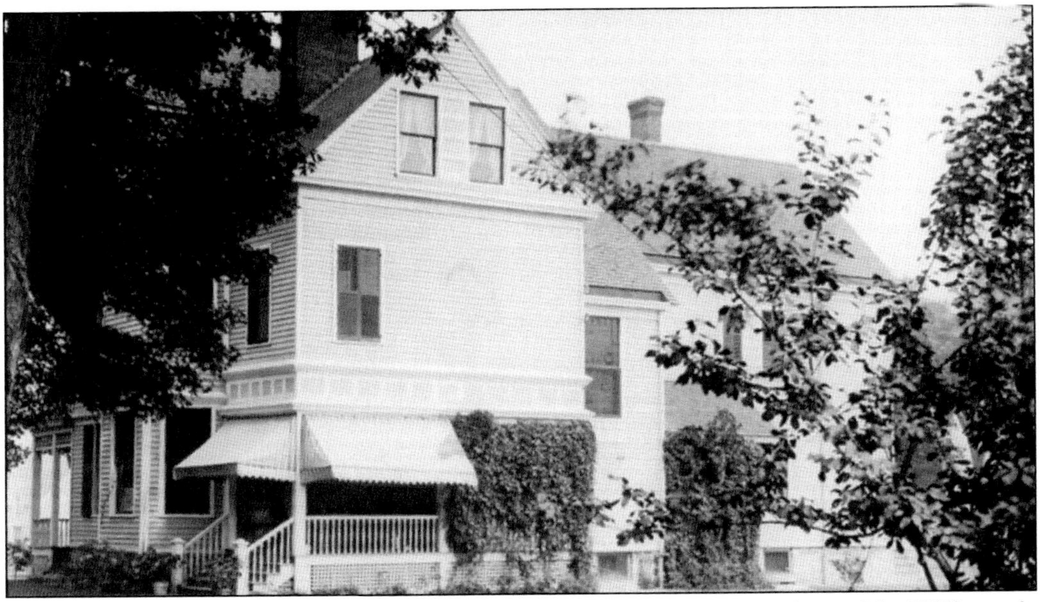

A spacious home was provided for Mr. MacManus, who was superintendent of the Willowvale Bleaching Company. Subsequently, it became the Ononda Club, a boardinghouse for female employees of the bleachery. A cafeteria occupied the lower floor, where the residents and bleachery employees could get their lunch. In later years, the Suplee family occupied the residence when Frank Suplee became superintendent. Later converted to apartments, the structure was razed in the 1960s after a fire. Joan's Diner and a shopping center now occupy the site.

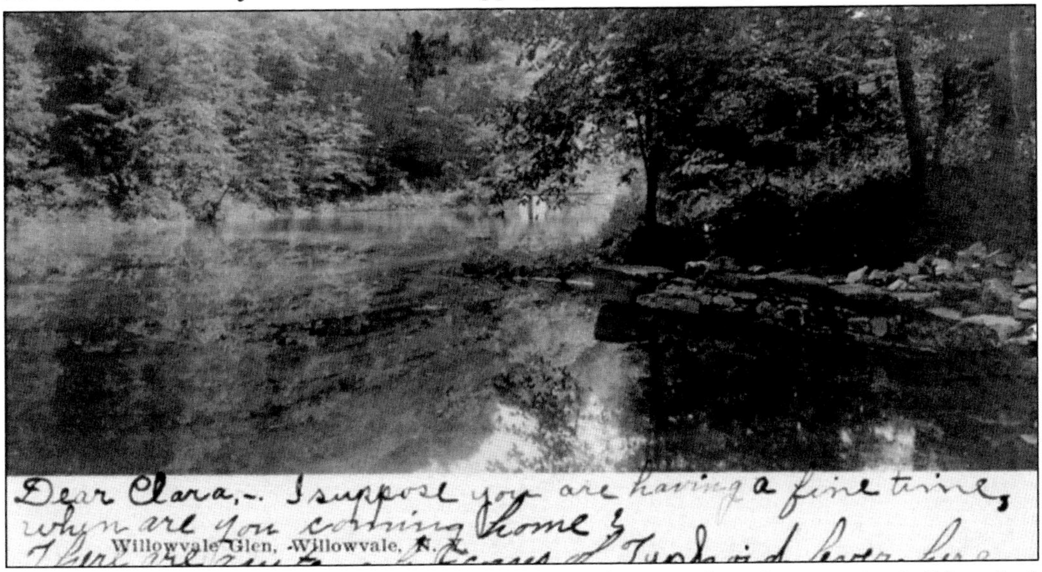

An undated booklet prepared by Project RACE (Regional Approach on Conservation in Education) while the Willowvale Glen was owned by Utica College provided a history and geology of the glen. Deeded to the college in 1959 by the Willowvale Bleaching Company, the tract of land was about 65 acres in a near natural state and was to be used as an outdoor laboratory. In the glen were three man-made ponds that offered an aquatic environment, natural woodlands, and a "field in secondary secessions." Clinton beds in the glen yielded a variety of fossils, plants, and numerous other organisms.

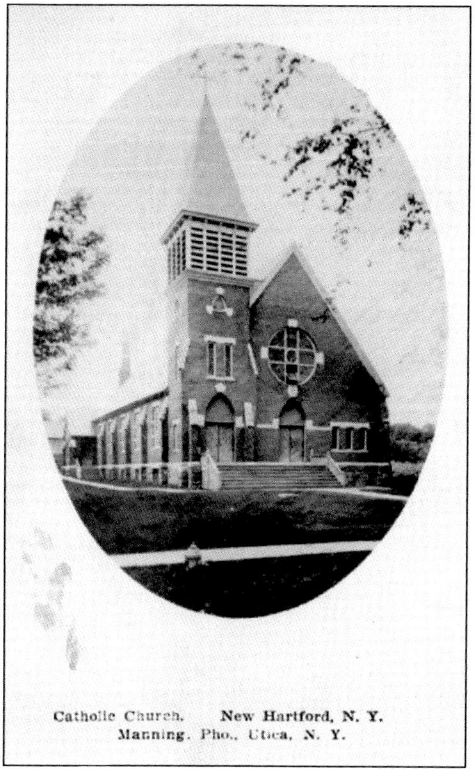

A new Saint John's Evangelist Catholic Church on the southwest corner of Oxford Road and Sherman Street has replaced this earlier one built on the northwest corner, now the church parking lot. The new church is on the site of a house once owned by the family of James Schoolcraft Sherman, vice president under William H. Taft. The Sherman home was torn down to build the new structure. The new church, with seating for 1,000 people, was dedicated on January 23, 1966.

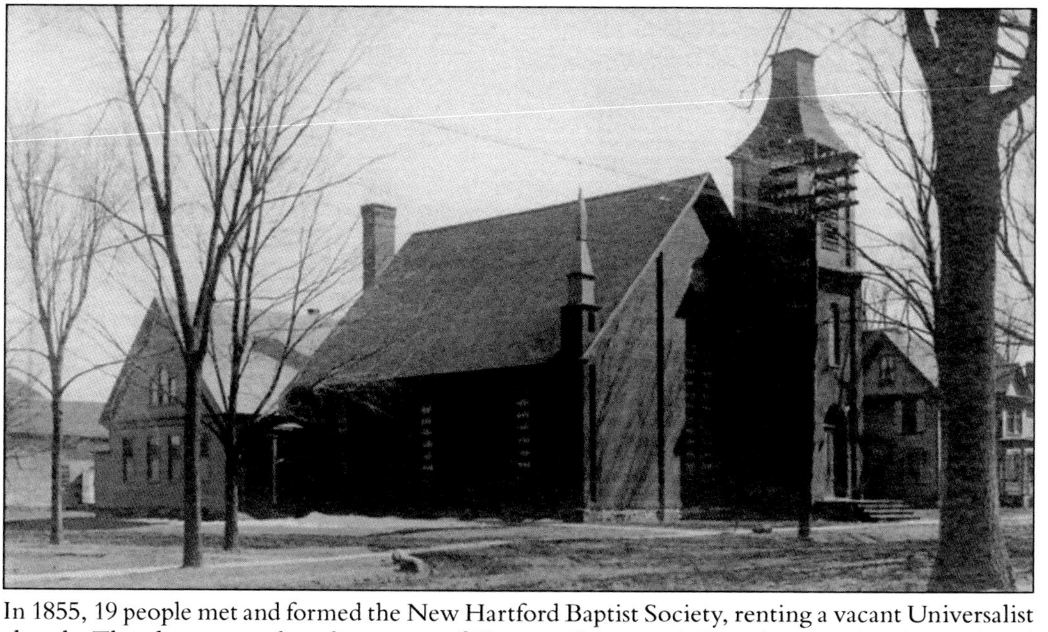

In 1855, 19 people met and formed the New Hartford Baptist Society, renting a vacant Universalist church. They later moved to the corner of Genesee Street and Campion Road and worshiped there for nearly 30 years. In 1885, the Baptists built a new church on the corner of South and Mill Streets with a tower and bell that were removed in the early 1900s and a four-room Sunday school addition was built at the rear. A Sunday school building was added in 1923.

Judge Jedediah Sanger, founder of New Hartford, donated land for the Presbyterian church. Originally Congregational at its dedication in 1797, they voted in 1801 to become Presbyterian. In 1827, New Hartford was set off from Whitestown. William Curtis, a resident and merchant, disagreed with this development, perhaps because he was the town clerk of old Whitestown. Villagers celebrated by shooting off a cannon near the point of Genesee Street and Paris Road, angering Curtis. He responded by having the bell in the church steeple tolled. In turn the cannoneers threatened to fire into the belfry. The bell ringing was soon stopped, saving the belfry from annihilation.

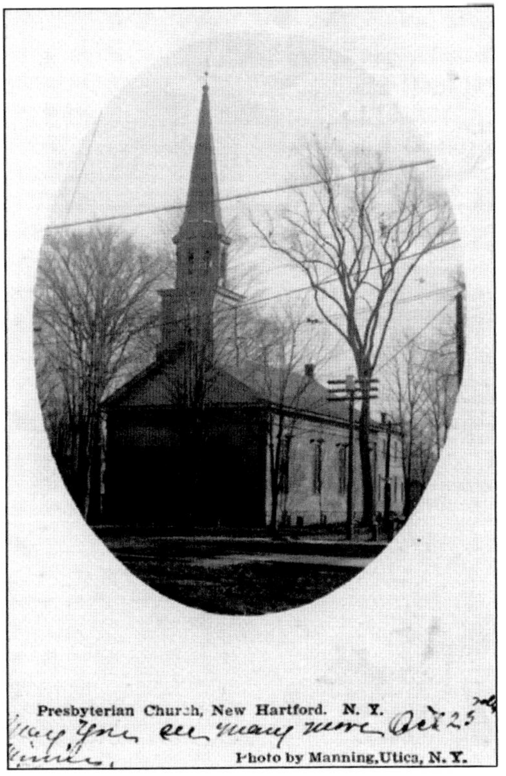

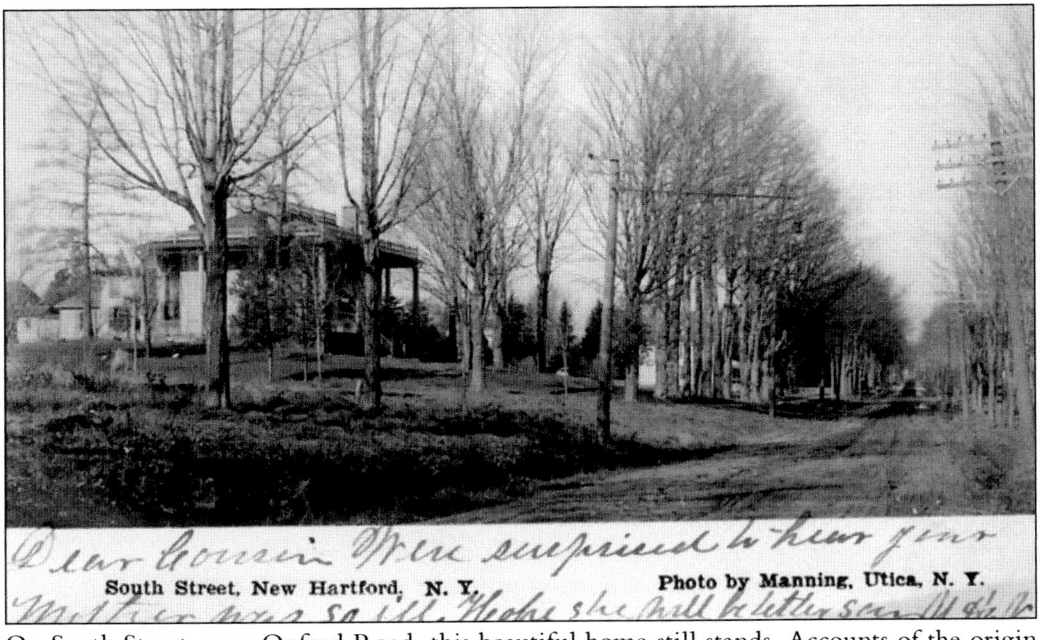

On South Street, now Oxford Road, this beautiful home still stands. Accounts of the origin of the mansion vary. It is believed to be built by Judge Jedediah Sanger in 1793 and 1794 as a wedding gift for his daughter Sarah and son-in-law John Eames, who were married in 1794. Later damaged by fire, it was rebuilt in 1830 by Sanger's grandson Walter Eames. A rear addition was built about 1920.

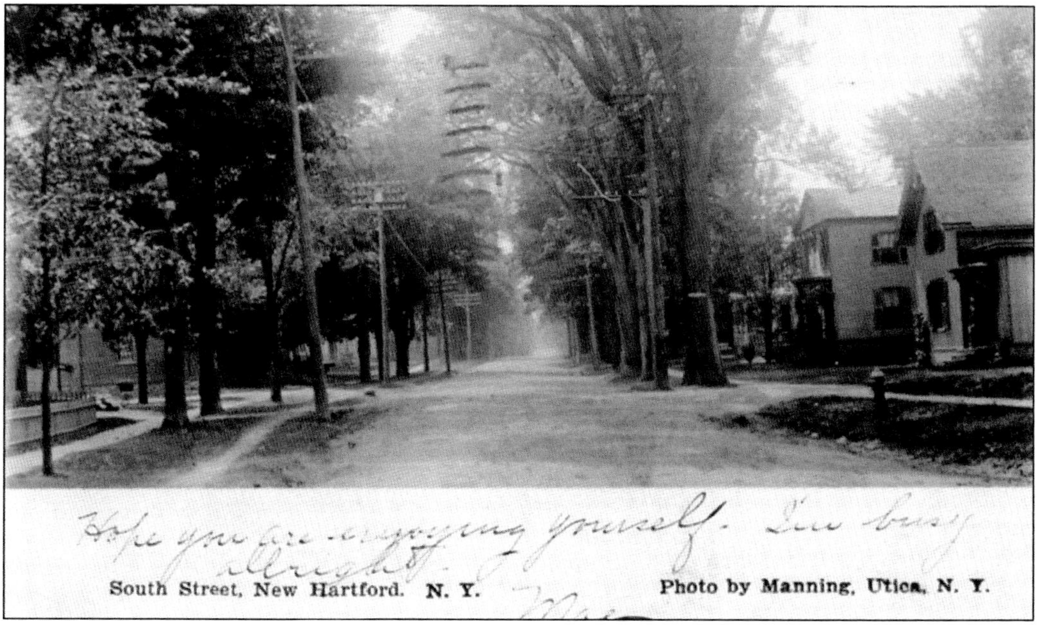

No longer unpaved or known as South Street, this is now Oxford Road looking south from Genesee Street. In 1906, the villagers petitioned to have the street name changed. On the corner of South Street and Park Street (at right) was a unique home with board-and-batten siding in the early Gothic Revival style, built about 1853. Now the site of the New Hartford Fire Department, this home was moved about 10 miles south to the Cassville area.

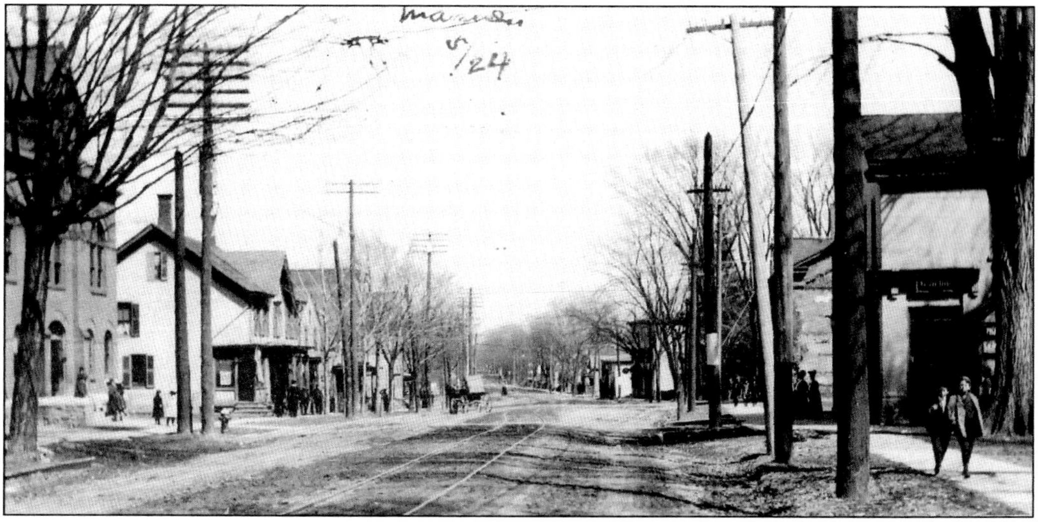

In the center of the village is Butler Hall (at left), given to New Hartford in 1890 by Morgan Butler. Originally the hall included a post office, justice office, public library, reading room, a room for ladies' gatherings, a gymnasium, bowling alleys, a kitchen, and a large hall that seated 450. There was also a stage for dramatic productions, minstrel shows, and other offerings. Recently remodeled, it now houses town and village offices. The trolley tracks were removed in 1941. The block on the right was once a solid row of businesses until a fire in the early 1900s destroyed many of them. (Courtesy NHHS.)

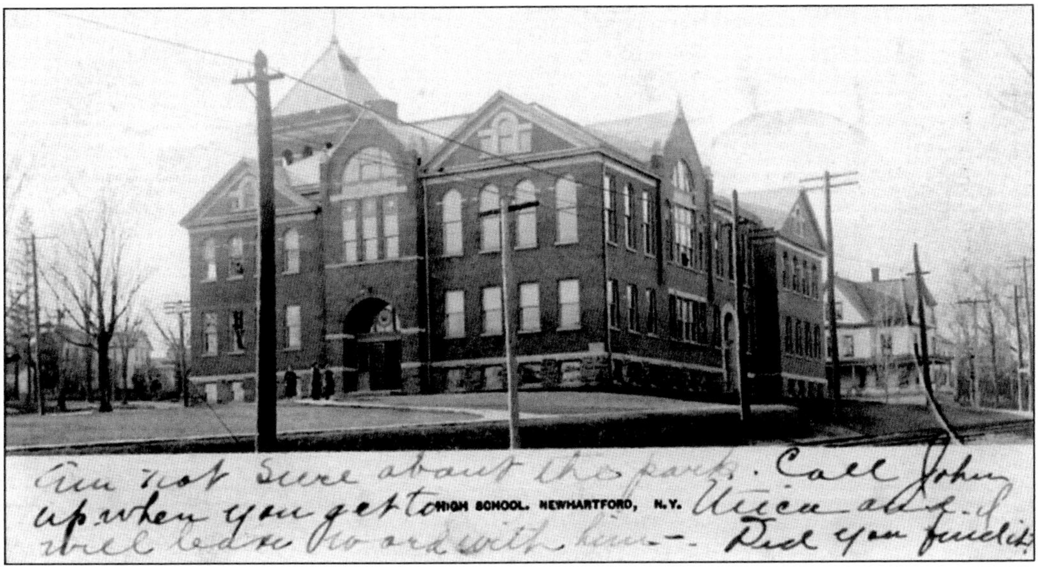

This red brick school at the junction of present-day Genesee Street and Paris Road was built in 1901 and opened to students in September 1902. The building of Romanesque design accommodated 600 pupils. Principal Arthur M. Scripture campaigned for a larger, better facility, which resulted in it being one of the best schools in the state. Additions were made to the building in 1921, doubling its capacity and adding a gymnasium. The school is now an apartment complex for senior citizens. The New Hartford Historical Society occupies rooms in the basement. (Courtesy NHHS.)

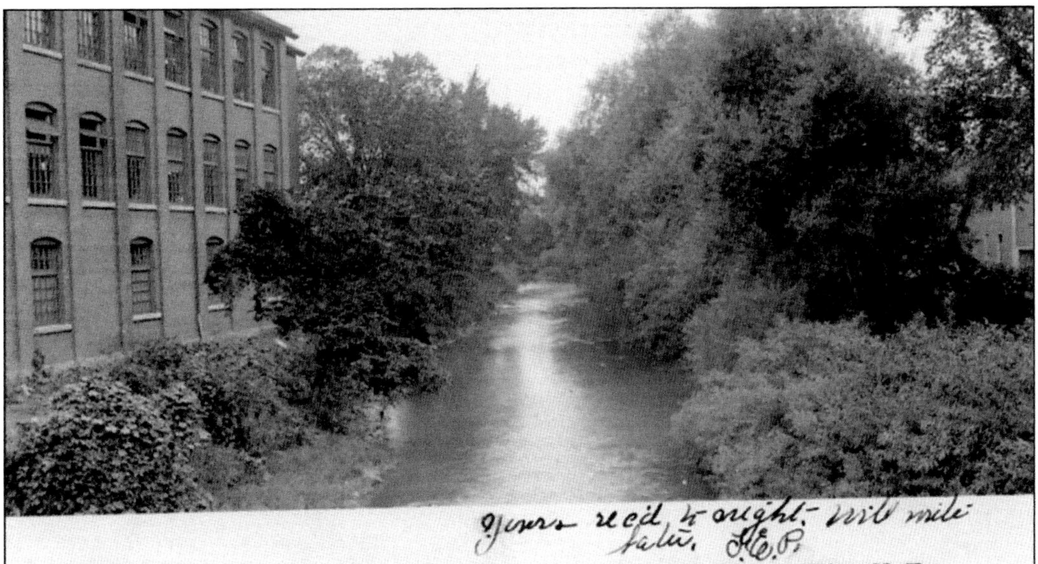

Pictured on this pre-1907 real-photo postcard, this factory was one of many situated on the Sauquoit Creek. It may be the New Hartford Cotton Manufacturing Company that appears next to the creek on both the 1874 and the 1907 maps. In 1788, Judge Jedediah Sanger bought 1,000 acres of land along the creek. In 1789, he erected a sawmill and in 1790, a gristmill. Numerous other mills located in New Hartford resulted in "a healthy and rapid progress in population and wealth."

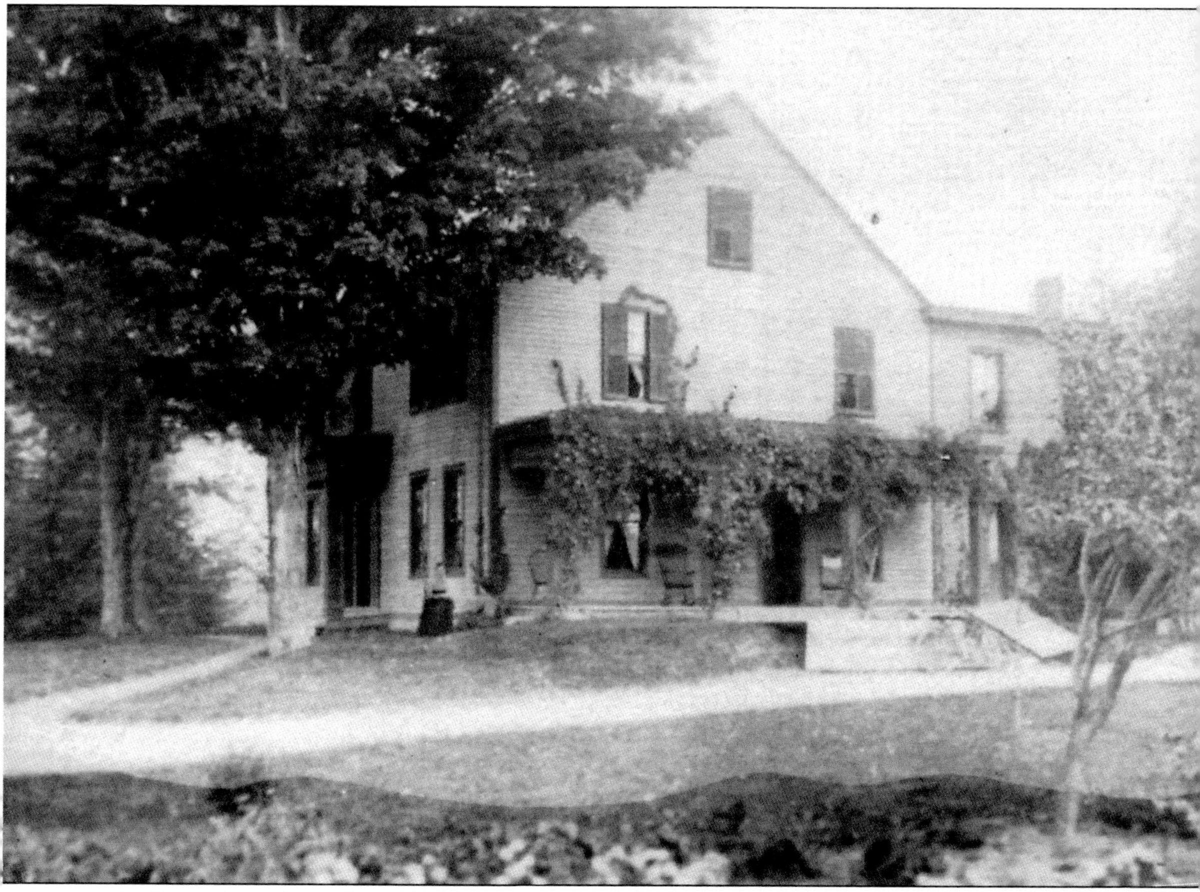

In 1905, the Yahnundasis Golf Club purchased the 90-acre Sherrill Farm on the Clinton Road (now Seneca Turnpike, State Route 5) for $11,250, and part of the adjacent Moore Farm for $2,400. In 1906, they voted to remodel the Sherrill farmhouse for a clubhouse. In 1920, an additional 100 acres of the Moore Farm were added. The Sherrill farmhouse, located where the Wedgewood Apartments are today, was remodeled, enlarged, and opened in May 1907 as the clubhouse. Originally the golf course was laid out with nine holes, and in 1911, nine more were added. In 1920, plans were begun for the present golf course and clubhouse. Thirty-five acres were sold to the Utica Country Day School. A new school was built, and the club shared the property with the school until the new clubhouse was built, just west of the old one. It opened in April 1924. Sherrill Sherman, son of James S. (Schoolcraft) Sherman, was president of the club in 1918. (Schoolcraft was James's mother's maiden name.) Sherrill Sherman was also related to the Sherrill family, previous owner of the club's original property. James S. Sherman was one of the founders of the Yahnundasis Club.

Three

City of Utica

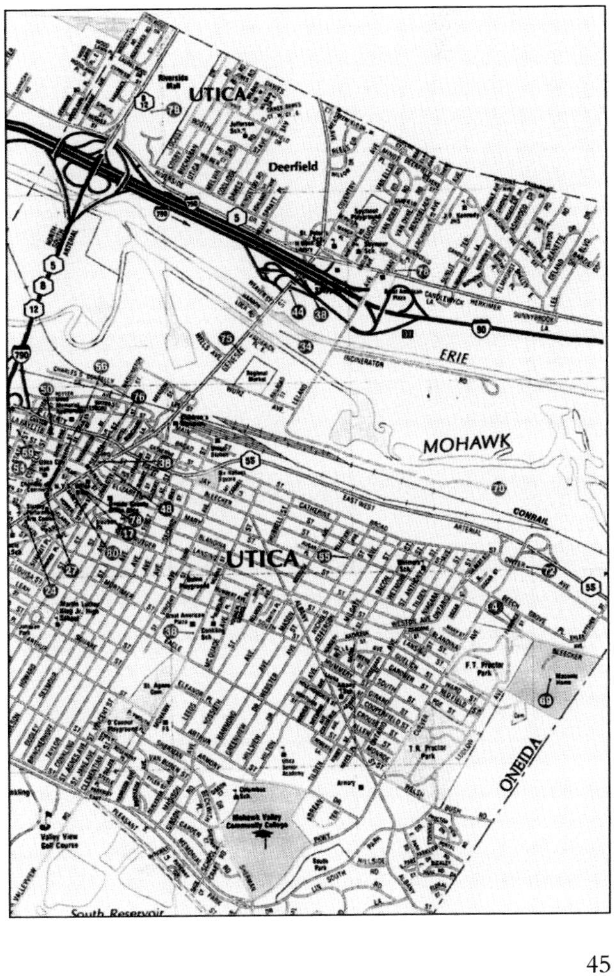

This map of the city of Utica is from 1995.

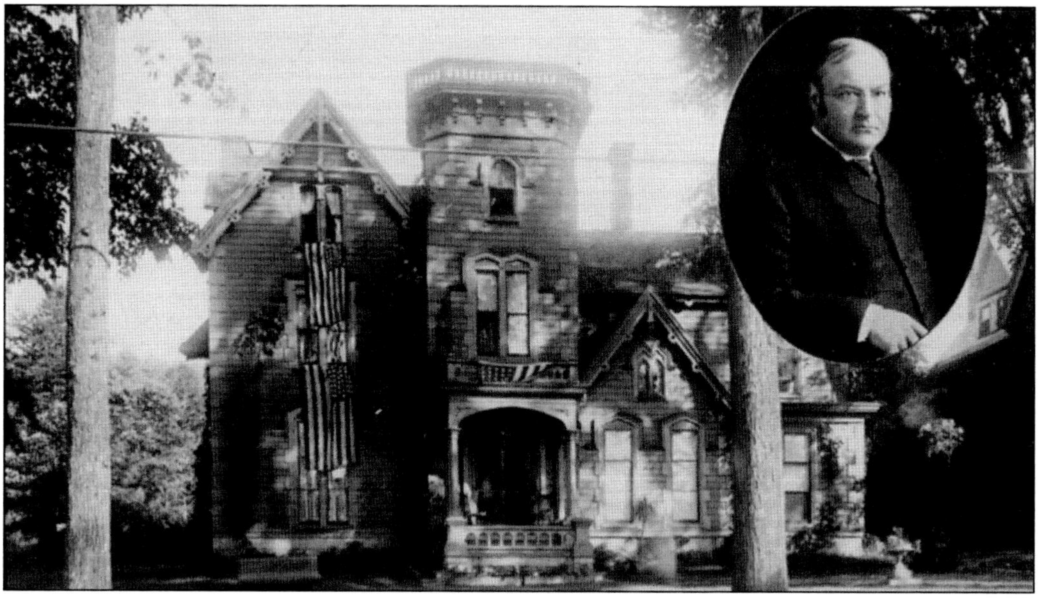

In the national election of 1912, James S. (Schoolcraft) Sherman was running for his second term as vice president under Taft but died just five days prior to Election Day. Sherman's residence was located on the east side of Genesee Street near Clinton Place. Many years later, the Sherman house was vacated and eventually torn down. Historians and the Landmark Society bemoan its razing. The property became a parking lot for an A&P Store. Later tenants were a drugstore and an automobile parts store.

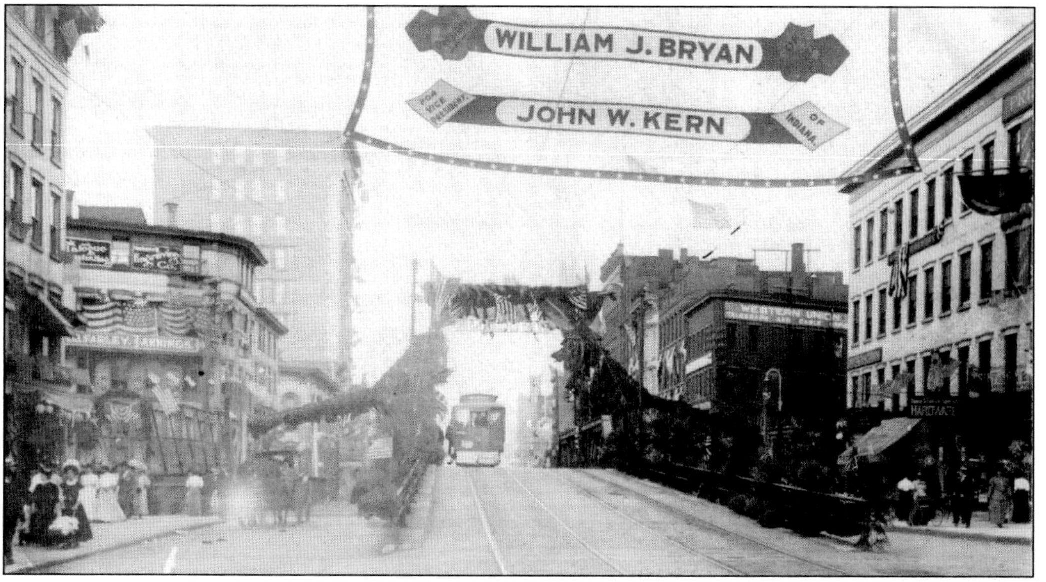

A trolley crosses the bridge on Genesee Street under a banner promoting Taft's and Sherman's opponents in the 1908 national election, William Bryan and John Kern. One who attended the Sherman Day festivities wrote a postcard to a friend saying, "This is the auto parade on Sherman Day – autos are carrying the statesman. It was a very large day." Another postcard with a picture of Sherman's Utica home informed the recipient, "Lula Younger Mason, a girl I went to school with worked here for the Shermans." (Courtesy OCHS.)

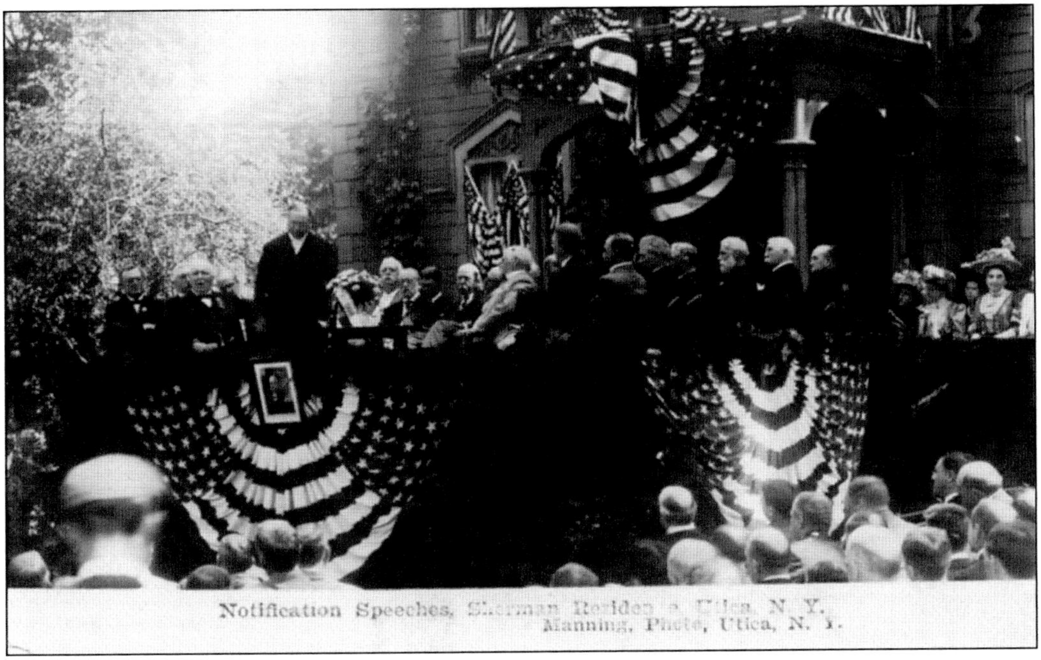

James S. Sherman addresses a large crowd in front of his Genesee Street home at Utica's celebration to honor him. An informal reception was held on July 2, 1908, followed in August by an elaborate Notification Day celebration held on the Utica Baseball Grounds in East Utica. A postcard written by one who attended the event relates, "Yesterday was Sherman Day. I never had such a time in my life."

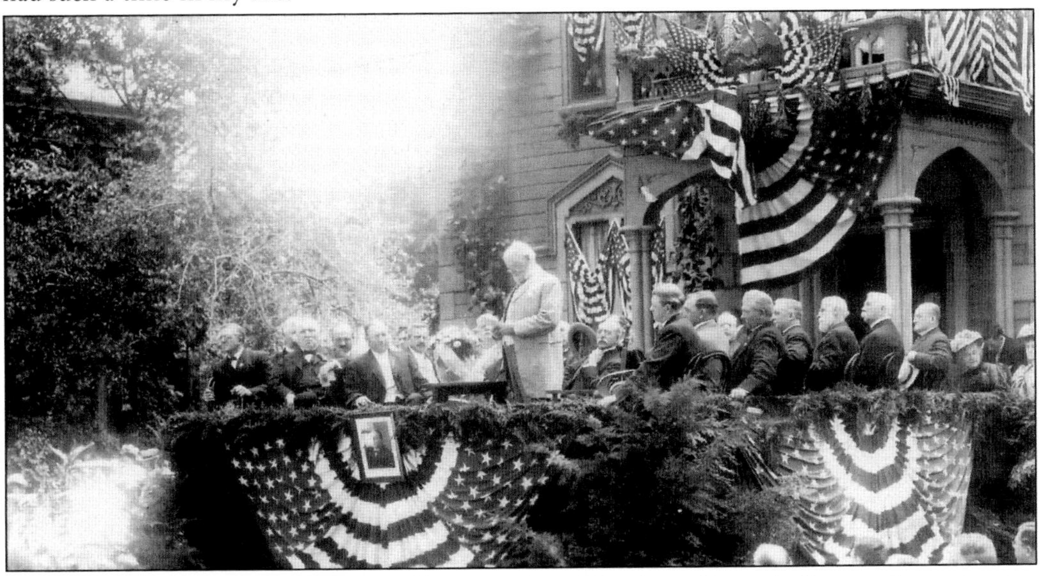

On August 18, 1908, a gala day was held in Utica in celebration of James S. Sherman's nomination as vice president of the United States, as the running mate of William Howard Taft. Many distinguished citizens appeared at the event, including local businessman and philanthropist Thomas R. Proctor (possibly the speaker in front of the Sherman home) and Secretary of State Elihu Root of Clinton. Sherman is seated to the left of the speaker, just above the framed picture. Taft and Sherman won the election. (Courtesy OCHS.)

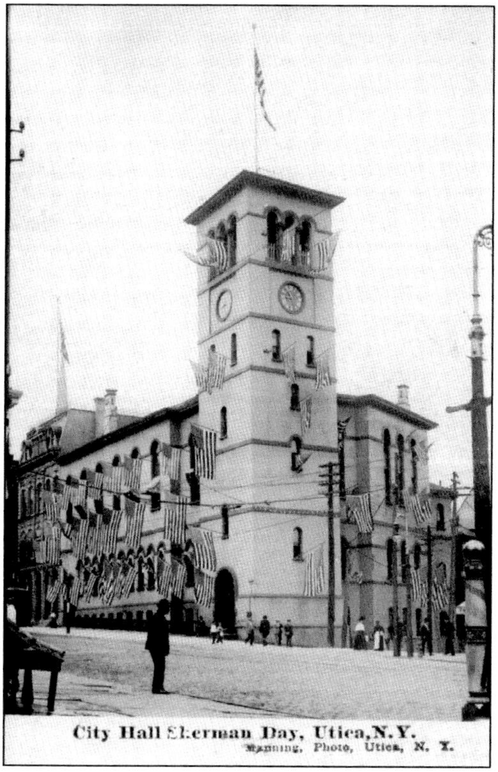

Utica's city hall is festooned with flags to celebrate Sherman Notification Day. Constructed in 1849 and designed by Richard Upjohn, it was completed in 1853 and demolished under the guise of "urban renewal" in 1968. The clock was salvaged and installed in the Tower of Hope at the new city hall, built nearby in 1975. The loss of this distinctive building inspired a movement for preservation of the city's historical and architectural heritage resulting in the formation of the Landmark Preservation Society. (Courtesy OCHS.)

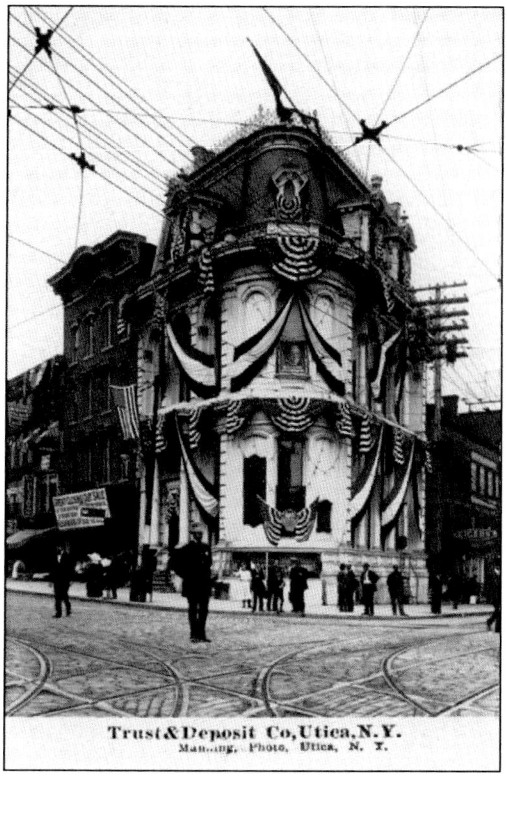

Decked out for Notification Day, the Utica Trust and Deposit Company stands on the southwest corner of Genesee and Lafayette Streets. It was modernized sometime between 1900 and 1915, changing the Mansard-style roof and eliminating the rounded corner. Incorporated in 1899 with James S. Sherman as president, it merged with two other banks in 1931 due to the Great Depression. It later relocated to the corner of Seneca and Columbia Streets. The building pictured was razed and replaced by a new building that became home to Liggett's Drug Store for many years. (Courtesy TPHS.)

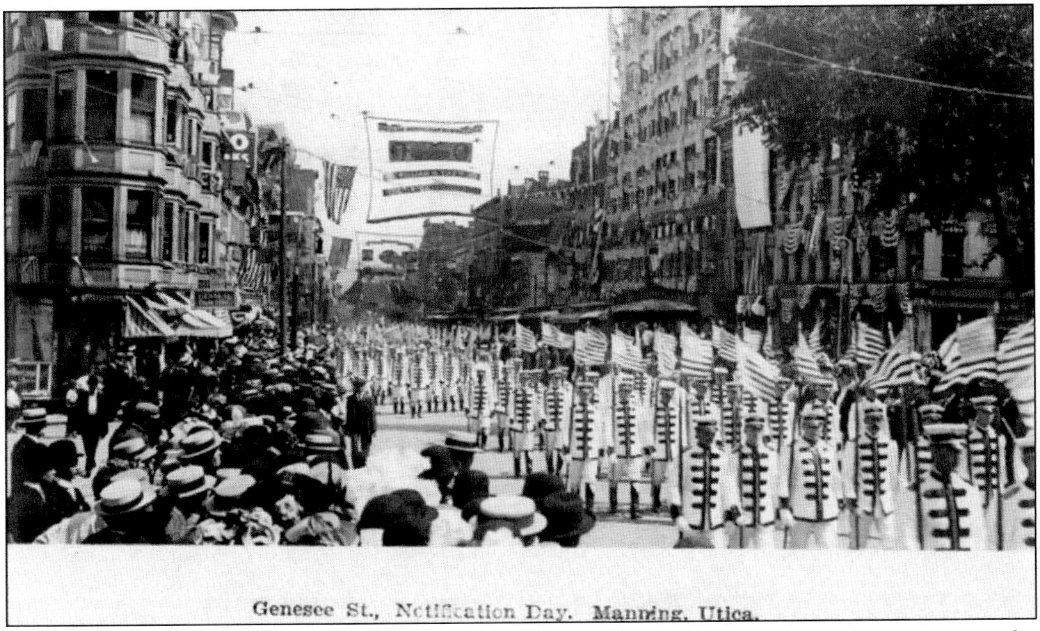

Utica Republican's marching club, the Conkling Unconditionals, strut down Genesee Street for the Sherman Notification Day parade. The group, named for prominent Utica resident United States senator Roscoe Conkling and his good friend Pres. Ulysses S. "Unconditional Surrender" Grant, was called by the *New York Times* "the best drilled marching club in the country." They wore white uniforms trimmed with black and gold.

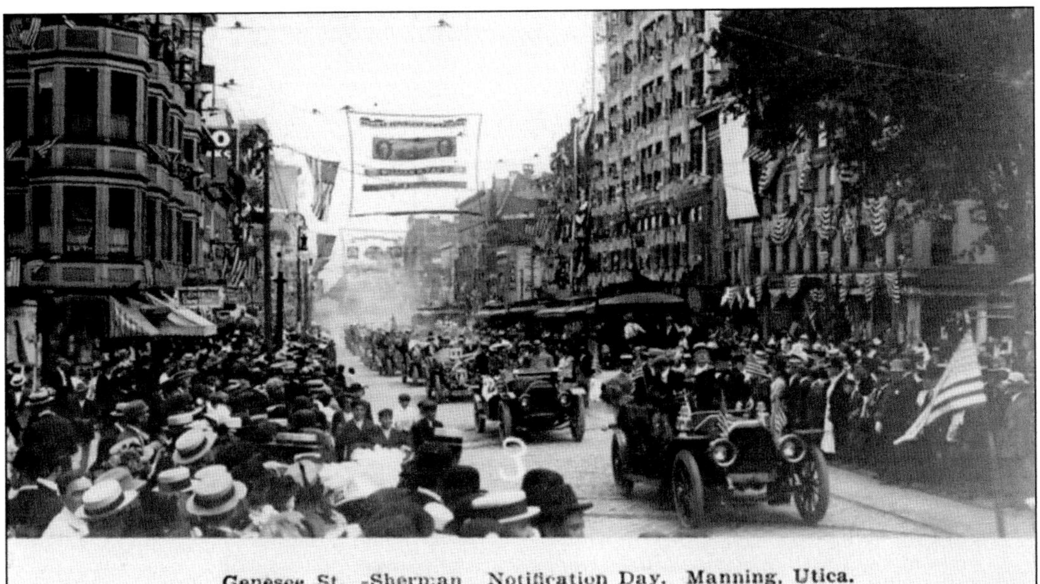

Early 1900s automobiles join the parade to honor James S. Sherman. Buildings along Genesee Street were festooned with patriotic buntings and flags. Sherman rode in an open car, accompanied by noted Utica resident Thomas R. Proctor and Utica's mayor F. J. Baker. A Utica newspaper article of the day reported, "The celebration extended over 2 days and thousands of people poured into the city by train and trolley" to honor the distinguished Utica resident. (Courtesy OCHS.)

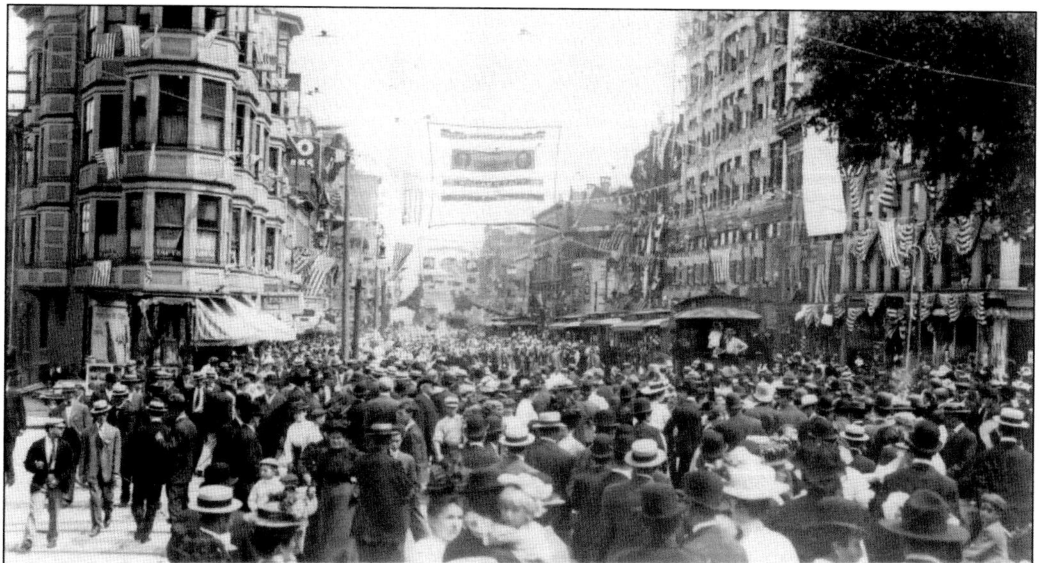

Genesee St., -Sherman Notification Day. Manning, Utica.

Wall-to-wall people are crowded between the buildings on Genesee Street to honor James S. Sherman. His public career included his election to Congress in 1886. He represented his district, except for 1891 through 1893, up until 1908. Sherman, an 1878 graduate of Hamilton College in Clinton, became active in public service soon after his admission to the bar in 1880. (Courtesy OCHS.)

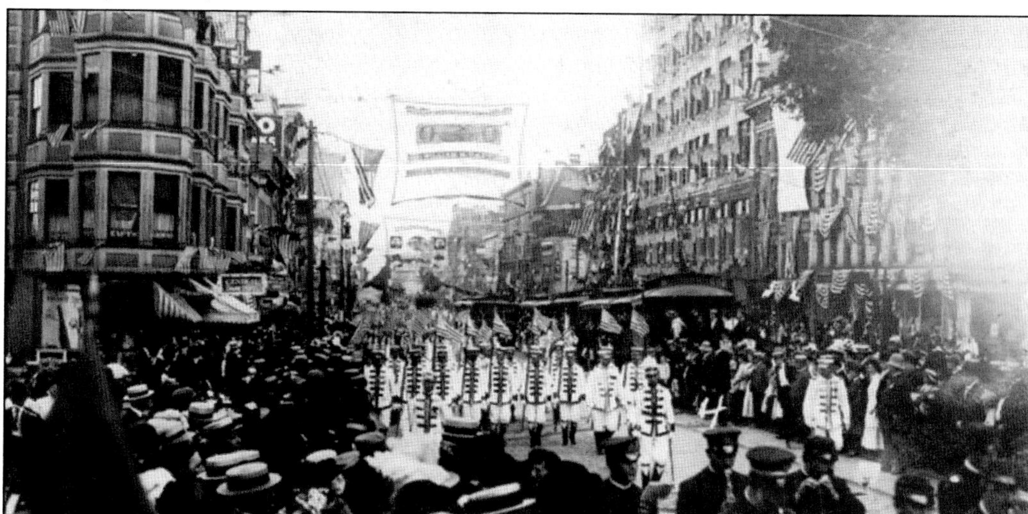

Genesee St., -Sherman Notification Day. Manning, Utica.

James S. Sherman was no stranger to the people that lined Genesee Street to celebrate Notification Day. Born in Utica, he began his study of law there, and on admission to the bar, became a partner with his brother-in-law Henry J. Cookingham. In 1884, the Republicans elected him mayor of Utica. At the end of his two-year term as mayor, he ran for representative of the United States Congress, where he continued except for one term until 1908. He was then honored with the nomination as vice-president under William Howard Taft.

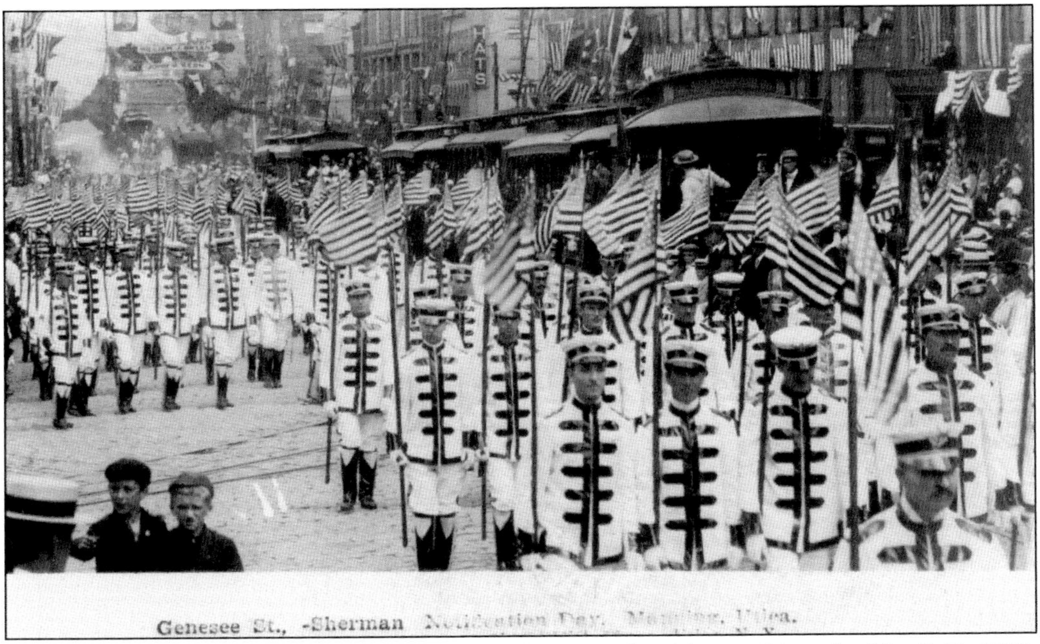

In Frank Tomaino's "This Week in History" column in the *Observer Dispatch* of April 11, 1976, he recalls that a Utica newspaper article of the day reported that "The Conkling Unconditionals – that high-stepping, fast-stepping Republican marching club – would lead the way up Genesee Street, followed by the Knights of Columbus, 120 employees of a Little Falls Manufacturing Company and village bands from the surrounding area." (Courtesy OCHS.)

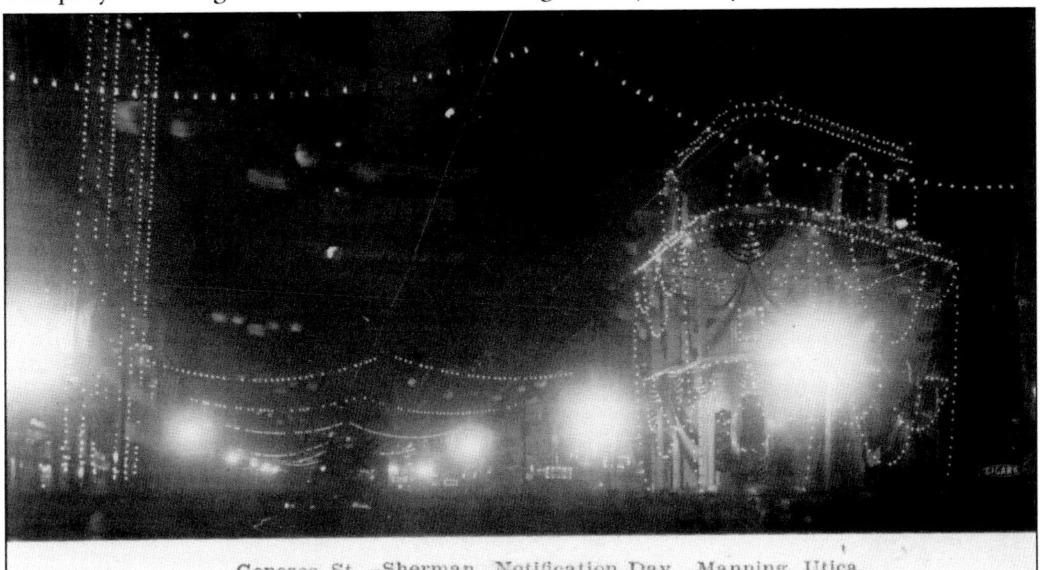

The celebration continued as Utica's Trust and Deposit Company and Genesee Street are brightly illuminated by hundreds of lights. The day's events included notification ceremonies held at the parkway. United States senator Sutherland, chairman of the Notification Day Committee, "eloquently complimented" James S. Sherman. Sherman died on October 30, 1912, at age 57, five days before the election. He is buried in Forest Hill Cemetery in Utica. A memorial statue of him at Parkway West and Genesee Street was dedicated in 1923. (Courtesy OCHS.)

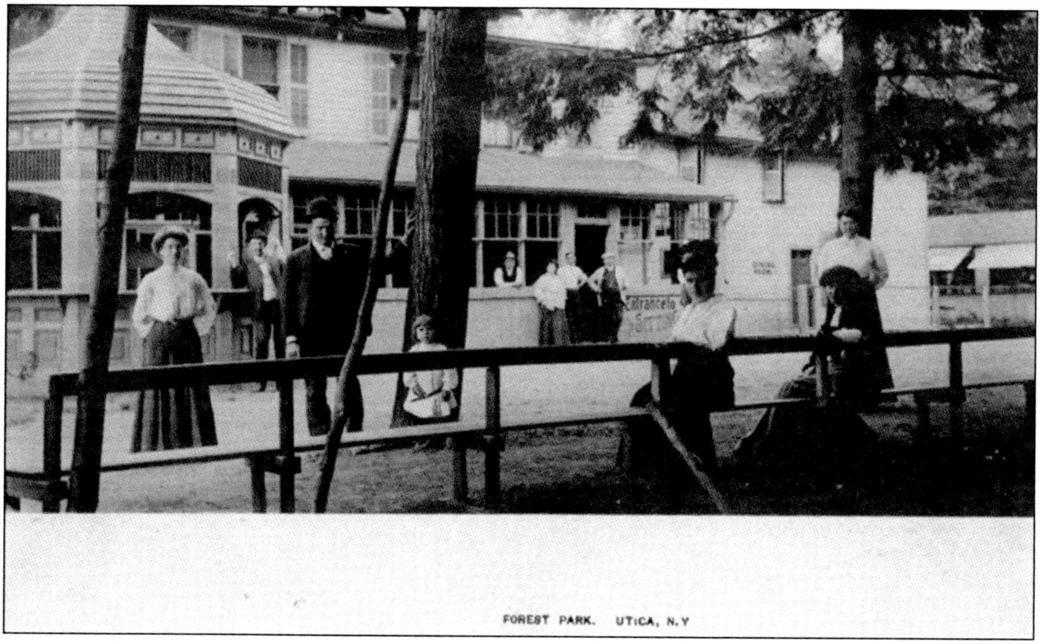

Visitors of all ages relax while visiting Utica's Forest Park. The park-goers dressed up for the occasion, a sharp contrast to today's more informal dress. Trolley service provided access to the park, a Utica recreation area located just south of Proctor Boulevard on the western side of Oneida Street. During the 1920s, more people acquired automobiles and were able to travel longer distances for recreation. Trolley parks became less profitable, resulting in the closure of this and other area parks. (Courtesy OCHS.)

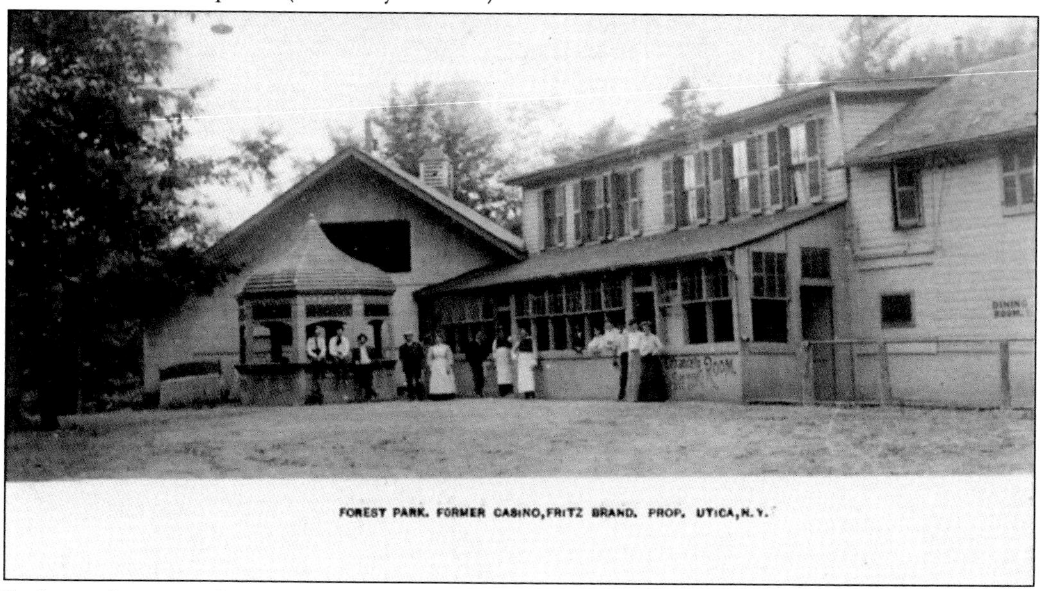

Park employees wait to greet park-goers at Forest Park, the former Casino Park and Hotel. According to an early-1900s Utica City Directory advertisement, Fritz Brand was the proprietor. Attractions such as fine Vaudeville, a concert, and dancing were held every afternoon and evening throughout the summer season, and a fine orchestra was in attendance. Trolley cars ran every 10 minutes until midnight.

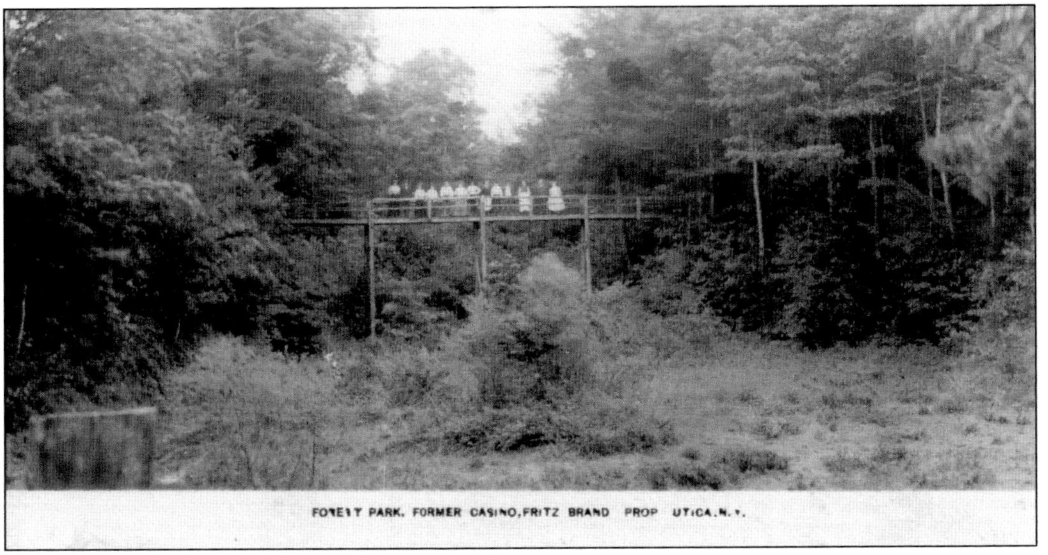

Park-goers line a bridge in scenic Forest Park, enjoying a view of the surrounding woods and waterways. This park, which opened in 1891, is often confused with the Utica Park that was located at the east end of Bleecker Street, near where the Masonic Home property and the Charlestown business complex is today. This East Utica location was first named Utica Park but changed its name to Forest Park in 1925. The East Utica Park closed in 1934. Possibly the Oneida Street park had closed by 1925, when the Utica Park changed its name. (Courtesy OCHS.)

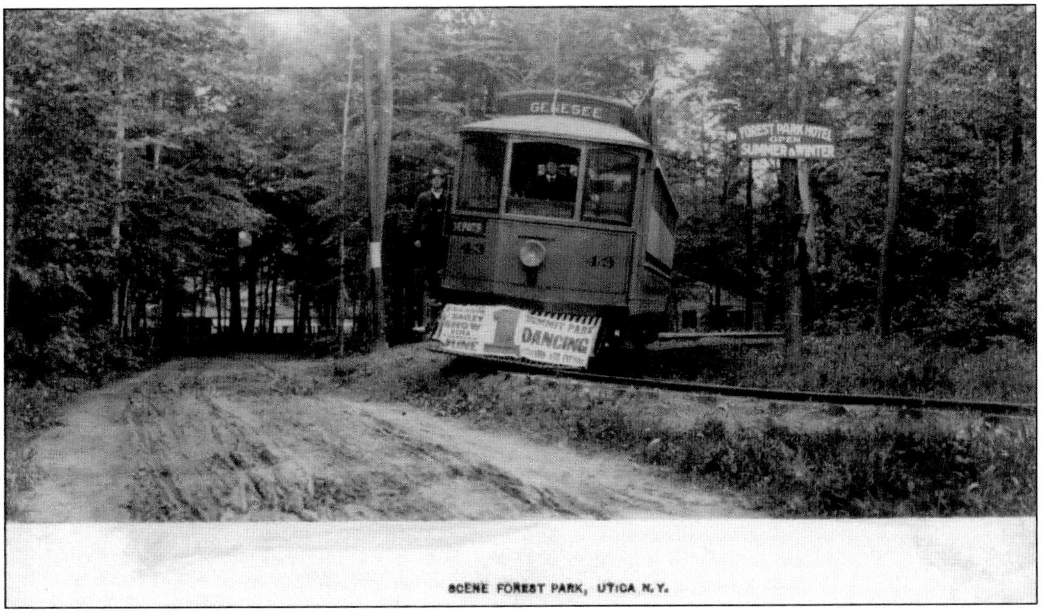

The sign reads, "Forest Park Hotel, Open Summer & Winter." The trolley, on its cowcatcher, advertises the Barnum and Bailey Circus and dancing at Summit Park in nearby Oriskany, another popular recreation area with trolley service. The Jewish Community Center, Georgian Court Estates, and the Brook Apartments now occupy land on Oneida Street that was once part of the former Forest Park. (Courtesy OCHS.)

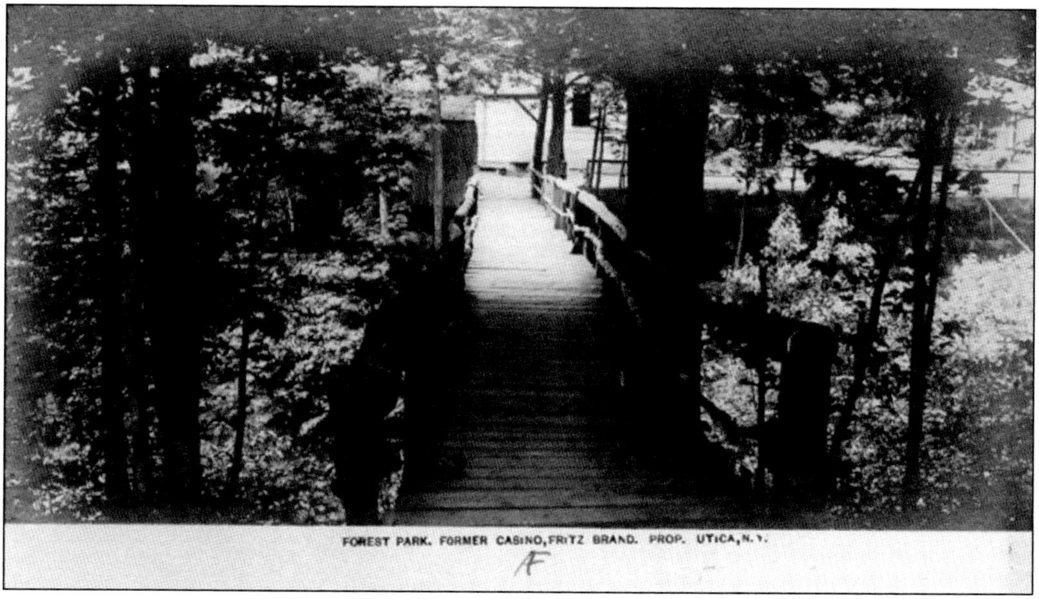

Paths and bridges in Forest Park offered visitors a quiet retreat. Most of this area from Prospect Street south to the Sauquoit Creek in New Hartford village and west to an area known as Capron was called "No Man's Land." In 1921, New Hartford residents voted to turn over a large section of this land to the city of Utica. This became official in 1922, and Utica's southern boundary then stretched south to the Sauquoit Creek bordering New Hartford.

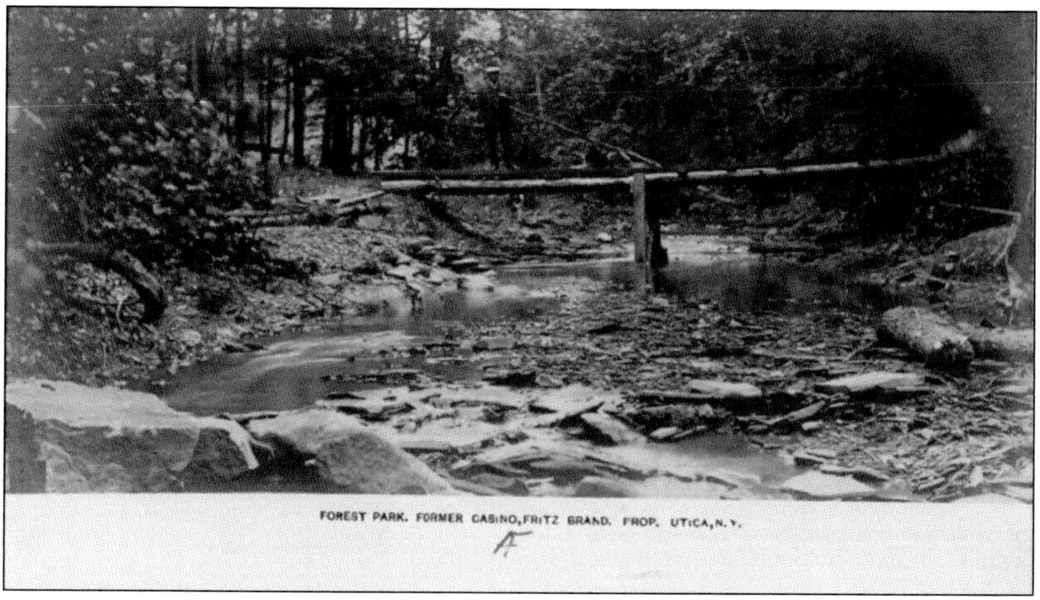

An alternative to the available amusements was nature walks through the woods and along the streams. From old maps, it appears that Forest Park was located in or near Halleck's Ravine, south of Proctor Boulevard. The area behind the apartment buildings and Jewish Community Center on Oneida Street, once recreational, is now residential.

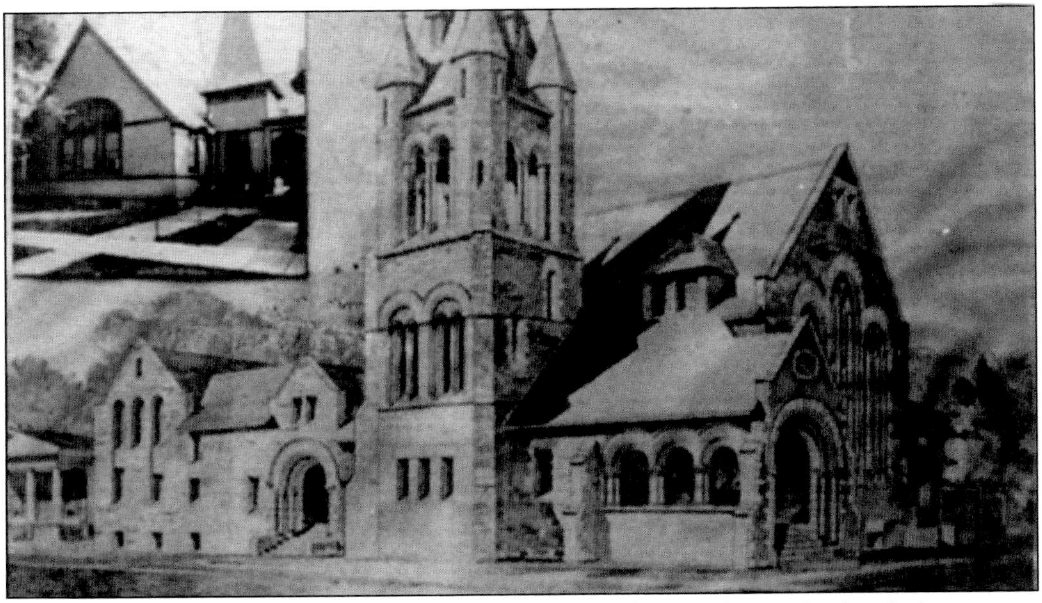

On May 13, 1883, Congregational services for 40 people were begun in the city's common council chamber. After deciding to form a Congregational society, the group was organized in September 1883 as the Plymouth Church. In 1884, property was purchased for $14,000 at the corner of Plant and State Streets and a small chapel was built. In 1905, a larger stone church was built at a cost of $70,000. This church was dedicated in June 1906. A church house was built in 1928 that in 1946 was used as temporary quarters for the newly organized Utica College.

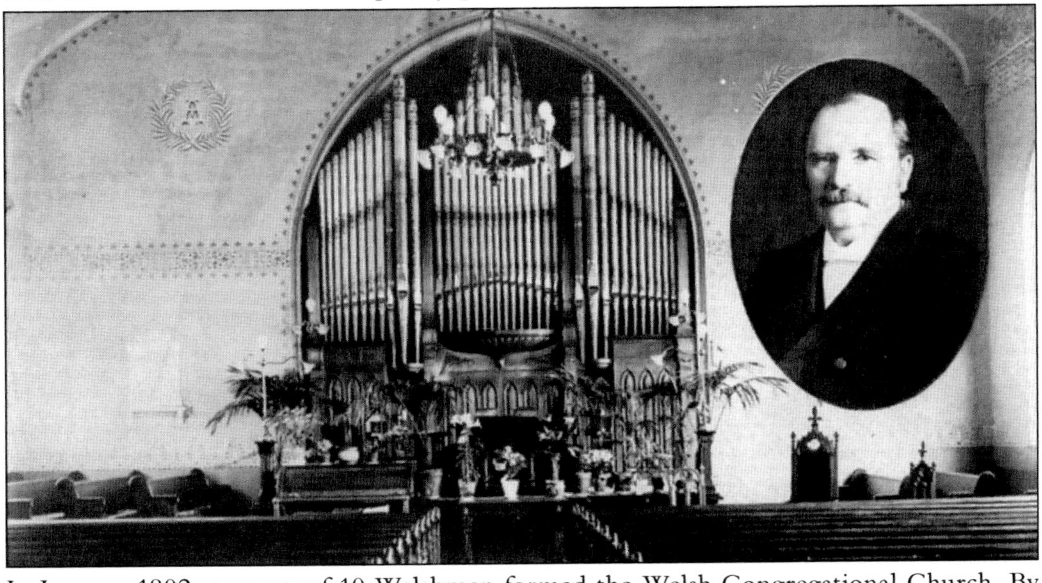

In January 1802, a group of 10 Welshmen formed the Welsh Congregational Church. By November, there were 28 members. Until a small wooden church was built in 1805 on the corner of Whitesboro and Washington Streets, services were held in members' homes. In 1836, a larger church was built near the first one. In 1872, a brick church was built on Washington Street and the name was changed to Bethesda Congregational Church, to honor a pastor from that village in Wales. Pictured is the Reverend W. Caradoc Jones, who served the church from 1902 to 1915.

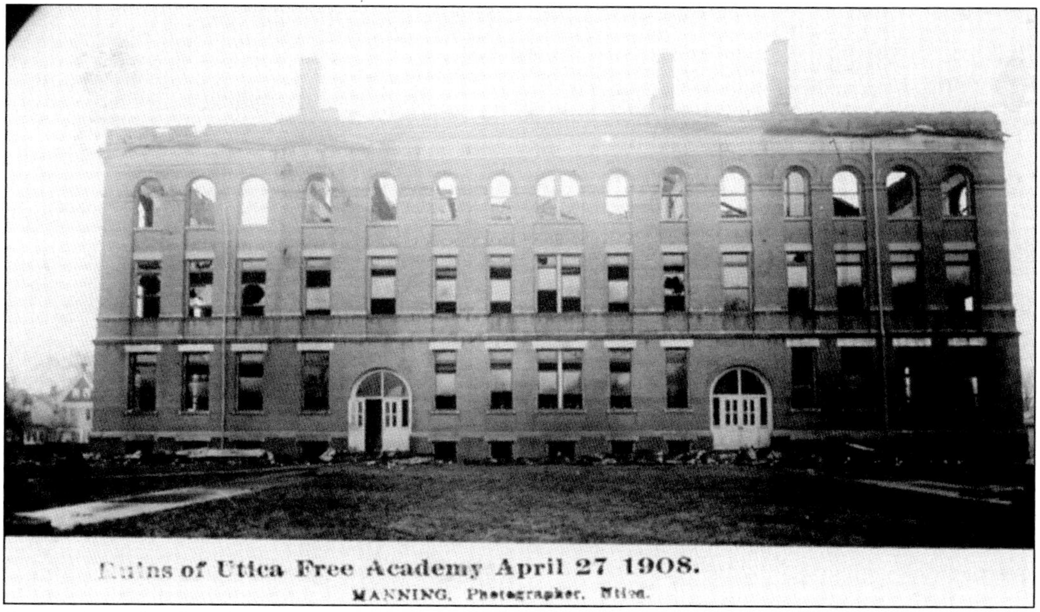

Ground was broken for the new Utica Free Academy on Kemble Street in 1896. In 1898, when almost completed, it was destroyed by fire. It was rebuilt and opened in 1899. The school was again struck by fire in April 1908, and was again rebuilt. Crowds of people filled the streets to witness the conflagration. A Utica Free Academy teacher who lived nearby sent in an alarm and ran to the school, broke glass in a door to enter, and turned on a stream of water from a standpipe (a vertical pipe extending from a water supply.) Joined by the school janitor, a former firefighter, they went from floor to floor turning on the standpipes.

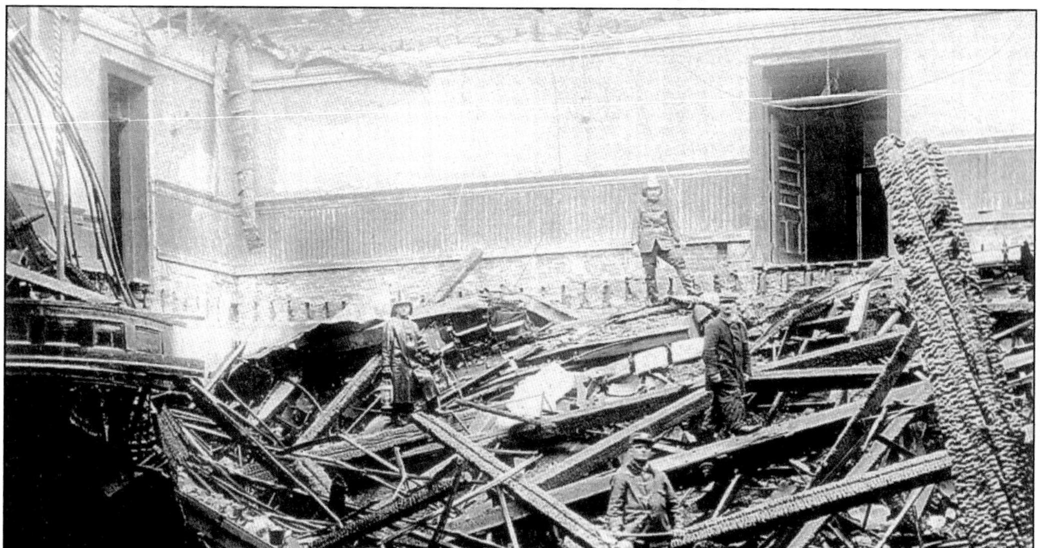

On this postcard, a chaotic scene of tangled timbers is surveyed by fireman. Starting in the attic, the flames spread quickly to the lower floors. The entire roof fell in, completely ruining the first-floor auditorium. The fire was brought under control at midnight. The damage to the structure and contents was estimated at $100,000. The school cost $175,000 to build. No definite cause of the fire was ever determined. (Courtesy OCHS.)

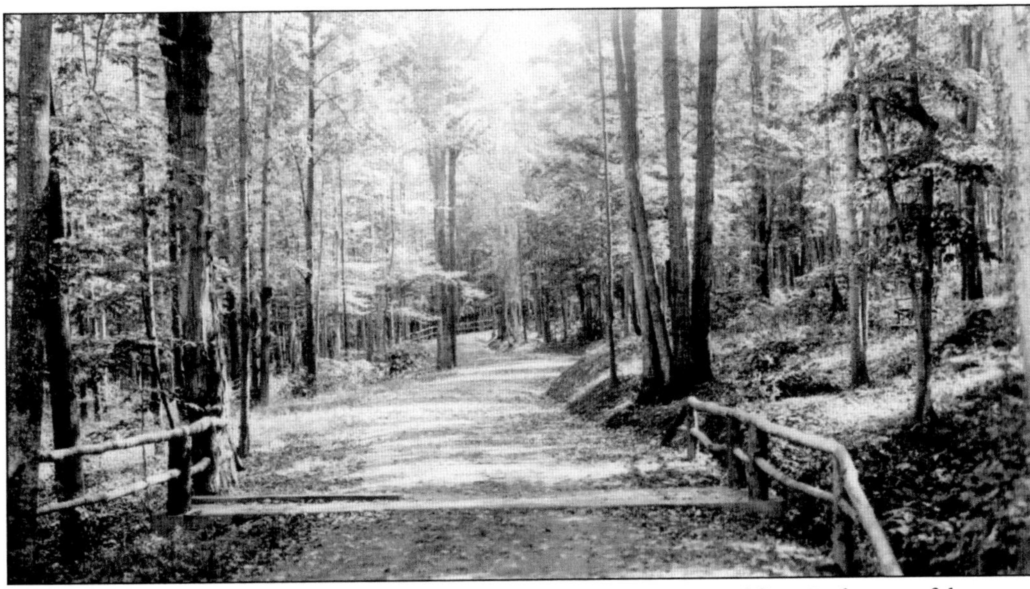

Dirt roads and rustic bridges welcome visitors to Utica's Roscoe Conkling Park, one of the many Utica parks. The land for this and other Utica parks was donated in 1908 by the Thomas R. Proctor family, which was well known for its generosity to the city. It is the largest city park at more than 400 acres. The park was named for prominent Utica resident Roscoe Conkling, who became Oneida County district attorney at age 21, Utica's mayor in 1858, a United States Congressman from 1859 to 1863, and a United States senator from 1866 to 1881. (Courteous OCHS.)

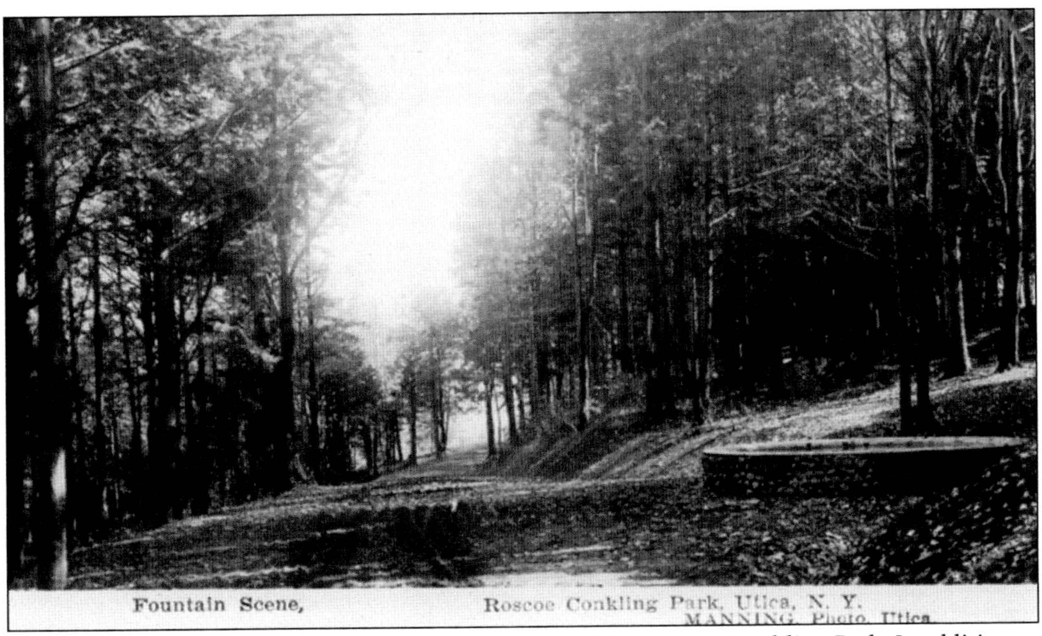

An attractive stone fountain stood along this scenic road in Roscoe Conkling Park. In addition to this park, dedicated in 1909, the Proctor family also donated land for Frederick T. Proctor Park and Thomas R. Proctor Park. In 1923, the 50-acre Frederick T. Proctor Park, the last privately owned park in the city, was given to Utica by Maria Proctor, wife of Thomas. She also paid the taxes on the land for the year and sent a $2,500 check for expenses as well.

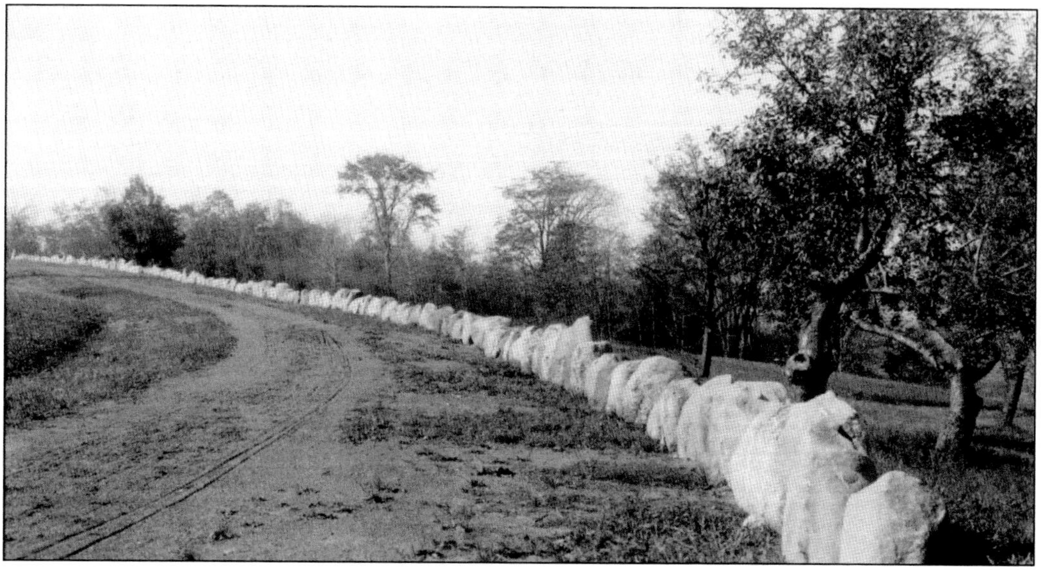

A series of articles in Utica's *Observer Dispatch* newspaper in 1992, titled a "Special Report: Utica's Decaying Legacy," indicated problems with Roscoe Conkling Park and both F. T. and T. R. Proctor Parks. Vandals smashed bathroom fixtures and fireplaces. A pavilion with a cracked concrete floor was the only intact structure. Glenn Coin of the newspaper talked to a local visitor to the park who commented, "I wonder if Conkling and Proctor would be turning in their graves?" The article states, "Beauty and neglect mingle on scenic hillside." Attempts were being made to spruce up the park. (Courtesy OCHS.)

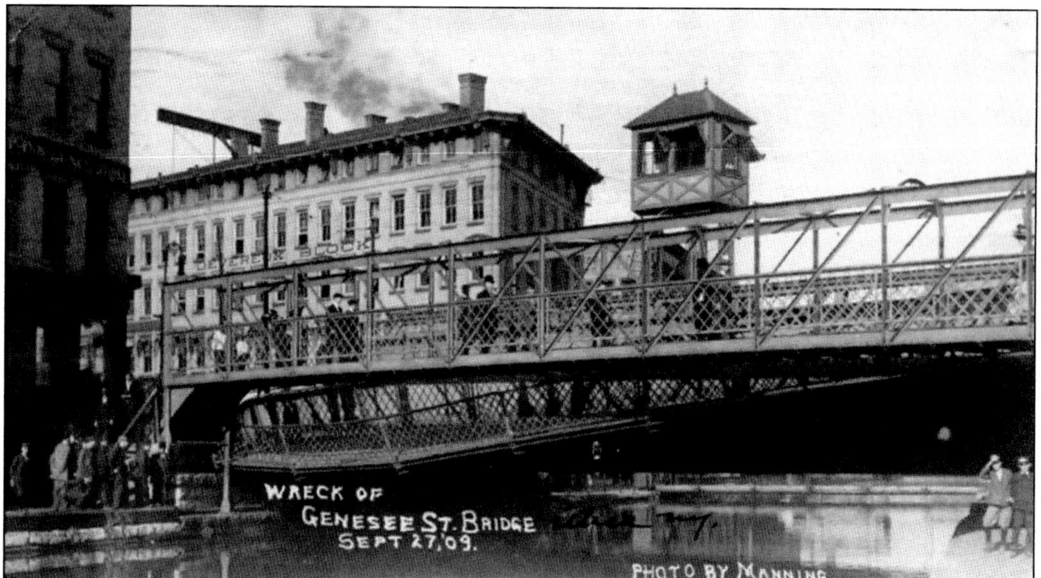

This 1909 real-photo postcard taken by Allen J. Manning was also written by him or a partner and sent to Lynn Walters, who was apparently a customer. It read, "Our Business Friend Arrived in Utica, NY all safe and we are still making photos & postcard(s) at our old stand - 124 Columbia Street. Regards and Success. Earl D. Williamson and Allen J. Manning." The Genesee Street Bridge, an old lift bridge over the Erie Canal at Genesee Street, bore the nickname "the Green Elephant," as it was a source of endless trouble and was frequently out of commission.

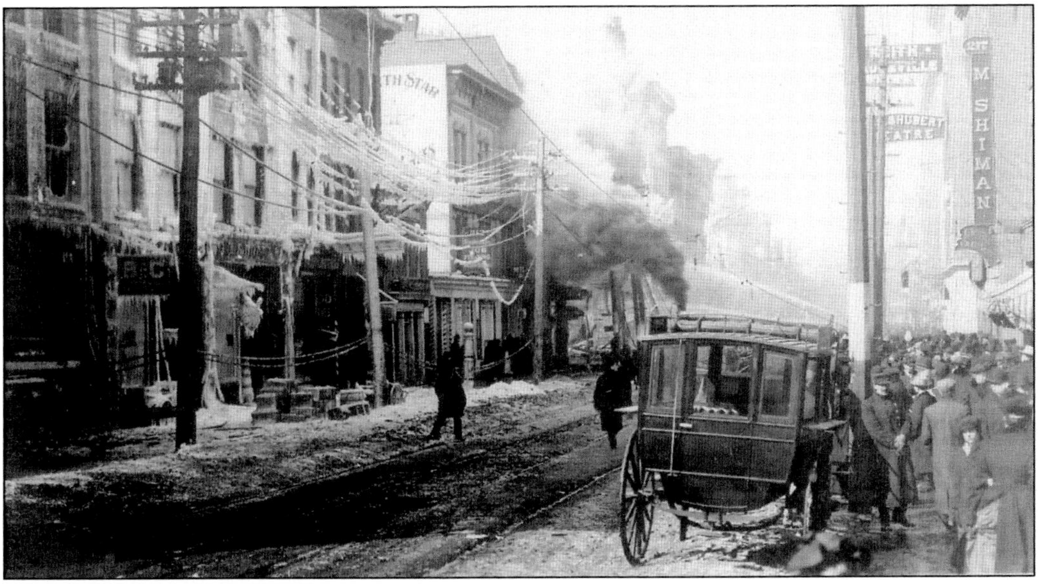

The YMCA building on the corner of Bleecker and Charlotte Streets was the site of a disastrous fire that totally destroyed the structure. Just before 3:00 a.m., a passerby noticed the blaze and turned in the alarm. The fire spread rapidly, with the heat so intense it melted the snow on the opposite side of the street. Live trolley wires created further problems. The origin of the fire was a mystery but was thought to be the result of an explosion. Spectators crowded the street to view the devastation. (Courtesy Tom Gates.)

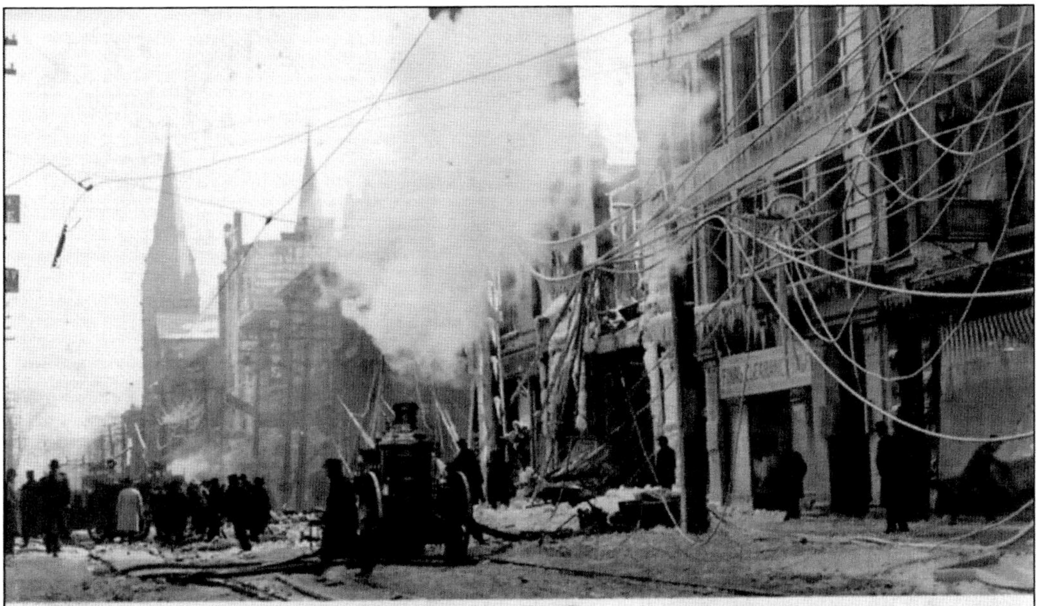

A hand pumper stands below a tangle of wires coated with ice along Bleecker Street. Dangerous circumstances were created when walls became shaky and began to fall. When the walls fell, a line of poles covering two blocks crashed to the ground. The breaking of the wires threw the street into darkness, greatly hampering the work of the firemen. Police were called to guard the wires, keeping firemen and spectators away from them.

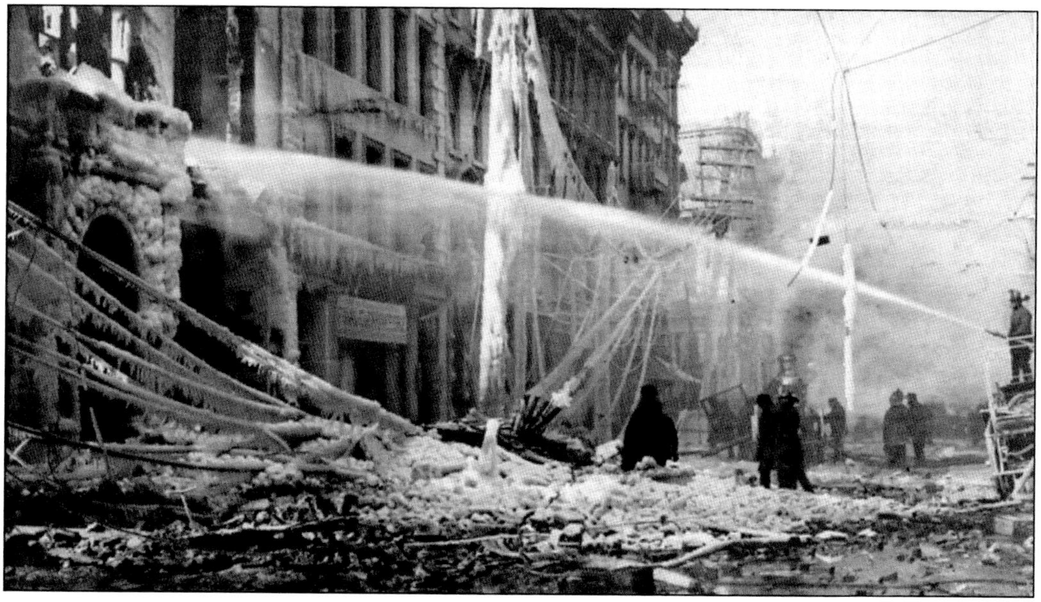

Lost in the YMCA fire was the stock of the nearby Thomas Maher clothing store and the A. Kidder Music Store. The beautiful YMCA building, erected in 1888 at a cost of $40,000, was designed by Fuller A. Wheeler, an Albany architect. The first floor contained YMCA offices, a board of directors room, reception room, parlor, reading room, library, and classroom, all newly furnished. The main assembly hall seated nearly 1,000. On the second floor was a dining room, a kitchen, locker rooms, and a bathroom. Four bowling alleys were located in the basement.

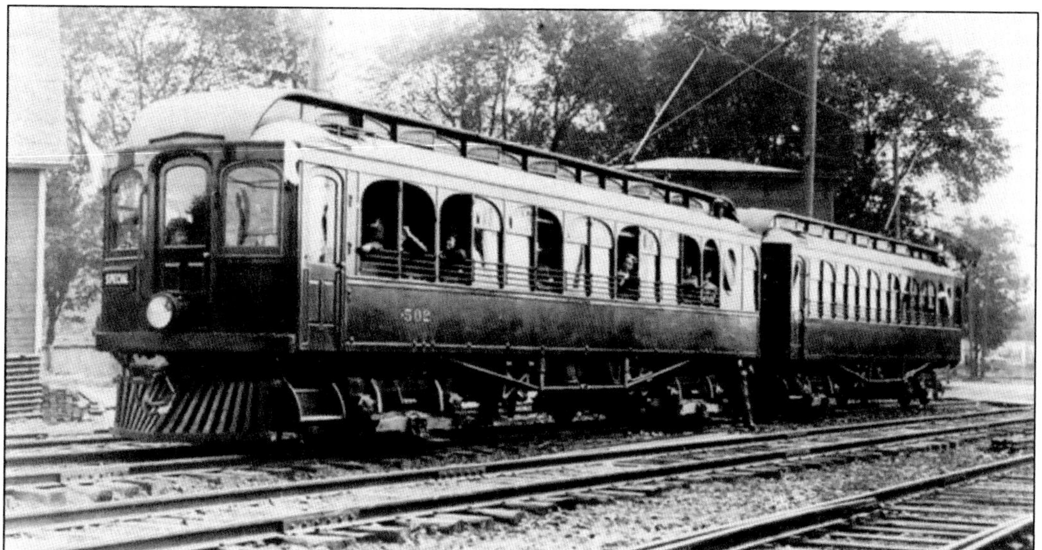

This electrified train traveling on the West Shore Railroad made its first official run on June 15, 1907. A third rail under the train was used instead of the usual overhead trolley wires. Cars made use of city tracks and overhead trolley wires to reach downtown terminals, then changed to third rail current on the West Shore's right-of-way. Electric lines dominated the rapid transit scene until the improvement of highways in the 1920s and 1930s when fast motor bus service was available and automobile use increased. By 1941, electrified trains and trolleys disappeared from the scene.

Four

Towns of Kirkland and Westmoreland

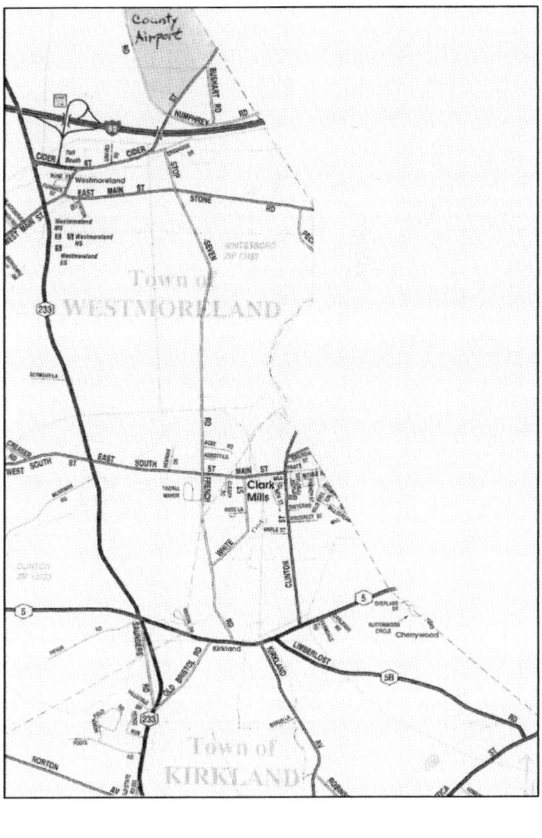

This 1995 map shows the towns of Kirkland and Westmoreland.

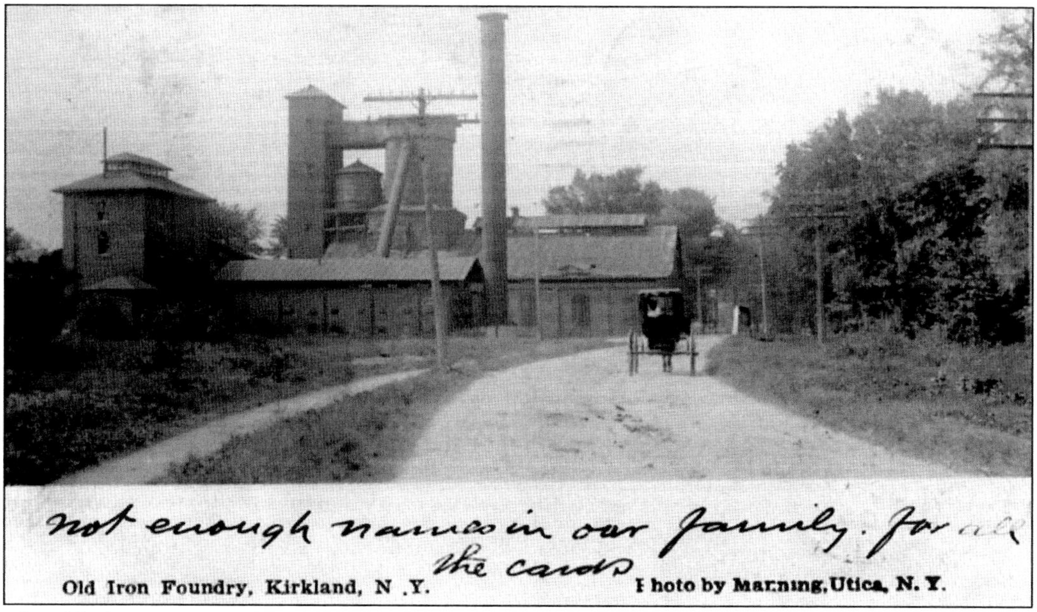

The old Clinton Iron Foundry once stood in the hamlet of Kirkland on what is now Route 5, Seneca Turnpike. Ore from the nearby Clinton Hematite Mines was used in the production of cast-iron products. Its first blast was in 1874. Never very successful, in 1878, it was renamed Kirkland Iron Company. In 1890, the company ceased production, and in 1913, the site was razed.

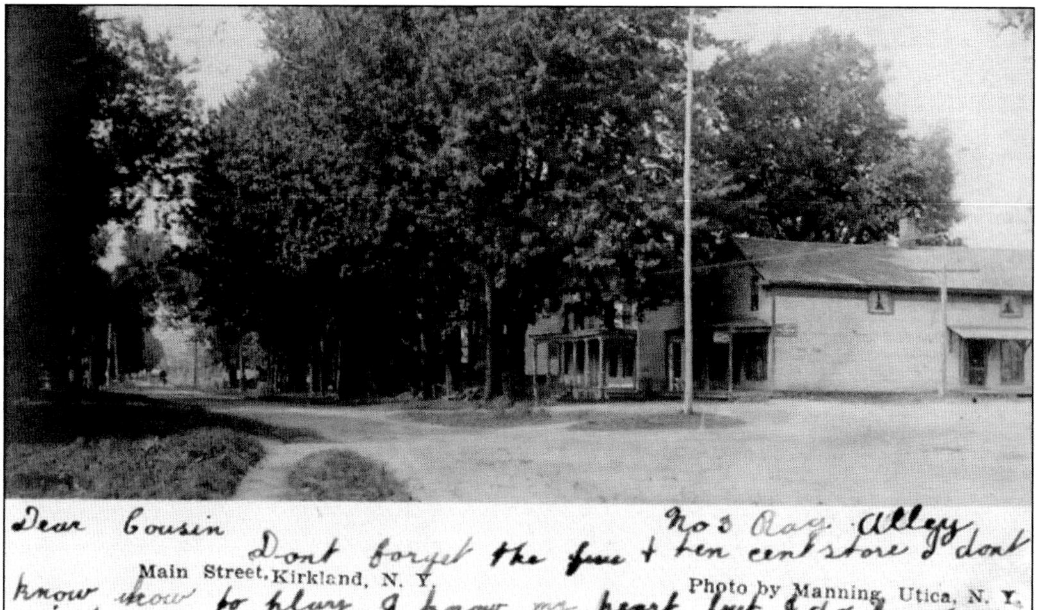

Main Street in Kirkland, State Route 5, and Seneca Turnpike was, until construction of the New York State Thruway, the main route between Utica and Syracuse. The poor condition of dirt roads caused motorists to complain that they were a menace to one's life, and they considered themselves fortunate to get through the day without a serious breakdown. Frank Tomaino's history column in the Utica *Observer Dispatch* states that in 1907, the state agreed to spend $133,000 for a 22-mile-long highway between Utica and Oneida Castle to replace the bumpy dirt road.

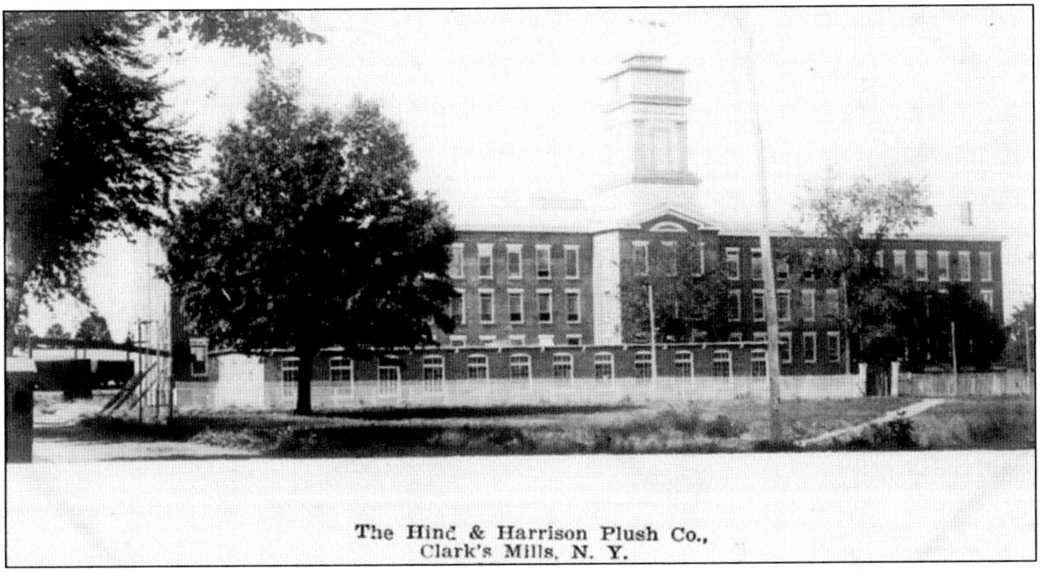

In 1891, the Hind and Harrison Plush Company was formed by Arthur Hind of England. He purchased an abandoned factory in Clark Mills, adding a dye house, weave shed, print shop, and a small general store to the original buildings. The mill's boiler and engine rooms provided power and electricity for the plant and the entire village. Hind imported workers from England and built about 200 houses and a recreation hall for his employees. The hall is now the American Legion Post. Hind's partner Harrison left the business in 1906. After Hind's death in 1933, W. R. Kennish bought the business and ran it until 1943. The mill closed in 1948.

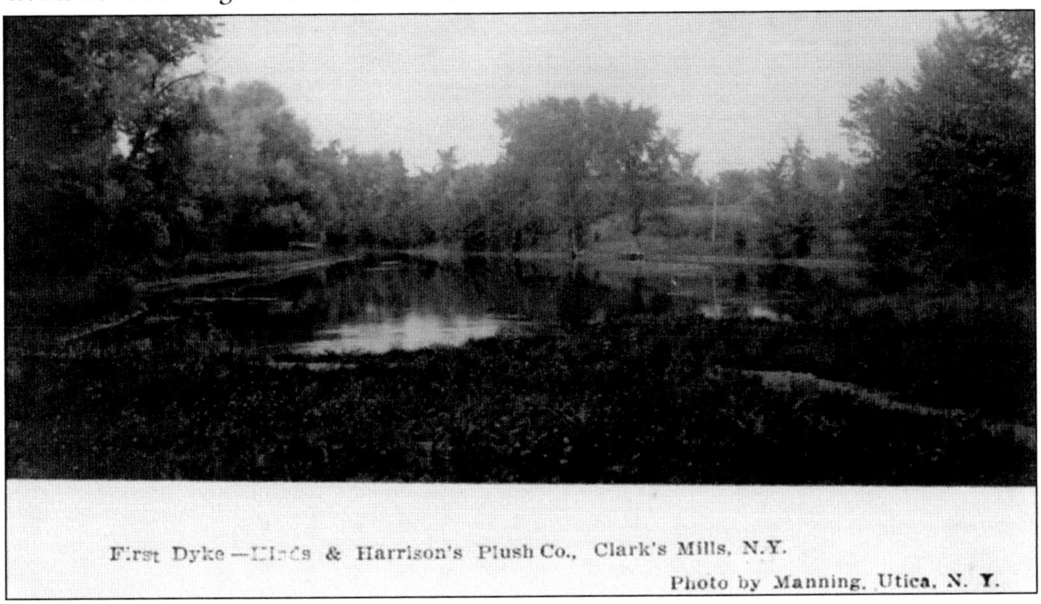

The dike system channeled water from the nearby Oriskany Creek and provided a haunt for local youngsters. At peak times, the Hind and Harrison Plush Company employed nearly 1,000 people, producing a couple million yards of plush annually. Plush is a velvet-like fabric with long, soft pile woven from silk, cotton, wool, or a combination of material. It sold from 50¢ to $10 a yard. Plush was used for wagon seats and upholstering, casket linings, coats, and automobile lap rugs and drapes, as well as for upholstery for Ford and Durant automobiles. (Courtesy OCHS.)

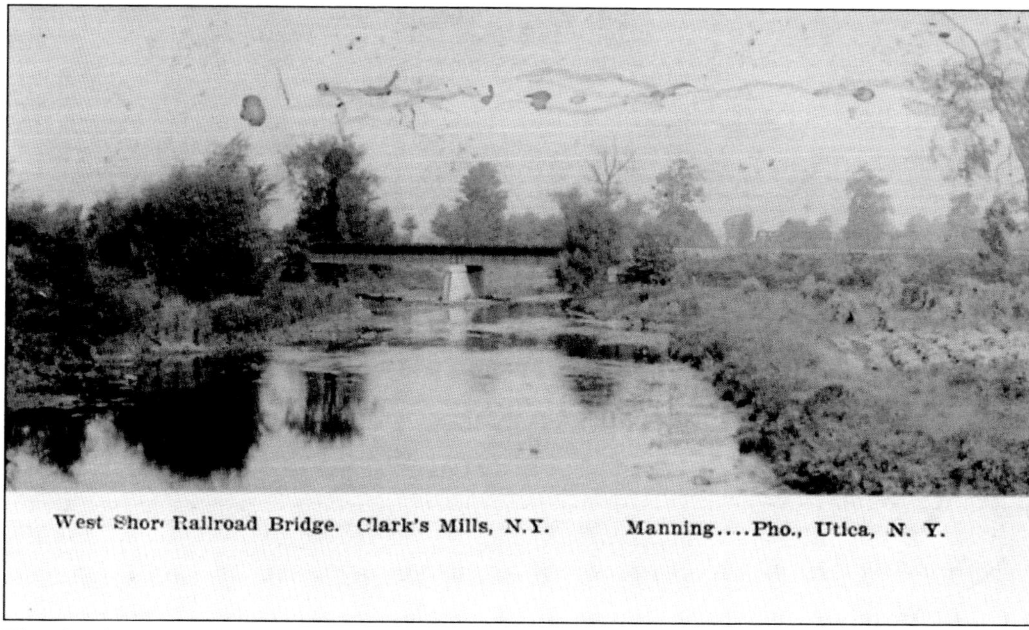

The Oriskany Creek flows beneath the West Shore Railroad bridge. In the distance at right is the tower of the Hind and Harrison Plush Mill. North of Clark Mills, the creek and the rails diverge with the tracks continuing on to Rome and the creek heading north toward the village of Oriskany, famed for the Revolutionary War battle fought there. (Courtesy OCHS.)

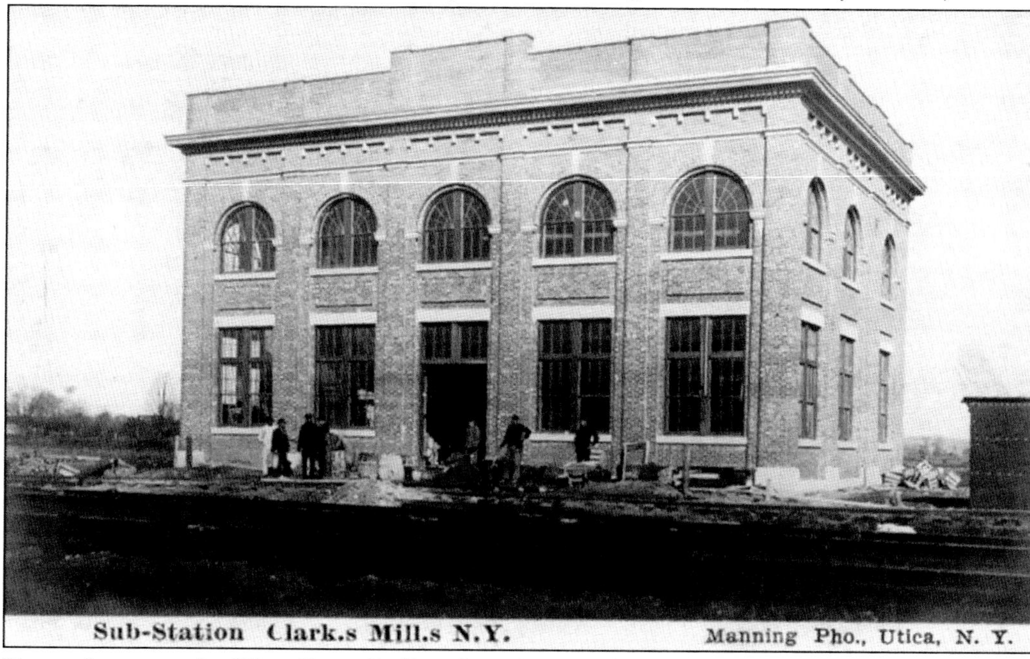

Situated next to the West Shore Railroad tracks was the third rail power station. It became the Acee Meat Company slaughter house for about 40 years. Later owned by Sunrise Mean Company, followed by Utica Veal Company, it burned down in the 1980s. A concrete slab is all that remains of the old power house, and the tracks have been removed. Treeless in this 1907 view, the area is now covered by a thick growth of trees near Acee Lane.

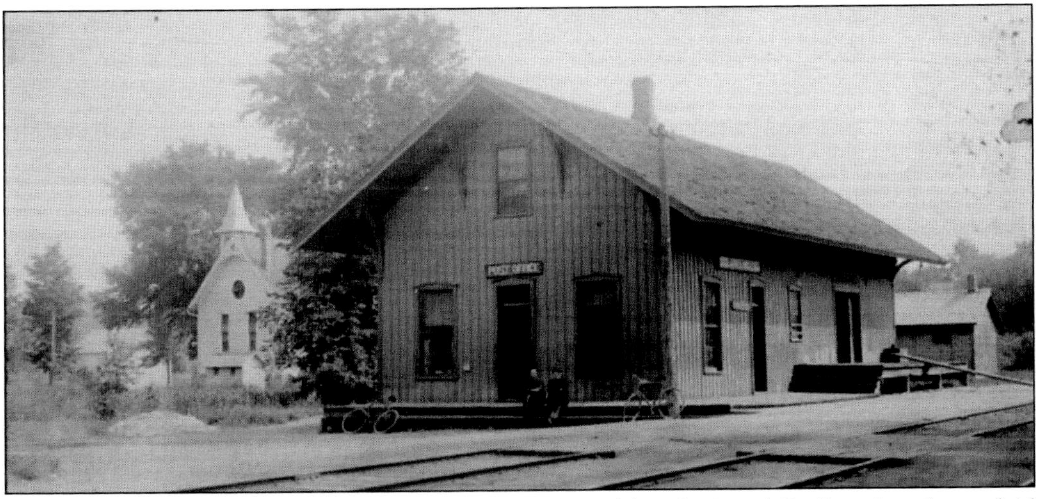

The 13-mile-long Ontario and Western (dubbed the Old and Weary) Railroad track was laid in 1870 at a cost of $250,000. The train ran the 45-minute, 13-mile round-trip between Rome and Clinton three times a day. Primarily a freight carrier, the train had, instead of the caboose, a combination car that accommodated passengers and served as quarters for the crew. The Great Depression, declining fortunes of the railroad, and the increasing use of private cars resulted in discontinuation of the passenger service in 1931. Soon after, the depot closed and was razed in the late 1940s. The Methodist church is left of the station. (Courtesy OCHS.)

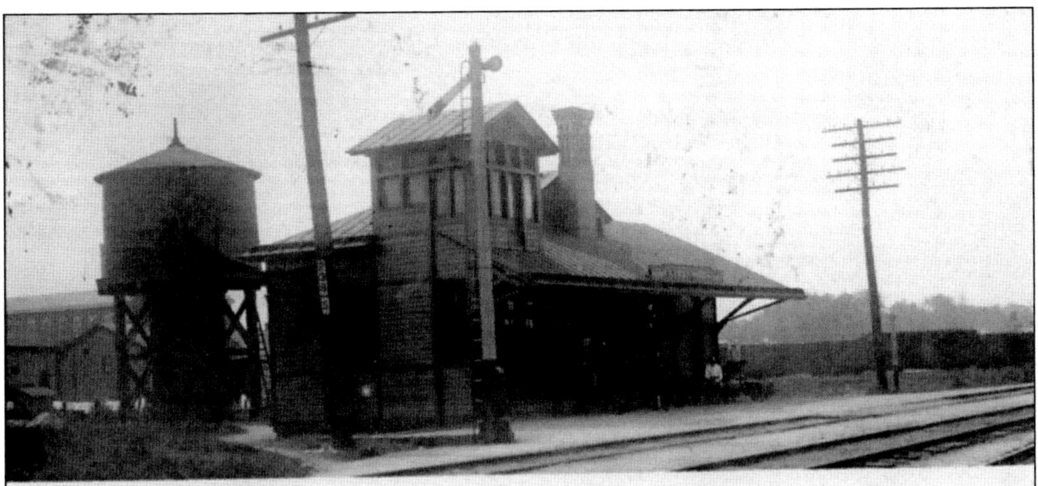

In 1907, third rail trolley service began in Clark Mills on the electric West Shore Line, operating until December 1930 and providing service between Utica and Syracuse. The West Shore Depot served the third rail trolley and the railroad. The West Shore baggage station remained open until 1950, and in 1957, was torn down.

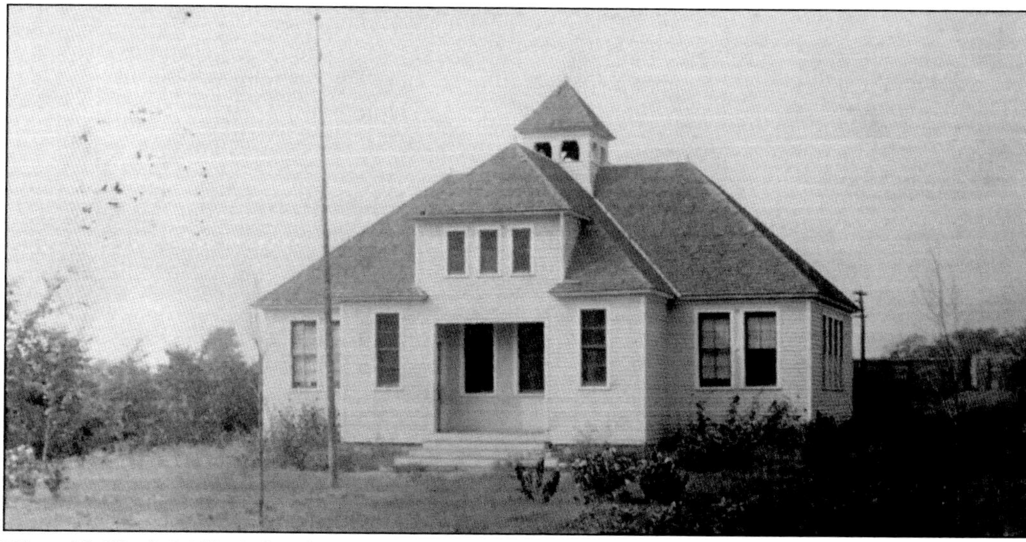

The old Clark Mills School was located where the Fireman's Field is today, adjacent to the lawn of the American Legion. Originally a two-room schoolhouse, it expanded over the years, adding a second story around 1915. In the 1930s, high school students became part of the Clinton Central School system. The Frances E. Rhodes Library occupied an addition at the rear. A new elementary school was opened on South Street in 1957. In 1980, the Clark Mills school closed permanently, and elementary students then attended Clinton Central School. The school building is now known as Cambridge Manor Apartments.

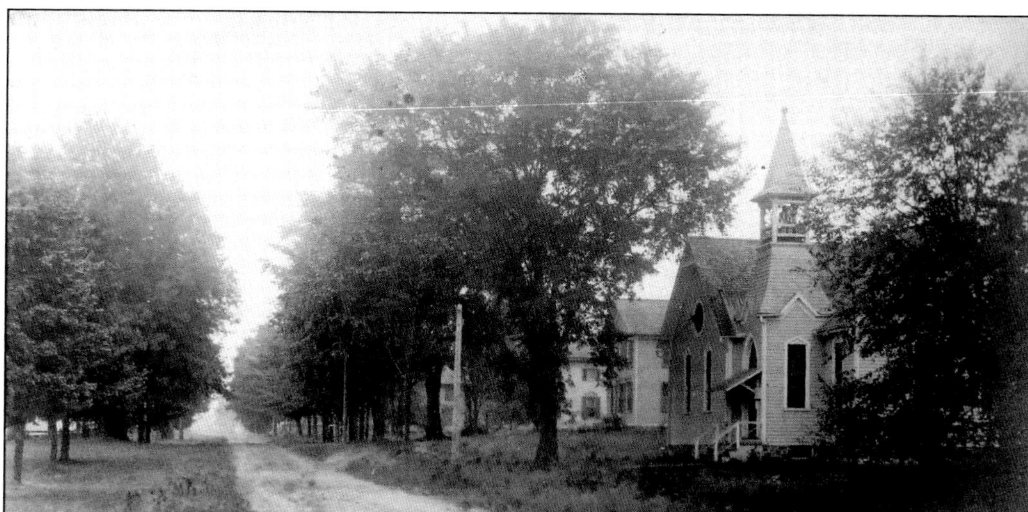

The first Methodist Episcopal church of Clark Mills was organized in 1894. Services were held over Lynch's Store. They resolved to build a new church and selected a lot between Clinton Street and the New York Ontario and Western Railway Station near the corner of Mill Street. The lot was purchased for $200. It was said the pastor, Rev. F. B. Stanford, drove his horse and buggy into the creek bed and with his own hands dug out the stones that were used for the foundation. The church was built in 1895. About 1914, an addition was built, providing room for the Sunday school and for social activities. The church is still active today.

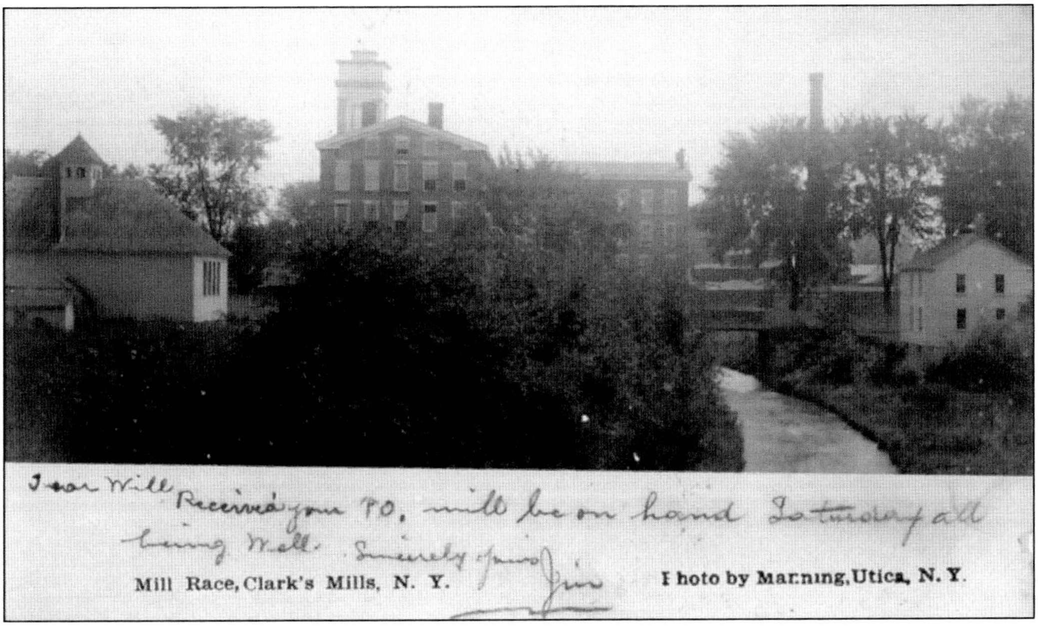

The Oriskany Creek provided the waterpower for the early factories in Clark Mills. At center is the Hind and Harrison Plush Company. The millrace diverted water from the creek to the mill and also provided summertime recreation for local children. At left is the Clark Mills School, around 1906, on the north side of Main Street. The building at right was Tony's Grill, known for its delicious spaghetti.

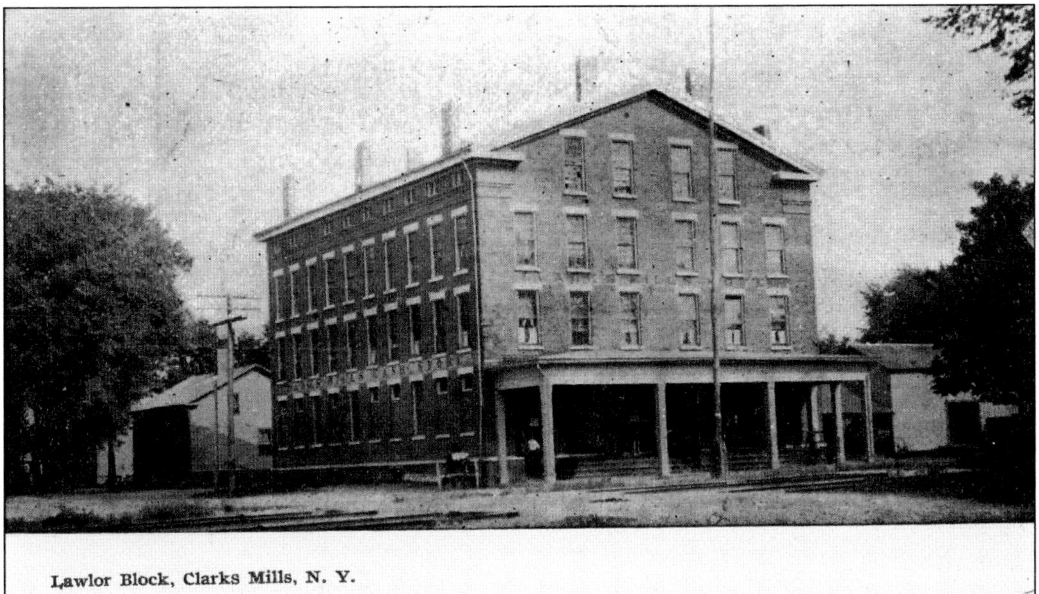

Although referred to as a hotel, this building was never actually a hotel. It once was Lawler's Store, an early department store, and O'Brian's Saloon. The O'Brians' living quarters were on the second floor, and apartments occupied the third floor. The top story was a dance hall. For a short time, the building was used for a school. The Hind and Harrison Company later bought the building and made apartments there. The building no longer exists.

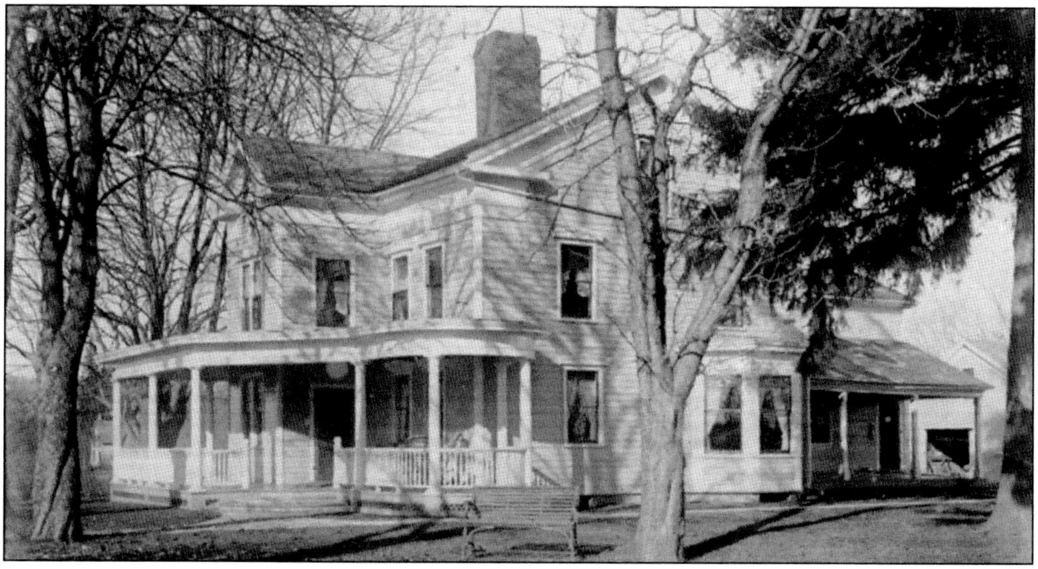

At the end of Maple Street, off Clinton Street, is the former Copeland residence. Originally Nathan Thompson had a gristmill and home there. At one time, the Clarks for whom Clark Mills was named lived here. When Arthur Hind owned the Hind and Harrison Plush Mill, he lived in the house and also had an apartment in Hotel Utica. When Hind moved out in 1909, P. W. Copeland, one of the original group from England and Hind's right-hand man, moved in and lived there with his family until he retired in the 1920s. The house was then purchased by the plush company and was rented until Dr. Louis Strobino bought it in 1948.

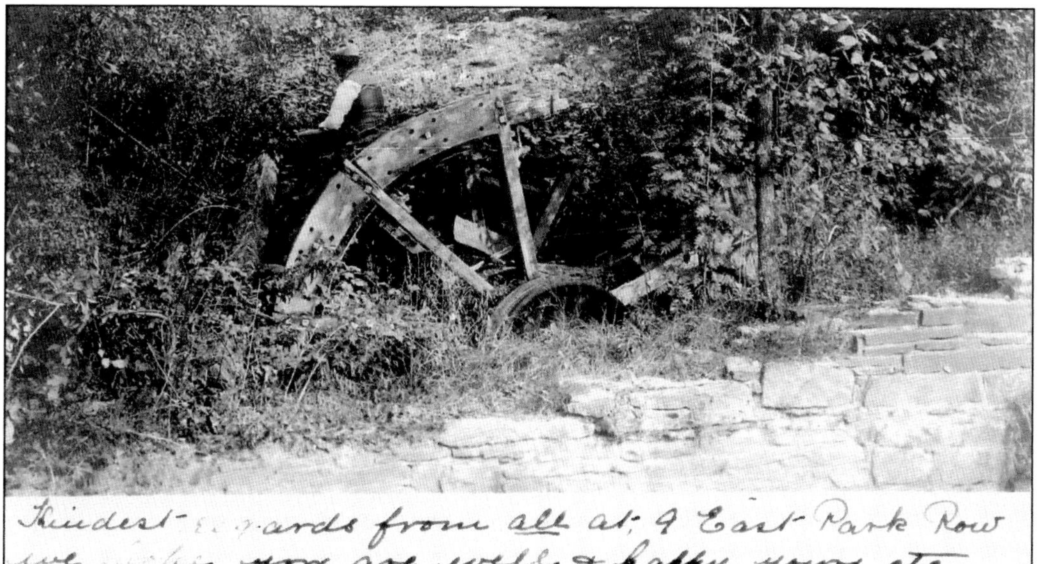

The ruins of an old waterwheel next to an old stone wall create a picturesque view along the Oriskany Creek. Sitting atop the wheel is Mr. Manchester, a resident of nearby Clinton Street. In the early 1790s, Nathan Thompson built a gristmill and a residence at the end of what is now Maple Street that runs west off Clinton Street. The waterwheel was from this early gristmill. The late Dr. Louis Strobino found a millstone at the site of the old mill and placed it in his garden where it still resides. (Courtesy Tom Gates.)

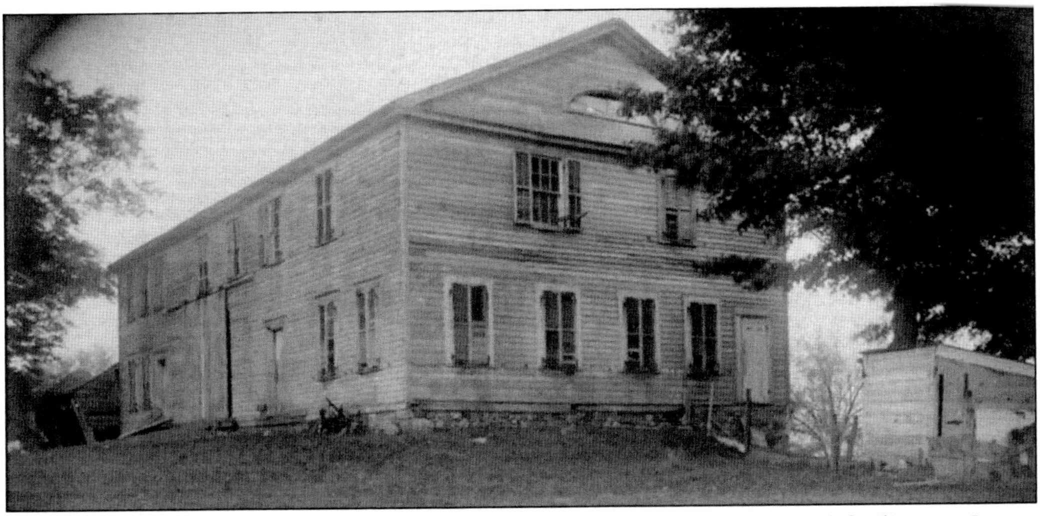

The Old Institute, once known as the DeLancey Institute, an educational facility on Graves Road in Westmoreland (then known as Hampton), was a boarding school for young ladies and gentlemen. Formerly a hotel operated by Samuel Halleck, it was situated in a grove of trees and was famous for the nearby mineral springs. Halleck sold the property in 1860 to A. G. Williams, who turned the hotel into an educational facility and named it Williams Collegiate Institute. The Graves family purchased the property in 1906 and used the former hotel and college for a barn. The main building was demolished in 1953 when the New York State Thruway was constructed nearby. It is said that Pres. Grover Cleveland attended this school and left his initials carved on a tree.

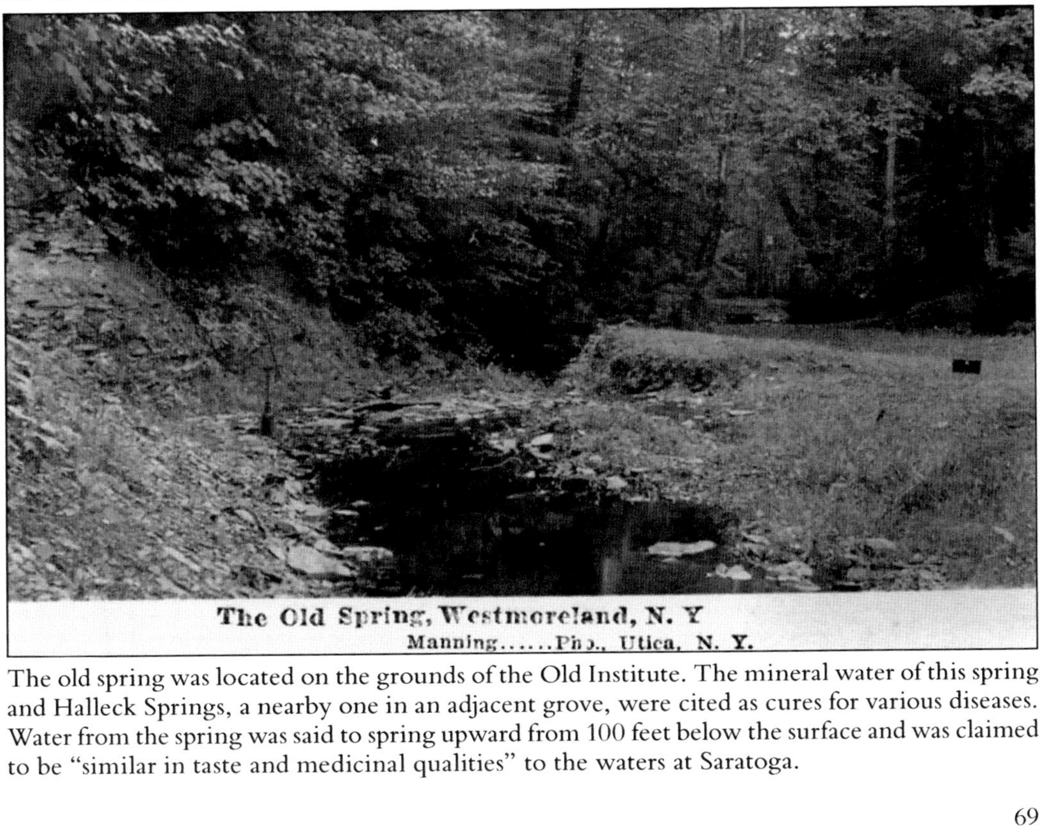

The old spring was located on the grounds of the Old Institute. The mineral water of this spring and Halleck Springs, a nearby one in an adjacent grove, were cited as cures for various diseases. Water from the spring was said to spring upward from 100 feet below the surface and was claimed to be "similar in taste and medicinal qualities" to the waters at Saratoga.

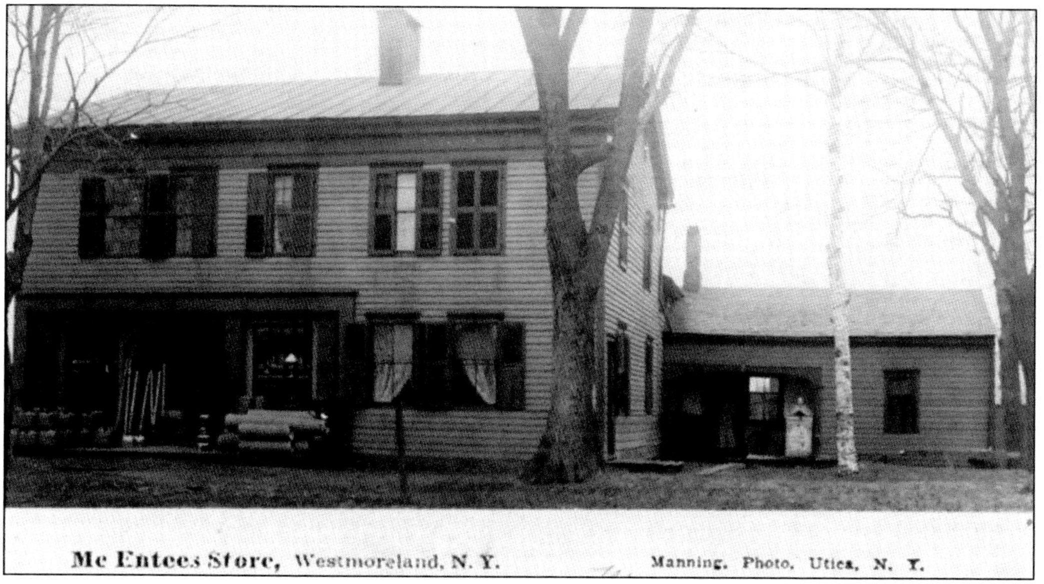

On the southwest corner of Route 233 and West Main Street, once the site of Madore's Texaco Station, there is now a Nice 'n Easy convenience store. The corner received its name from Arthur D. McEntee, who ran a hardware store and tin shop there earlier, previously established by Townsend and Bliss and later the Smith brothers. In 1927, Harold and Lloyd Storey Sr. operated a hardware store and Chevrolet sales business there. The hardware business, operated by the Storeys, moved across the road into a new building on the southeast corner. (Courtesy of Nancy Pritchard.)

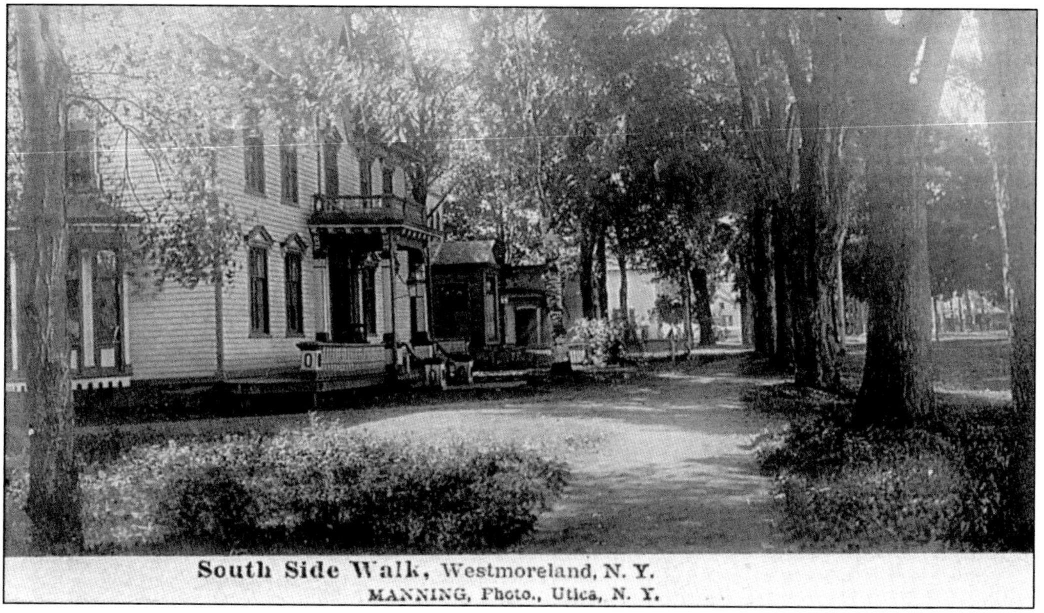

On the south side of West Main Street stood a local hotel shaded by towering trees. In subsequent years, it became a private residence. It was then used by the school district for a time before being converted once more into a private home, and it later became an apartment house. The building no longer stands on West Main Street. The corner is now a parking area for the Nice 'n Easy store. (Courtesy of Brenda Jones.)

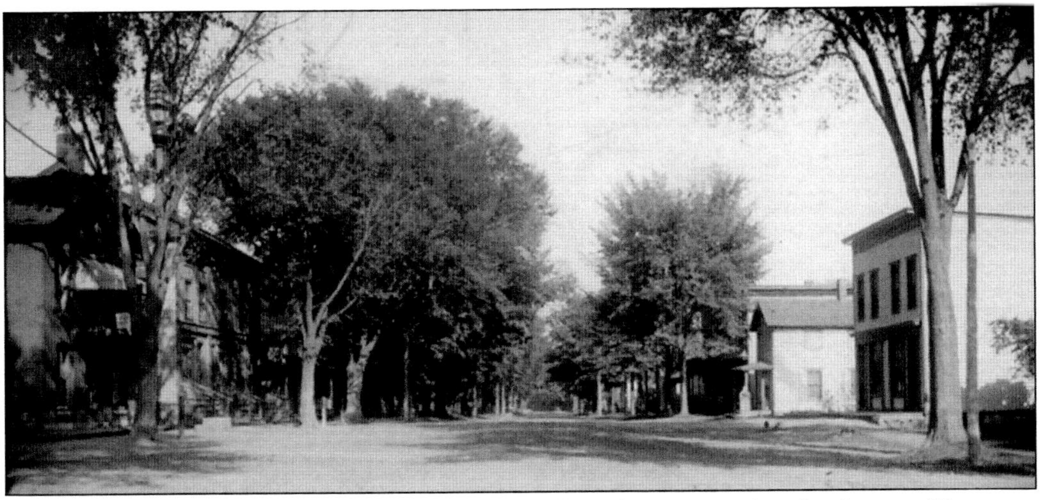

This building on the right, over 100 years old, has been home to various businesses. The many owners include Archibald McCostly, who first bought it in 1894. He was succeeded by many later owners. Tom Lawrence operated a tinsmith shop there in 1928, and by 1930, it was a poolroom and barbershop. In 1935, it was a barroom. Later the building housed apartments and the Westmoreland Post Office. In recent years, it was occupied by a real estate office, with a three-bedroom apartment upstairs. The real estate firm left, and the building has been remodeled into two apartments.

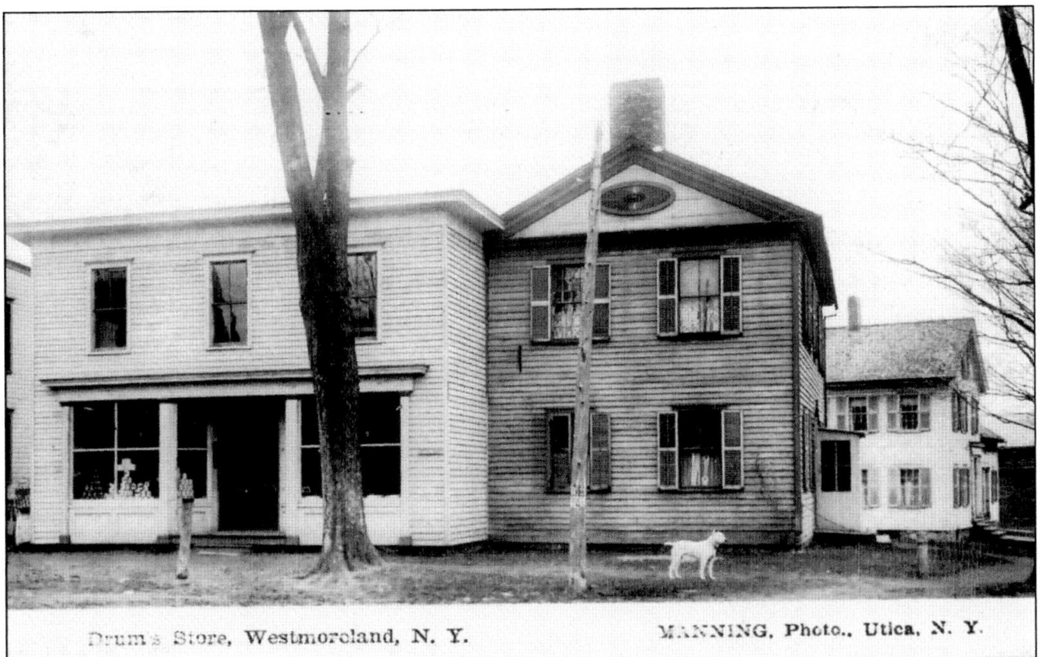

The Drum Building was located on the southeast corner of Main Street and Route 233. About 1900, George Drum quit the shoe business and opened a grocery store. After Drum died, Bernard and Helen McGinniss operated an ice cream and grocery store at the site pictured. This enterprise moved across the street, and the old Drum Store became an antique shop. Like many old buildings, this one, too, has been razed. (Courtesy Nancy Pritchard.)

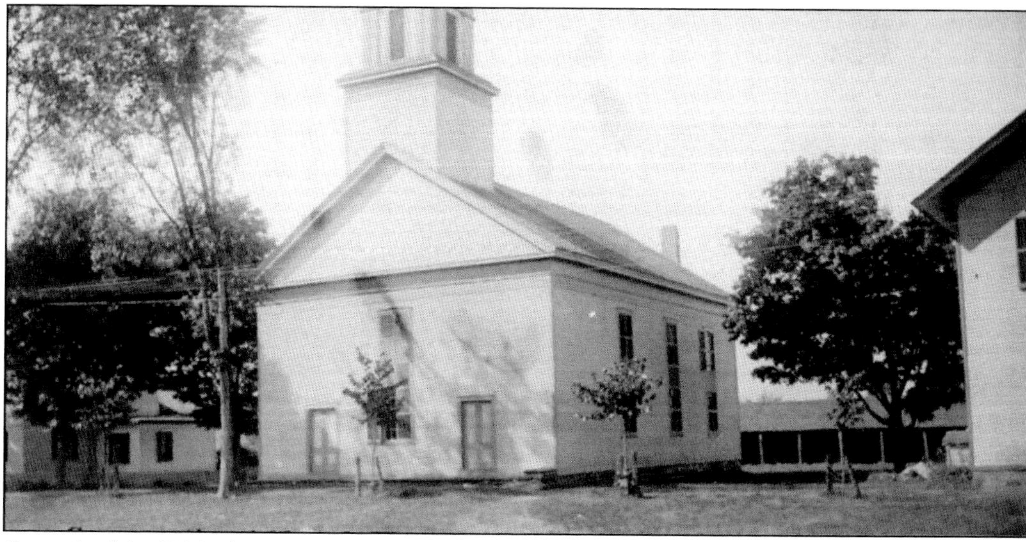

Organized in 1791, the Congregational church was active until the mid-1900s. One member was James Dean, the first settler in 1786 who had been trained as a missionary to the Oneida Indians. In 1867, his grandson, also James, became pastor of the church, serving until 1878. In the early years, disagreement as to a location for their meetinghouse resulted in a split, with both factions erecting a church. Reuniting in 1803, the South Street meetinghouse was sold to the Methodists. In 1817 and 1818, the church moved from the village green to northwest Main Street. In 1946, the Congregationalists sold their building to the Masonic Lodge with the stipulation that they be allowed to use it for services and meetings. Fire in 1960 destroyed the building. A new temple was built on the site.

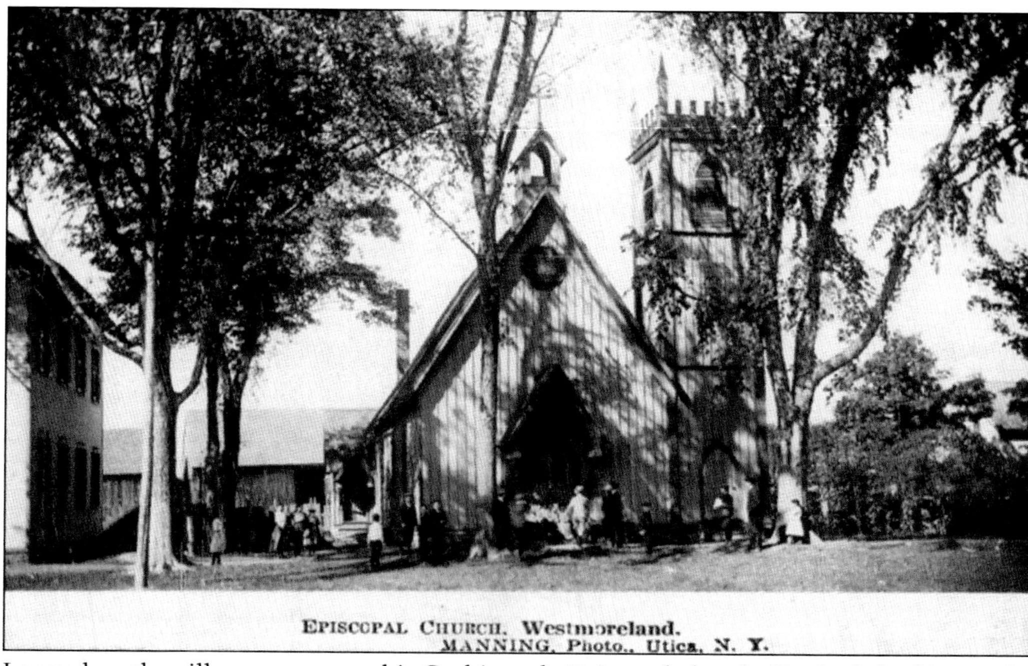

Located on the village green was this Gothic-style Episcopal church. To the left of it was the schoolhouse and the Congregational church. In 1924, the Episcopal church was dismantled and moved to Sherrill, where it still stands, now called the Church of the Gethsemanee.

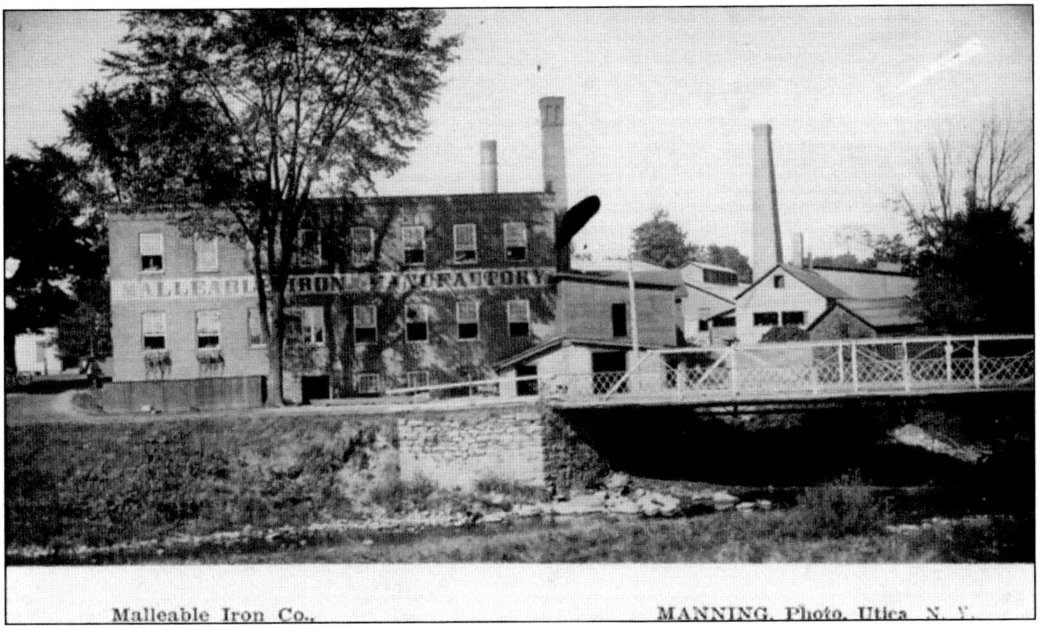

Westmoreland Malleable Iron Works was founded in 1850 by Erastus W. Clark. He was the business manager of the firm until he retired in 1871. At his retirement, his son, James M. Clark, became president of the company. In 1896, the business passed into the hands of Francis M. and Everett Metcalf, sons of Delia Clark and Nehimiah Q. Metcalf. Delia was the daughter of Erastus W. Clark.

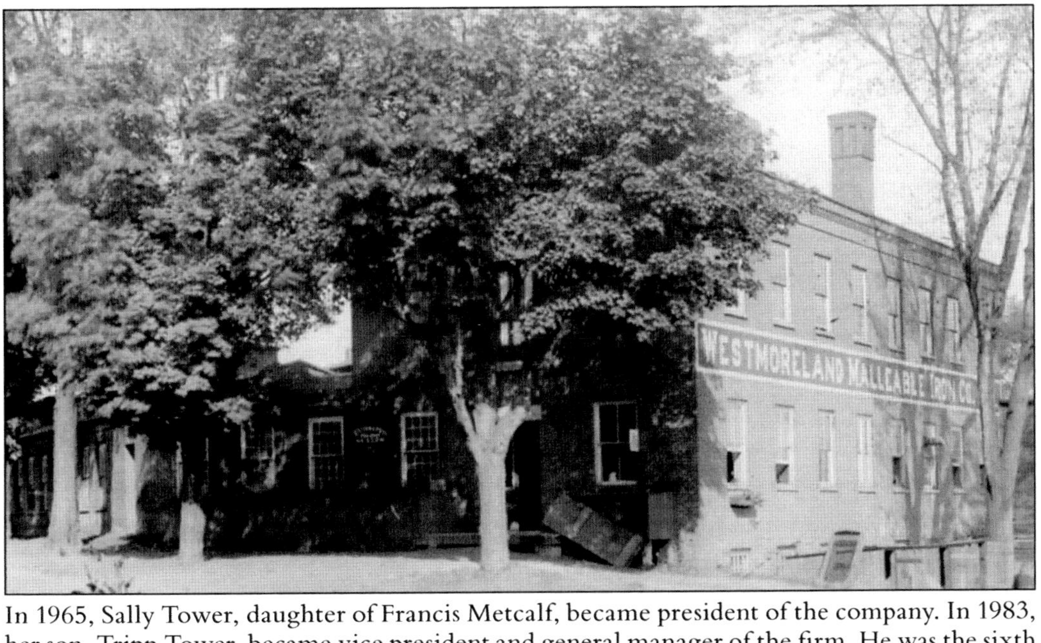

In 1965, Sally Tower, daughter of Francis Metcalf, became president of the company. In 1983, her son, Tripp Tower, became vice president and general manager of the firm. He was the sixth generation to be involved in the business. Westmoreland Malleable Iron ceased operations in 1989, and the factory was seized by Oneida County for back taxes in 1992. The building was demolished in 1994. In 1999, a historical marker was placed where the once-productive factory stood.

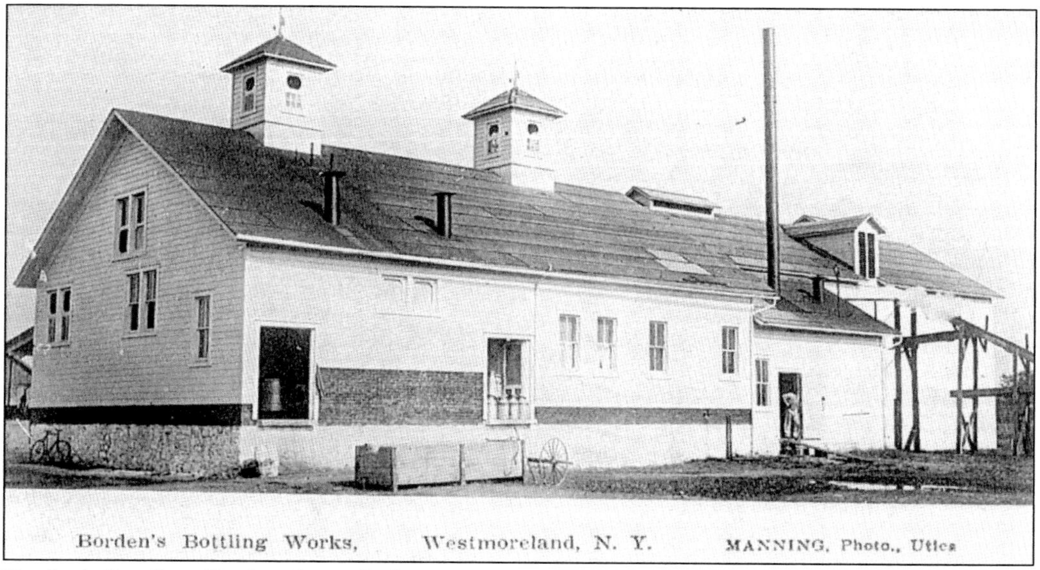

Borden's Bottling Works, also called Borden's Condensery, was on the present site of the town barn and offices. Established in the early 1900s, it was a huge structure with the top floor being used as an apartment for the plant superintendent and his family. One longtime Westmoreland resident recalled his early memories of waking to the rattle and bang of milk cans, the sound of wagon wheels, and the clip-clop of the horses as they rounded the bend in the road that led to the milk plant. (Courtesy of Brenda Jones.)

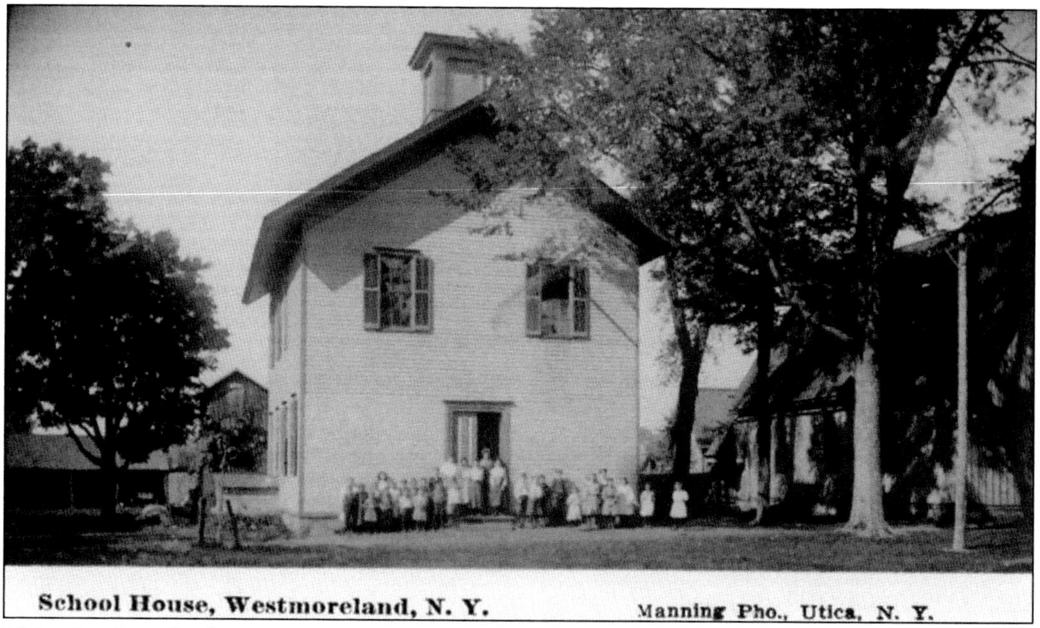

This school was built in Westmoreland in 1866. It was located next to the Episcopal church, on the site of an earlier school, which was a two-story wooden frame structure that existed until 1922. This earlier school was moved in 1886 to Cider Street and was converted to a two-family home. The new school was two stories high, with elementary grades on the first floor and high school on the second. The first graduation took place in 1904, with a class of two students. Westmoreland now has a modern school complex on Route 233. (Courtesy of Nancy Pritchard.)

Five

Oneida County Cities and Villages

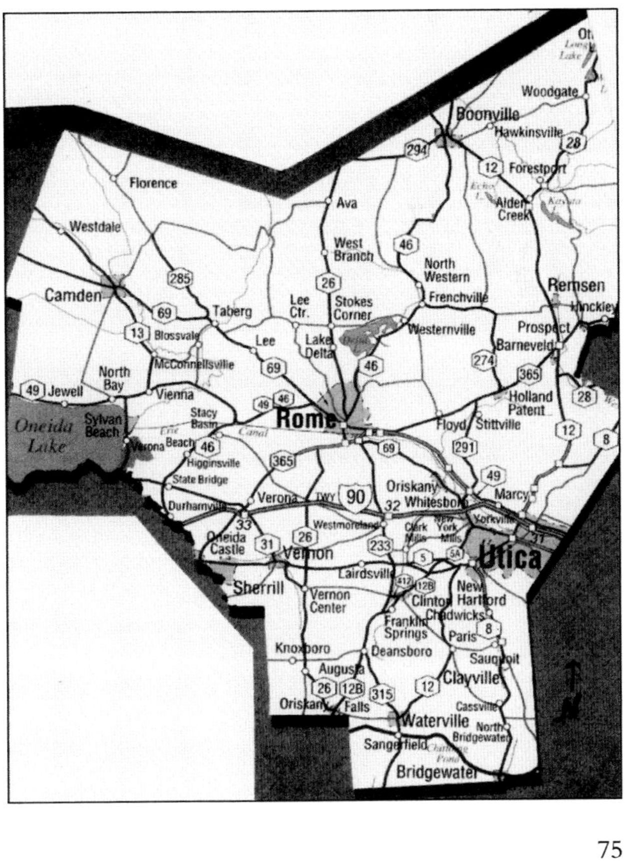

This 1995 map is of Oneida County.

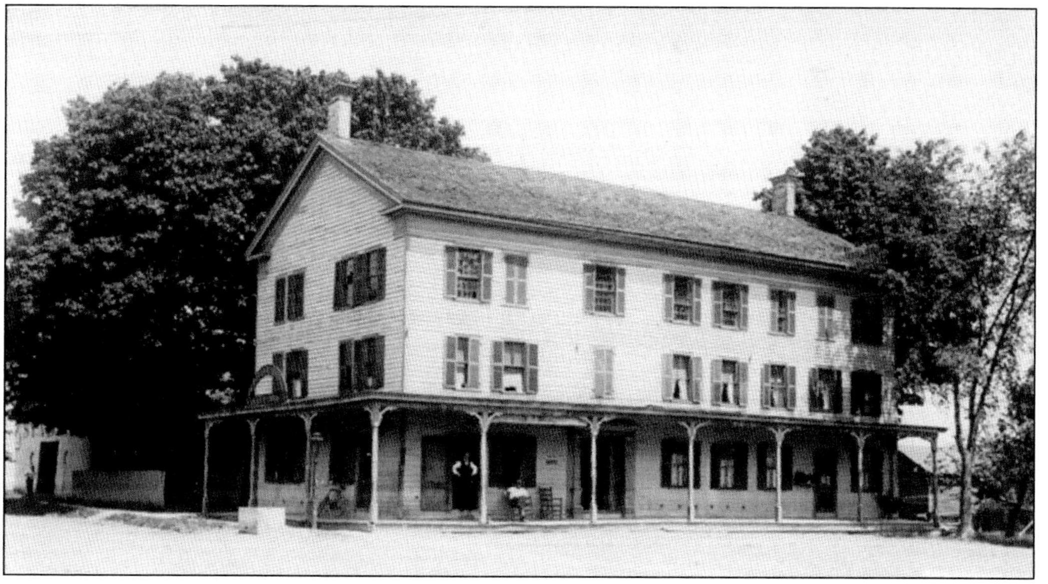

The first settlers appeared in Bridgewater about 1788. Active growth of the village began about 1810, following construction of the Cherry Valley east/west turnpike (now State Route 20). Levi Bostwick built what became the Hibbard House hotel about 1812. Later a third story was added. The hotel passed to A. C. Hibbard, and after his death it was operated by E. F. Saunders. In 1865, it was Beebe's Hotel, and at one time was called the Stage Coach Inn. Located on the northeast corner of Routes 8 and 20, it is now the site of a Nice 'n Easy convenience store.

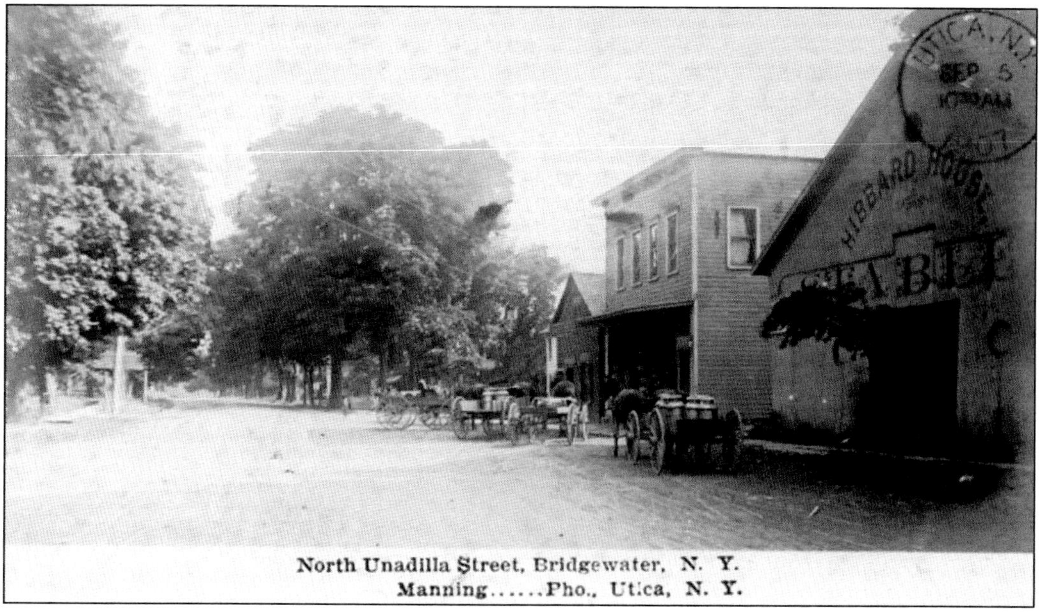

Stables for the Hibbard House, behind the hotel on North Unadilla Street, now State Route 8, provided a place where the hotel staff and guests could board their horses. It was once a stop for stagecoaches in need of repair or for coachmen to change their horses. This structure was lost to a fire in September 1913 along with two other nearby structures. A bucket brigade was formed to fight the fire. With help from the West Winfield Fire Department, the Hibbard House was saved.

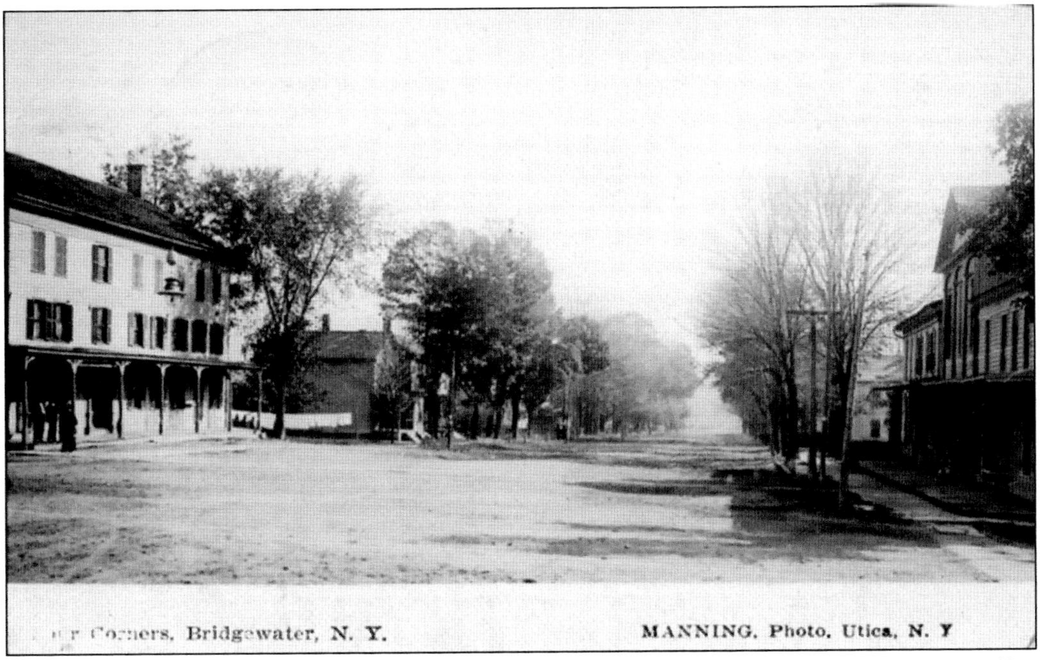

This view is looking east prior to the construction of Route 20, then called the Cherry Valley Turnpike. The tallest building at right is the Masonic hall. At left is the Hibbard House. Dirt roads were still unpaved in this *c.* 1907 scene. (Courtesy of Earl Allen.)

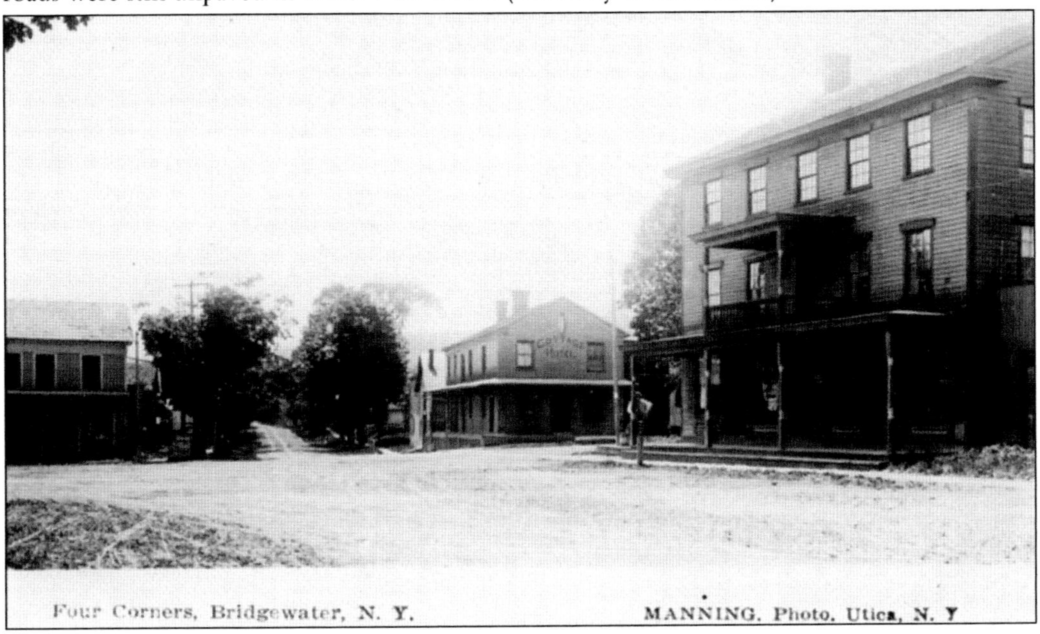

The hotel at right on the northwest corner of Routes 8 and 20 was the Shean Hotel, operated by Frank Shean. In earlier days it was known as the Bliven House and was later used as a grocery store by W. G. Roberts and W. O. Owens. The building was taken down about 1945. Across from the hotel on the southwest corner was the old brick store, originally operated by Allen Perkins and later by Albert Markel. It then became the Cottage Hotel. In more recent years it has been a used book store and antique shop. (Courtesy of Earl Allen.)

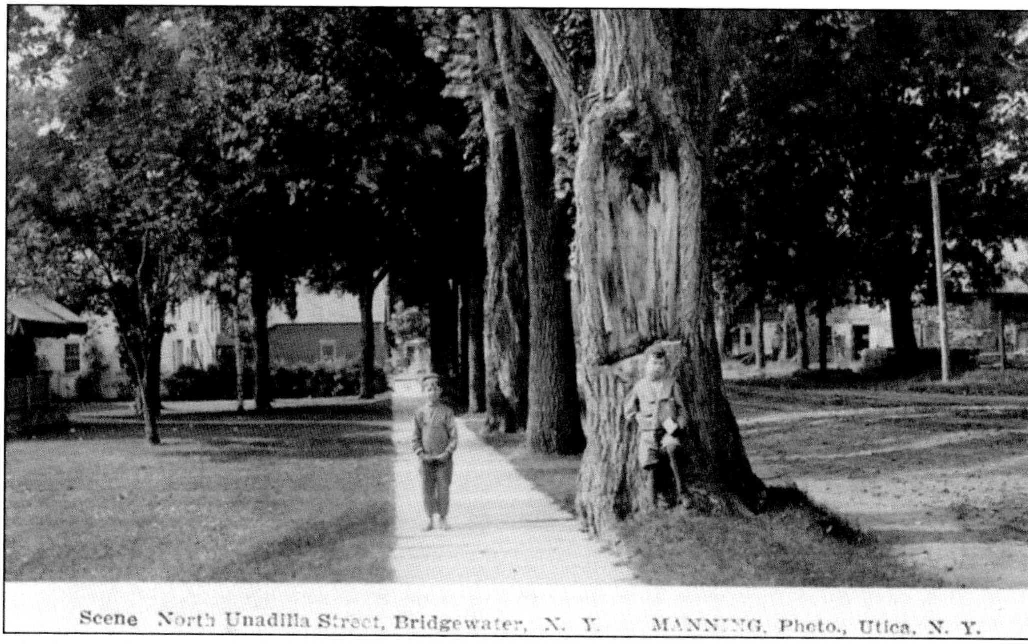

The huge elm trees dwarf the two young boys. The young lad leaning on the tree appears to have a strap over his shoulder and a box in his left hand, indicating he may have been a newspaper carrier. His barefoot assistant holds a tablet. Perhaps it was collection day and he was recording payments for his friend.

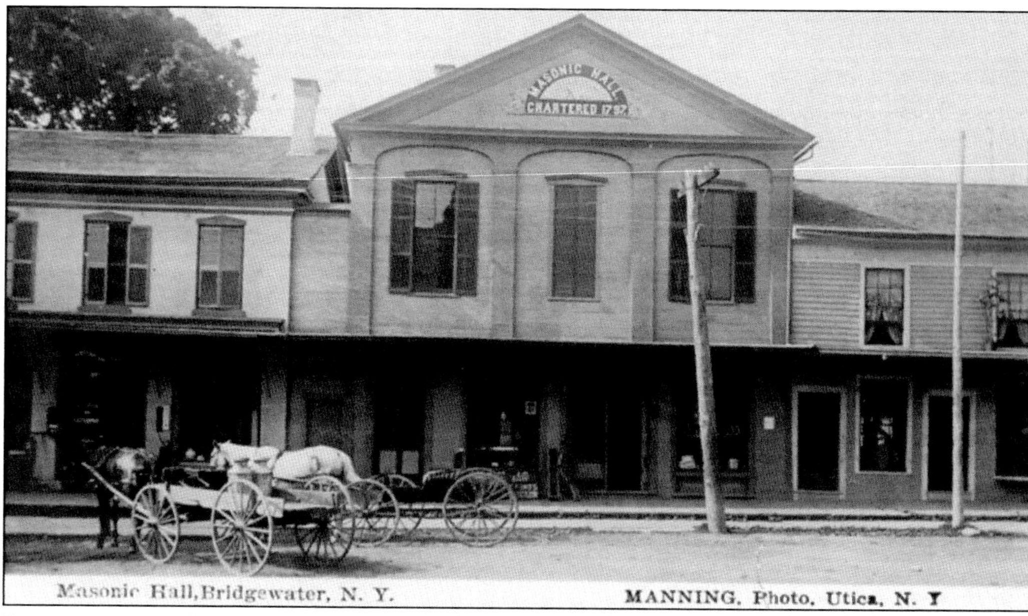

Western Star Lodge No. 15 Free and Accepted Masons was granted a charter in January 1797. There were 59 members. In 1878, the lodge was the oldest one in the county and 15th oldest in the state. At one time located on Route 8 behind the Cottage Hotel on the southwest corner of Routes 8 and 20, it was moved over to Route 20 on the south side of Main Street where it remains today. The building, still a Masonic lodge, now stands alone as the adjacent buildings that housed businesses and residences no longer exist.

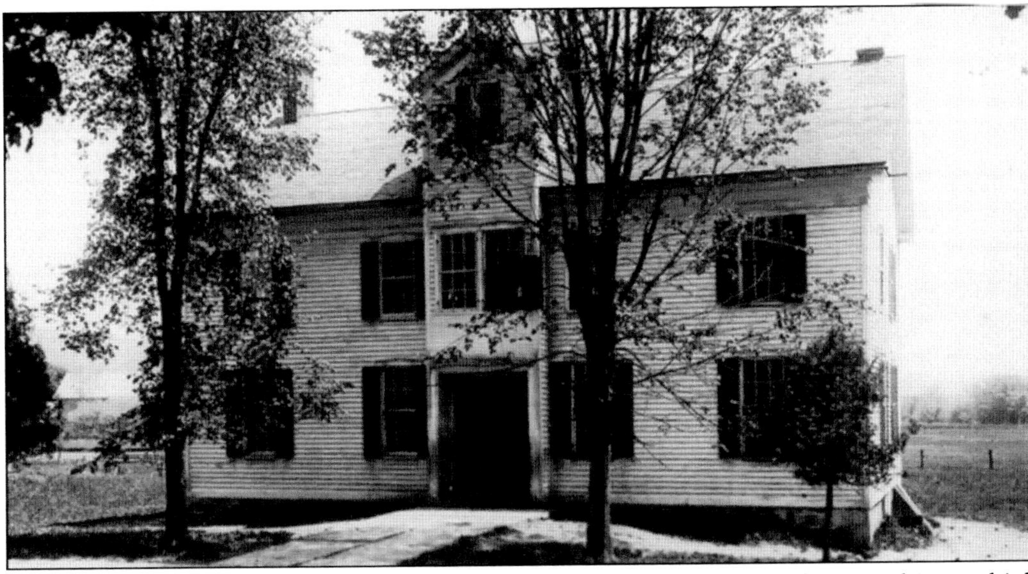

The Union School replaced the old red schoolhouse south of the center of town. This new high school on South Street was built by Sherman Stoddard in 1882. Located on the east side of Route 8 south, it still stands and is now an apartment house. A new larger Bridgewater Central School was built in 1931 and was used until 1969, when students began attending Mount Markham School District in West Winfield. The Central School was then used for a time as a grade school before closing permanently. The building is now a multiple-dealer antique store and an indoor skateboarding rink. (Courtesy of Earl Allen.)

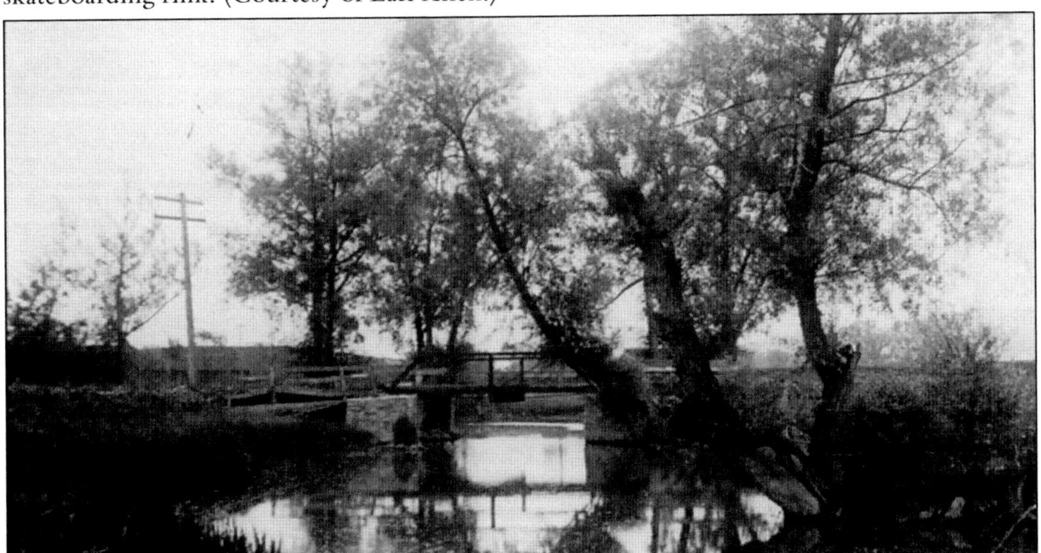

This popular swimming hole was on the Unadilla River at the Delaware, Lackawanna and Western Railroad bridge. Local boys preferred skinny-dipping. The boys had secret signals to alert their friends when a party was going to the river, and a signal to indicate whose turn it was to sneak soap and towels from home. Swimming instruction consisted of throwing a novice into the water to either sink or swim. One Halloween, a mischievous group shoved a piece of farm machinery into the pool that sank deeper than expected. As far as is known, it is still there. (Courtesy of Earl Allen.)

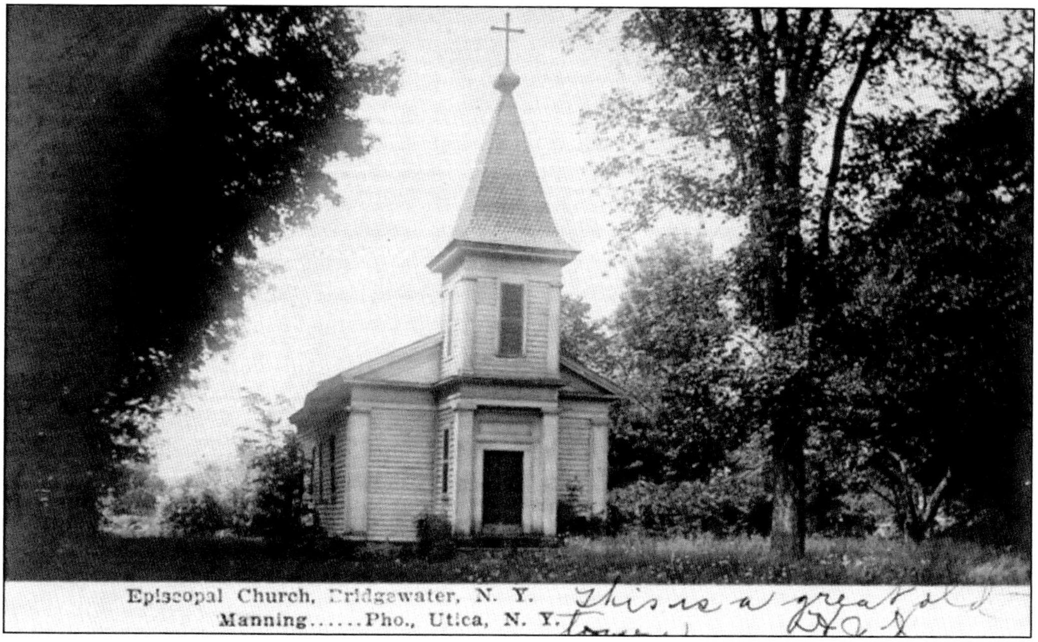

This *c.* 1908 real-photo postcard indicates the church was an Episcopal church. However, it was used jointly at times by Baptists, Methodists, and others. Later used for public entertainments, the old church fell into a state of disrepair and was torn down in the 1940s. Subsequently, a Kaiser dealership occupied the site that is presently home to Patty's Pub. A new Episcopal church was built in 1895 on Mill Street; it is now a private residence.

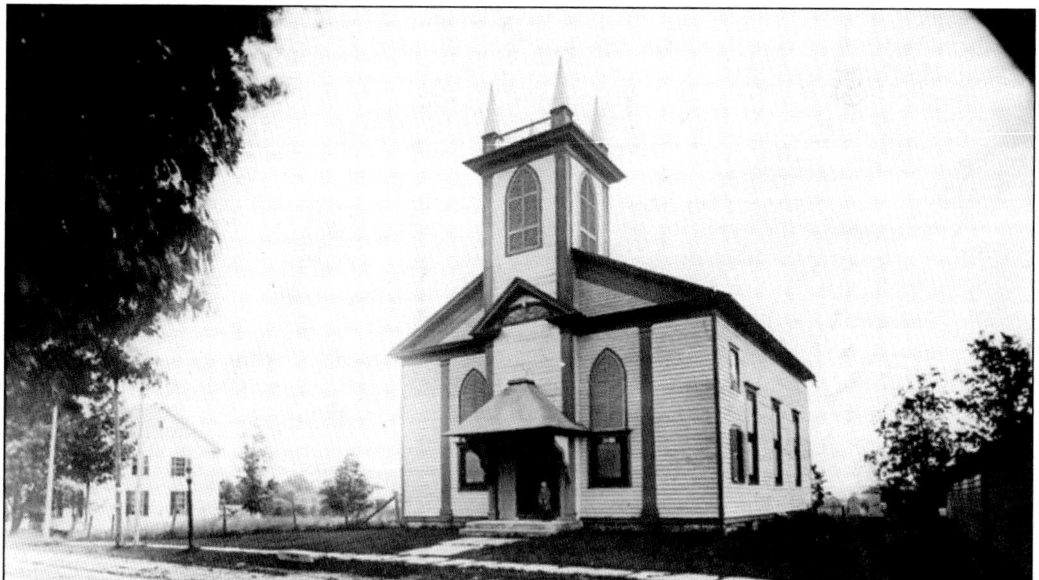

A society of Universalists was formed in the early 1800s. In 1834 and 1835, they erected a house of worship in the southern part of the village. By 1878, there was no regular pastor and meetings were not being held due to dissension created by the Civil War. Services resumed in the 1880s. Adjacent to the church is a small cemetery, which is still being used for an occasional burial. The church building was taken down in the 1940s.

The Congregational church was organized in 1798 with 13 members. A church was built in 1805 in the center of Bridgewater. The church divided in 1835, and a new society formed that built a new edifice on Route 8, just north of the four corners. It was repaired and remodeled in 1876. In 1902, a dining room and kitchen were added and a modern furnace was installed. In 1898, the Congregationalists celebrated their centennial, and in 1998, their bicentennial. It is still an active church.

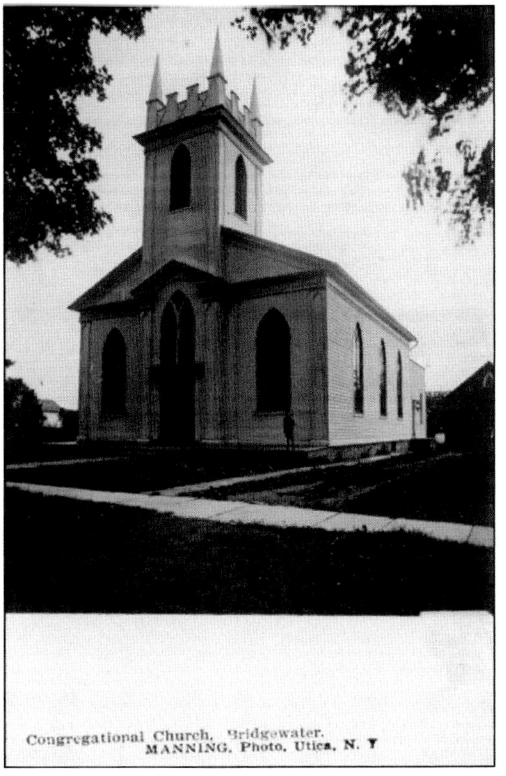

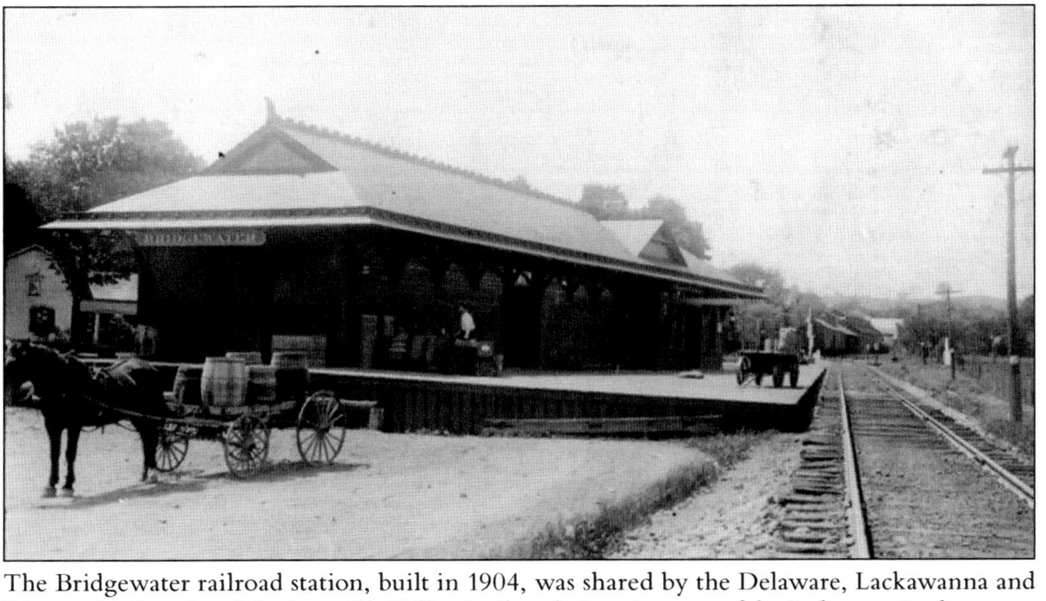

The Bridgewater railroad station, built in 1904, was shared by the Delaware, Lackawanna and Western Railroad and the Unadilla Valley Railroad. A major spur of the Delaware, Lackawanna and Western Railroad ran from Richfield Junction in Cassville to Richfield Springs, a popular resort in the early 1900s. Passengers traveled there on Sundays for the reputed health springs and to enjoy the amusement park at Canadarago Lake. Freight trains carried milk, livestock, feed, lumber, coal, propane, and carloads of cowhides to Hiteman Leather Company in West Winfield. The building on the right in the distance is the original station.

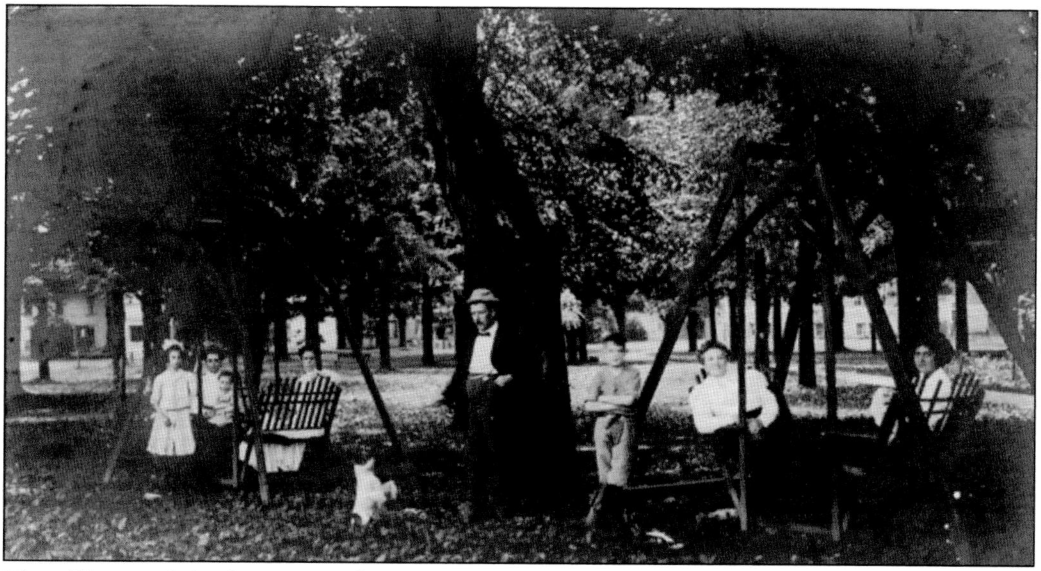

The village park in the center of Holland Patent still offers a pleasant retreat for the residents. On this 1907 postcard, the ladies enjoy the swings while the gentleman is entertained by his dog. Before any structures were built around the park, farm animals roamed the area, creating a nuisance to local citizens. At a town meeting in 1799, town officials voted to fine the owners of hogs, sheep, and horses found running loose. They would have to pay one shilling. A second offense would cost $1.

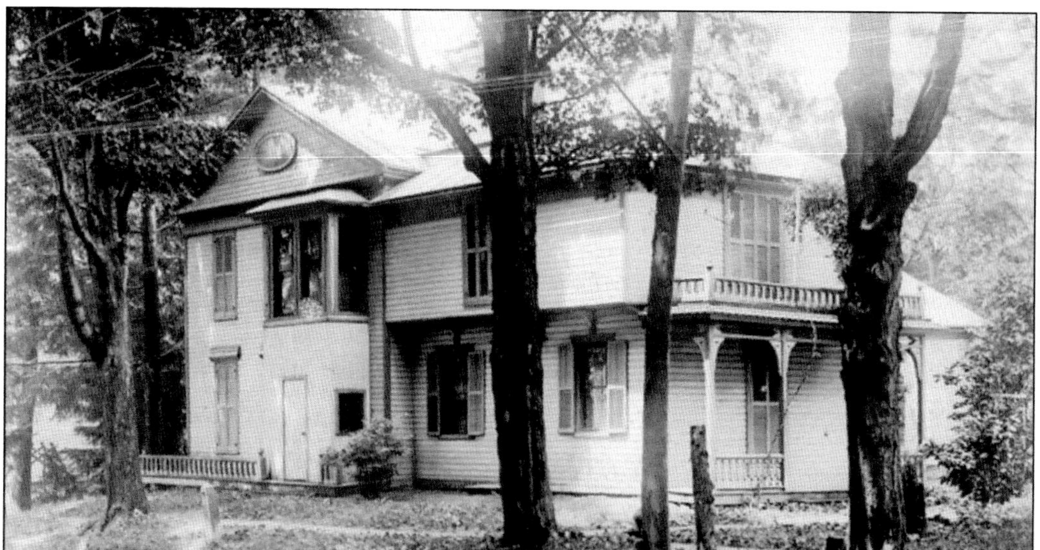

The Weeds, still standing at 9573 Main Street in Holland Patent, was once the home of the Reverend Richard Cleveland and his wife, Ann Neal. Ann and her family lived there for many years where Cleveland had been pastor of the Presbyterian church. They are buried in the village cemetery. The Clevelands had nine children, among them Grover Cleveland, the 22nd president of the United States. Grover lived in Clinton from 1851 to 1853, and attended school there. The Cleveland Home on Utica Street in Clinton, recently renovated, displays a historic marker.

Built on Church Street at the western side of the village park, the Baptists built their first church in 1813. In 1840, increasing membership resulted in building a new stone church, dedicated in 1842. The interior burned in March 1843 and was rebuilt at a cost of $3,300. A 1,565-pound bell was purchased in 1862, and from 1903 to 1908, stained-glass windows were installed. The church remained active until 1935.

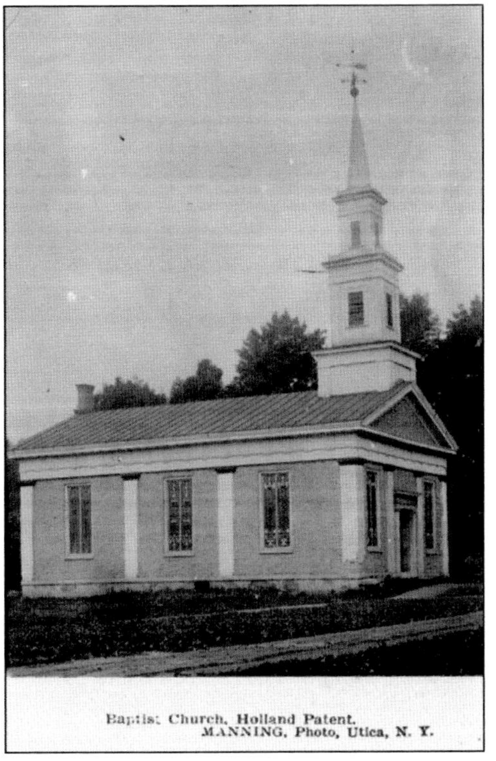

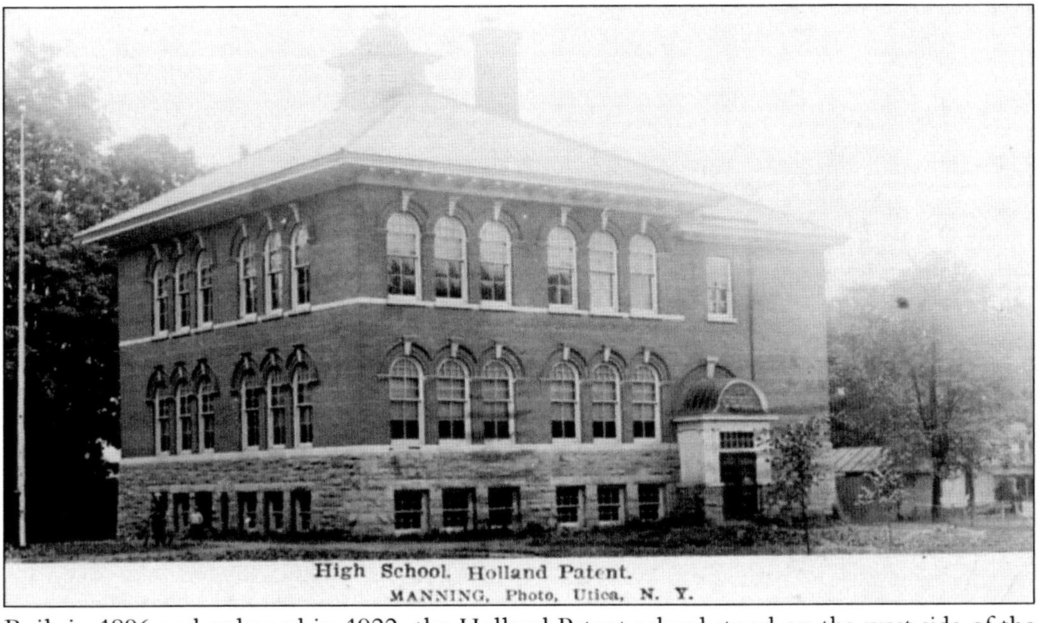

Built in 1896 and enlarged in 1922, the Holland Patent school stood on the west side of the park next to the Presbyterian church. It replaced an earlier school that was destroyed by fire in February 1896. An addition was put on in 1922, nearly doubling the size of the school. The last class of the original high school graduated in a new central school building in June 1937, leaving the old school empty until 1945, when it was sold to American Legion Post 161. There is now an empty lot where the school and American Legion once stood.

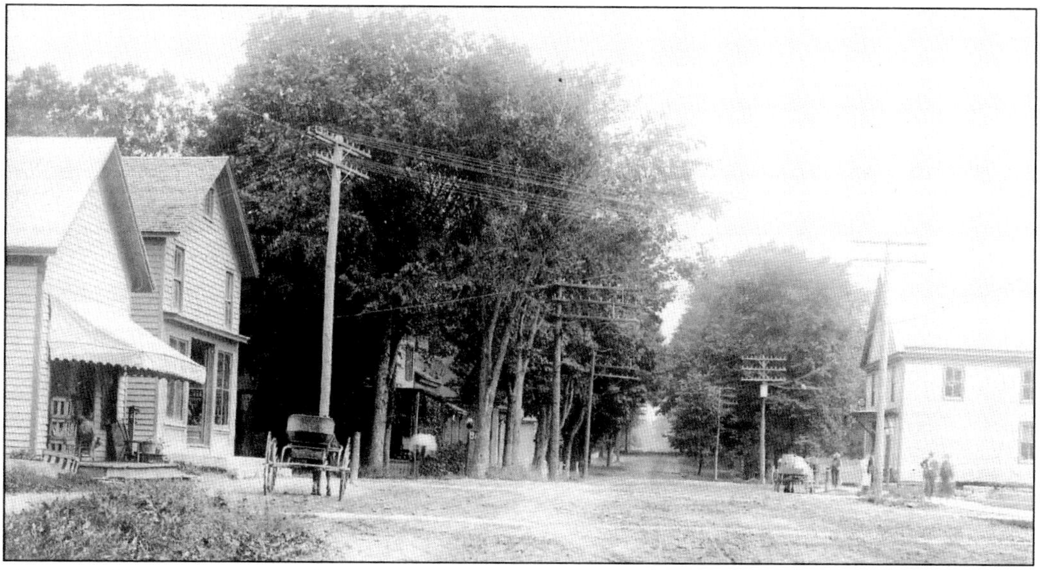

These buildings still exist on the corner of Route 274. The building at left was once Roberts Meat Market and today is Benny's Place, a bar. The building second from left housed a grocery store owned by P. O. Jones. His son Perewith Jones was a founder of the Victory Store grocery chain. Subsequently, Jones's store became a Victory Market. Later it became the Holland Patent Pharmacy and recently was converted to apartments. On the northeast corner was the former Powell Hotel that was moved on an angle in 1925 to accommodate gas pumps and a garage. (Courtesy Tom Gates.)

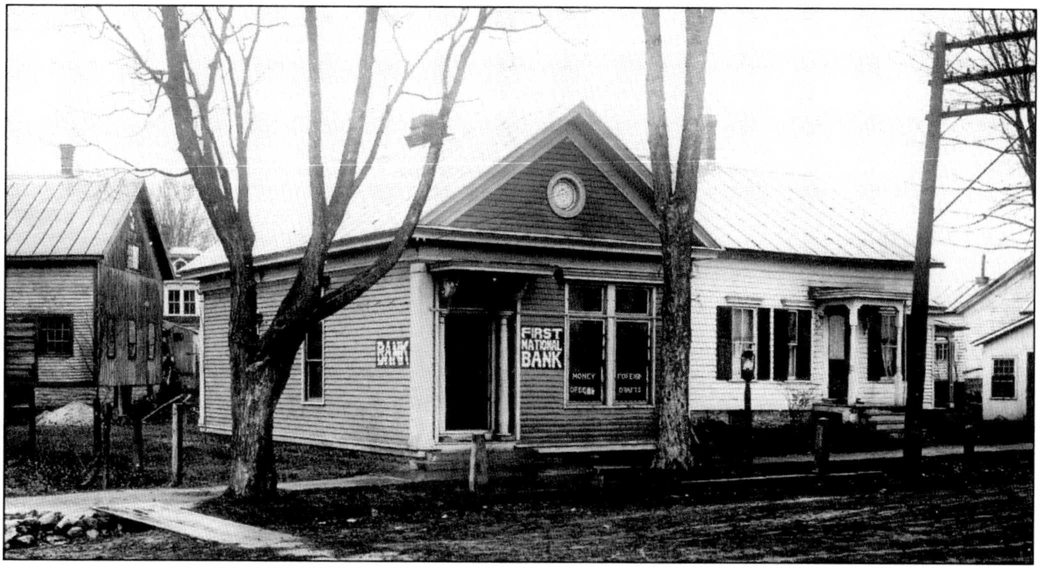

The First National Bank of Holland Patent, established in 1890, did business as a bank on Main Street (now Grande's Restaurant) until 1993. In January 1945, Oneida National Bank of Utica purchased the building. In February 1982, Oneida National merged with Norstar Bank. In January 1988, Fleet Bank purchased it, followed by Bank of America. After banks occupied the original Main Street location for 95 years, in May 1993, the bank relocated to a new larger building next to the library on Main Street, once the site of Kessler Insurance Agency. (Courtesy Tom Gates.)

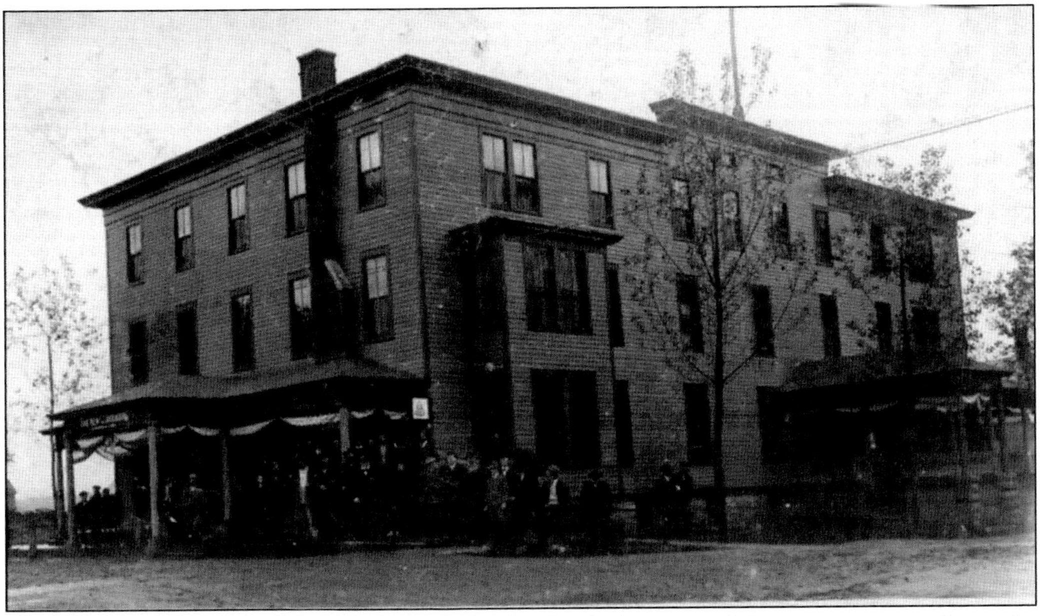

The Holland Patent community turned out for the dedication of the new waterworks at the rebuilt Clarendon Hotel on October 30, 1907. A fire in 1906 destroyed the original brick hotel, as well as many of the Main Street businesses, proving the water supply was insufficient for the village's needs. A village meeting produced a proposal to look into improving it. A $16,000 bond issue was approved for the project, and in 1907, the villagers celebrated its completion.

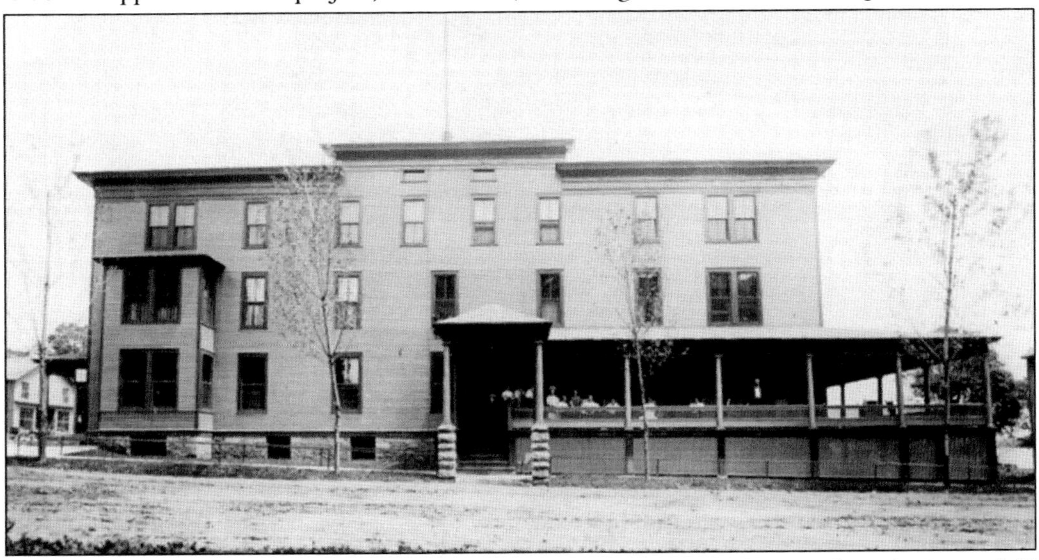

Erected in 1876, the Clarendon Hotel, a brick structure, was built on the site where the Butterfield House later stood. In 1889, twin brothers Charles and Ira Thomson rented the hotel. After the fire in 1906, Ira Thomson erected this three-story frame building, on the corner of Main Street and Park Avenue. Reed Thomson, son of Ira, took over the management in 1923 and changed the name to Thomson's Inn. In 1934, the hotel was sold to Eddie Martin of Utica who renamed it Martin Inn. In May 1938, the hotel and restaurant was sold to the Butterfield family. After several later owners, the property became an apartment house. The building still stands, albeit showing its age.

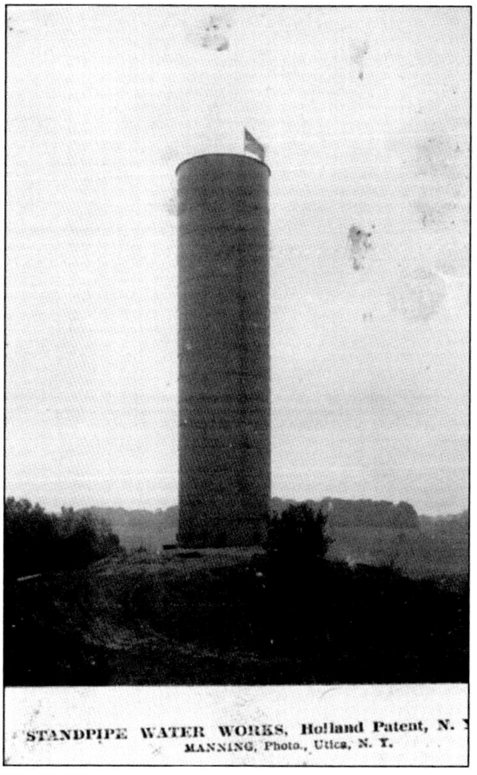

The Standpipe Water Works was located on Pride's Hill (now known as Barton's Hill) on an acre of land, purchased for $100 from Herbert Pride. Standing 80 feet tall, the standpipe was manufactured by a Virginia firm, Tippet and Wood, at a cost of $4,595. In subsequent years, improvements were made to the waterworks system that was used for about 60 years. In 1976, due to unsatisfactory water reports and boil water orders, a new water system was constructed. The old standpipe still rises over its now-wooded hilltop on Coates Road (once Center Street).

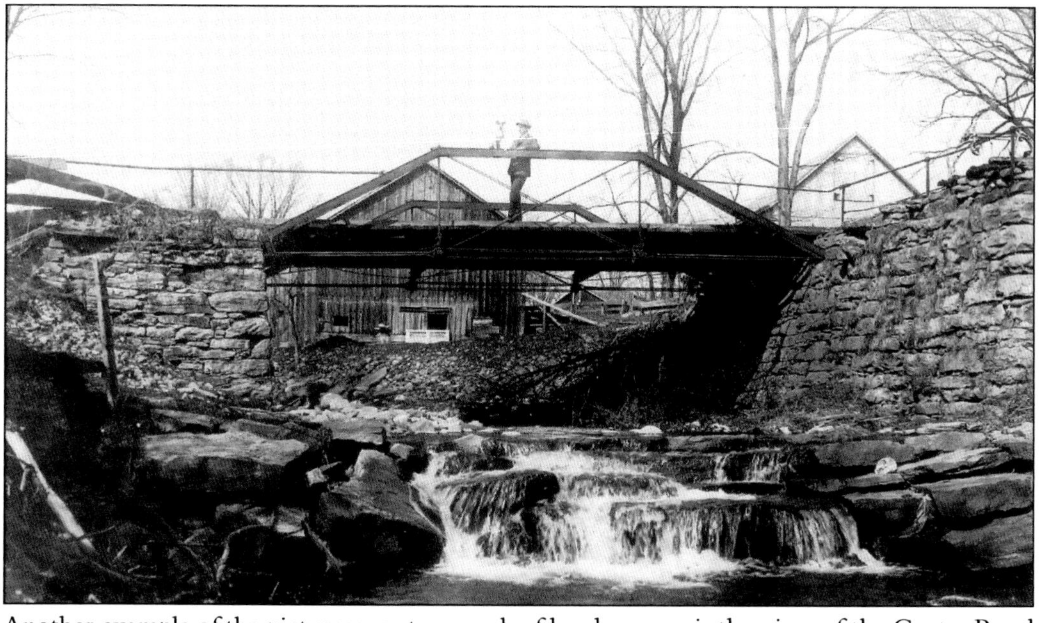

Another example of the picturesque stonework of local masons is the view of the Coates Road iron and stone bridge over Willow Brook (also known as Willard Creek) in Holland Patent. Local blacksmiths Griffith J. Jones and Joseph Davis made railings for the bridges. Willow Brook branches off Nine Mile Creek and flows west of the village park before heading north and flowing beneath the Coates Road bridge. (Courtesy Tom Gates.)

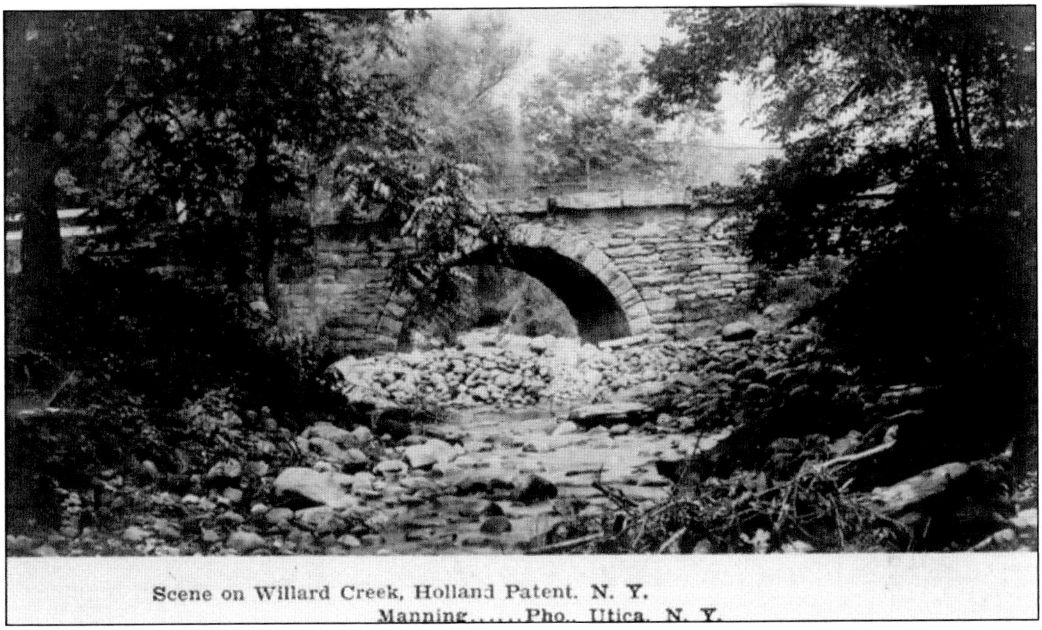

This early stone arch carried Main Street traffic (now Route 365) over Willow Brook. The beautiful stone bridges that spanned the creeks in Holland Patent were designed and built by local craftsmen. Stonemasons from nearby Stittville built the bridges from the 1850s to the 1890s. Local blacksmiths made the iron railings. A newer bridge incorporated this stone arch bridge into its design.

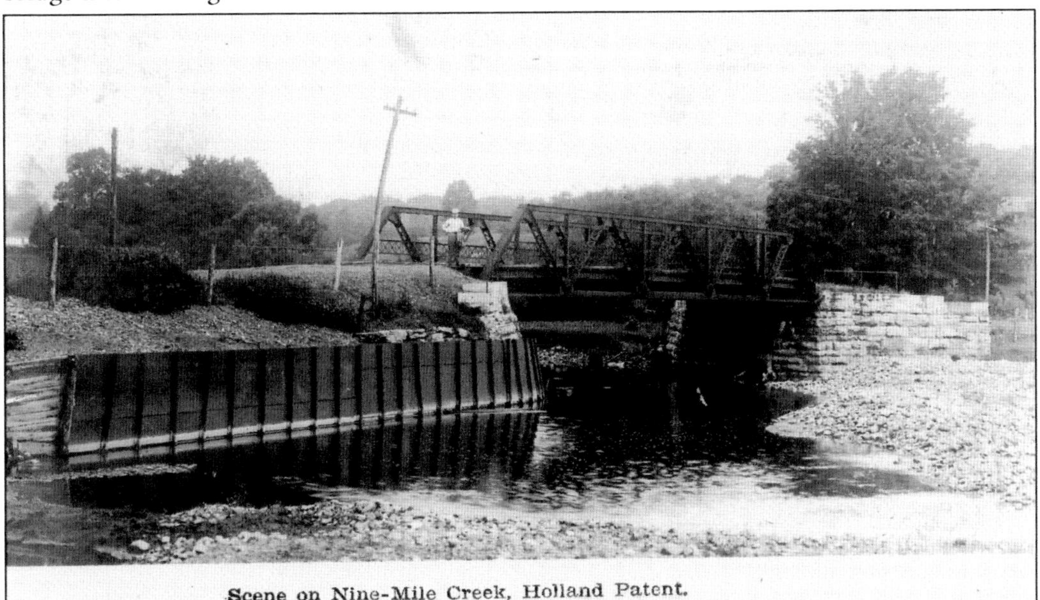

Nine Mile Creek flows south of the village park. Two branches fork off and head north. In 1797, Capt. Pascal DeAngelis built a gristmill and sawmill on the creek. Holland Patent saw its first settlers in the late 1700s. The village was named after Henry, Lord Holland of England, who was granted the land by the British Crown. He sold the tract, and later owners had it surveyed into lots of about 100 acres each. (Courtesy Tom Gates.)

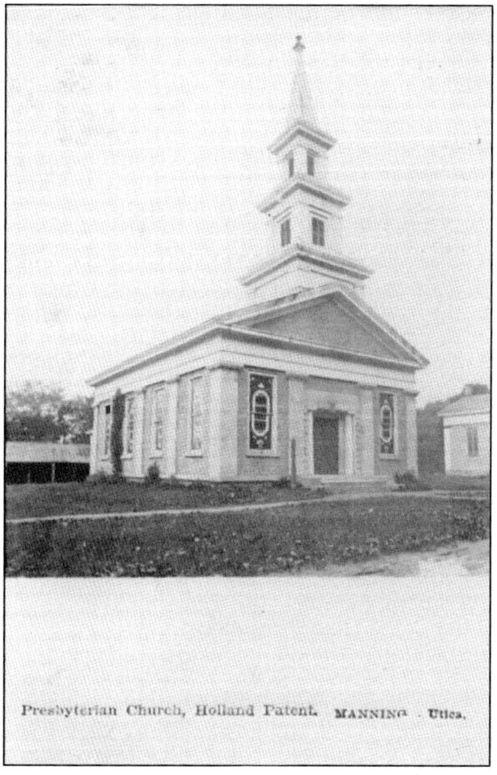

In 1799, the First Presbyterian Society was organized in Holland Patent. Worship was held in a community meetinghouse and school on the village green. A new $1,600 wood frame church was erected on the village square and was dedicated in 1823. In 1844, a new Greek Revival–style church was built on the village green. The previous wood frame church was purchased for an educational institution and was later moved to Main Street. It burned down in 1906. Grover Cleveland's father, Rev. Richard Cleveland, preached just one Sunday in this church, on September 14, 1853; became ill; and died on October 1. He now lies in the Holland Patent Cemetery.

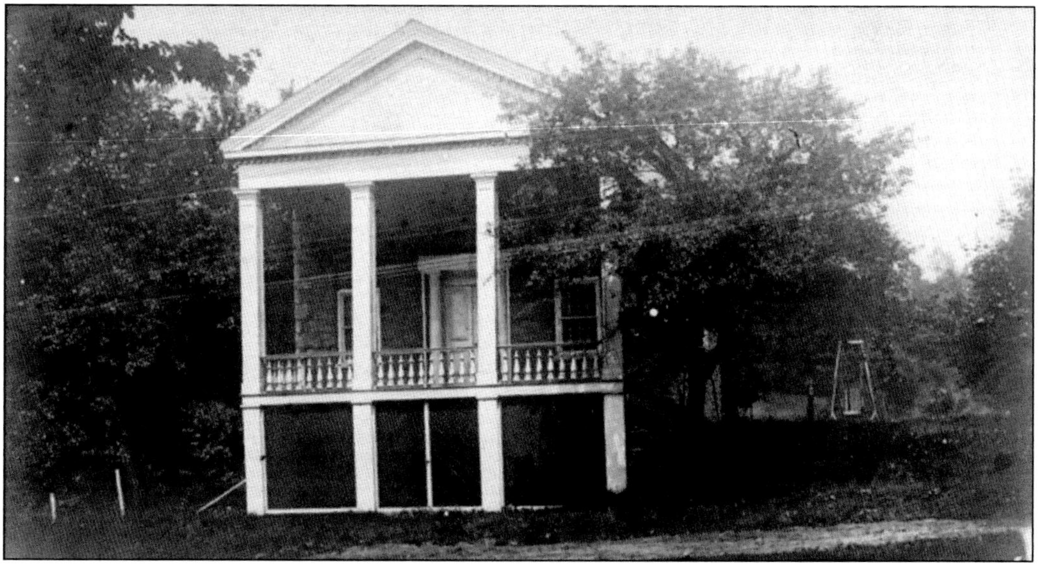

The Welsh Congregational Church, formed in 1842 on the north side of Main Street, faced the village green. A limestone structure with a front portico, it seated 200. Up until the 1950s, church services were in the Welsh language. Children of the members did not learn the language, however, resulting in a decreased membership. The church closed in 1956. The empty church was vandalized, and the stained-glass windows were damaged. In 1970, the former church was purchased and restored as a private residence.

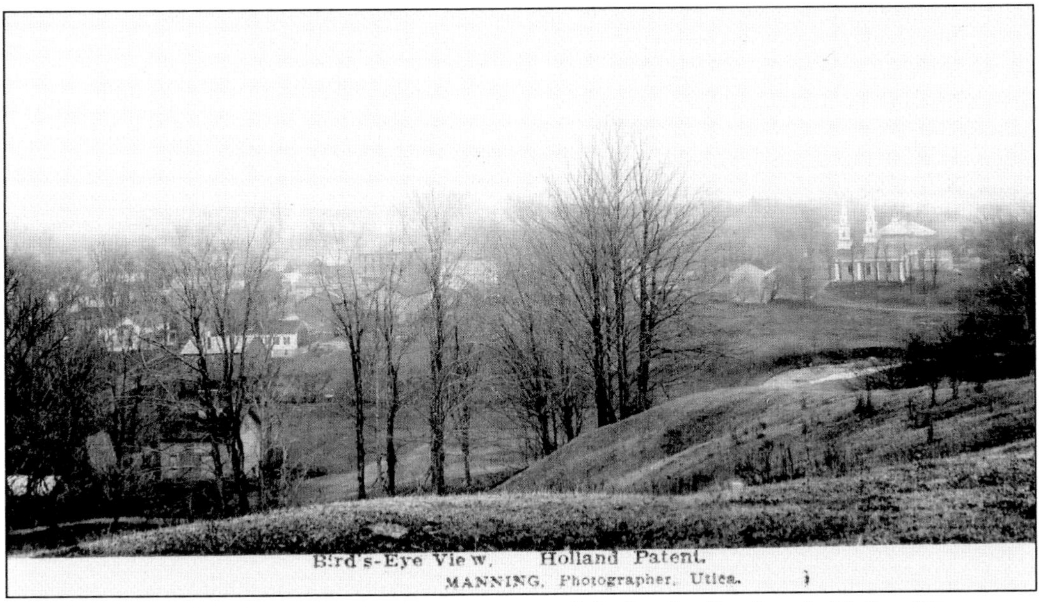

Seen at right is the old school on the village green and the Methodist church. Holland Patent was officially incorporated in 1885. A survey map by Henry Broadwell, dated September 1, 1885, established village limits as 300.82 acres. Incorporation was approved and officers duly elected. Ordinances and bylaws were passed for "the preservation of good order and the prevention of immorality" including profane or immoral language, causing a riot, and loud and boisterous noises. (Courtesy Tom Gates.)

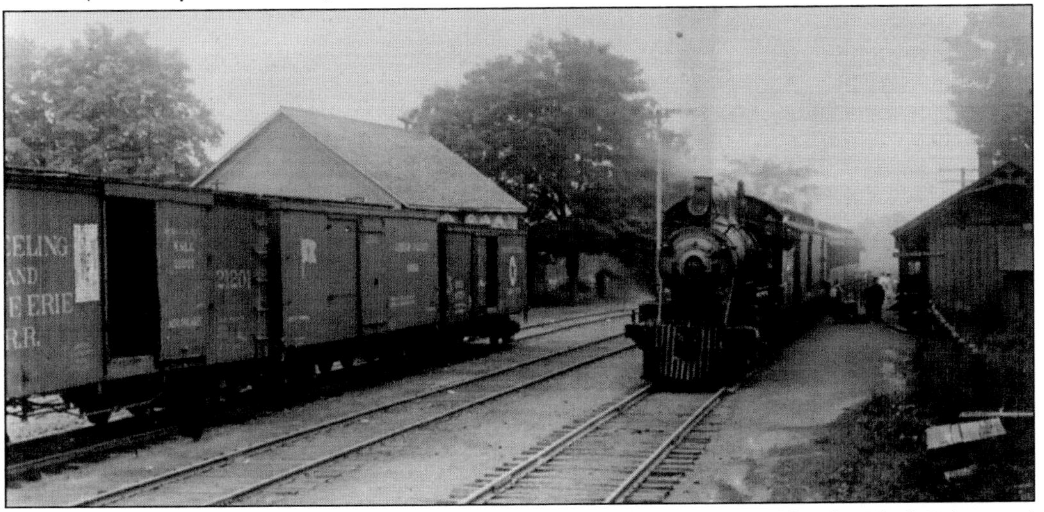

The Rome, Watertown, and Ogdensburg Railroad Company, preceded by the Black River and Utica Railroad System, reorganized as the Utica and Black River Railroad in 1860–1861 and continued operating until 1886, when it was sold to the Rome, Watertown, and Ogdensburg Railroad Company. The New York Central and Hudson River Railroad took over the routes and continued to run until 1968. They then merged with the Pennsylvania Railroad to form Penn Central. When they became bankrupt in 1972, Conrail continued operations. The depot currently houses the municipal offices, a meeting room, and a collection of local artifacts. During the Christmas season, the Adirondack Railway conducts trips from Union Station in Utica to the Holland Patent depot for children to visit with Santa.

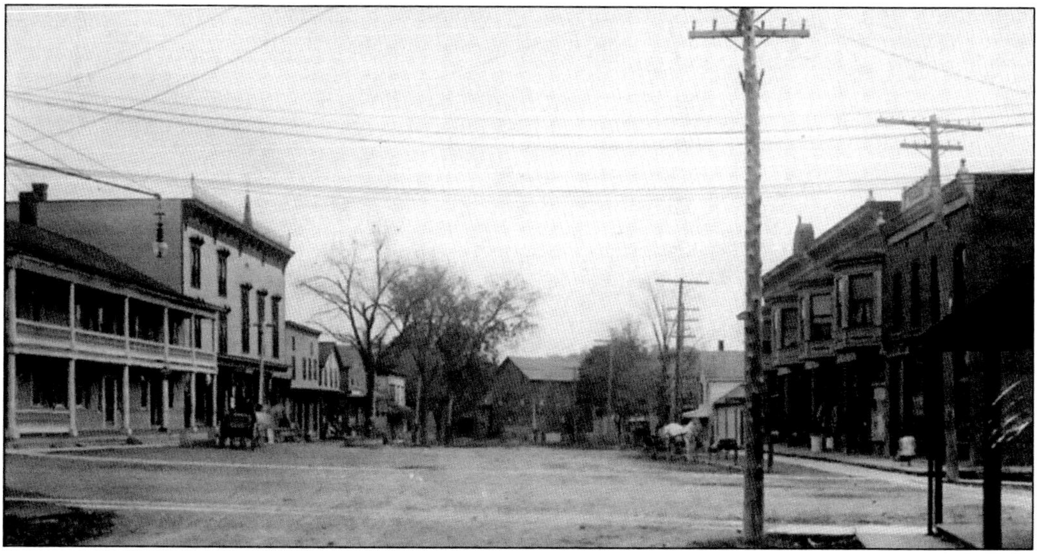

The village of Oriskany Falls, first called Cassety Hollow, lies between two ridges. In 1794, Col. Thomas Cassety settled here and built a sawmill. He was elected supervisor in 1798 at the first town meeting. Prior to his settling in Oriskany Falls, he had been imprisoned for three years in Canada for firing at a British officer who was ordering his father, James Cassety (a captain in the British Army), to take up arms against the colonies. He escaped and took refuge with a western tribe of Native Americans. At left is O'Neill's Hotel that was razed for a parking lot. At right are the City Bank, stores, and the post office.

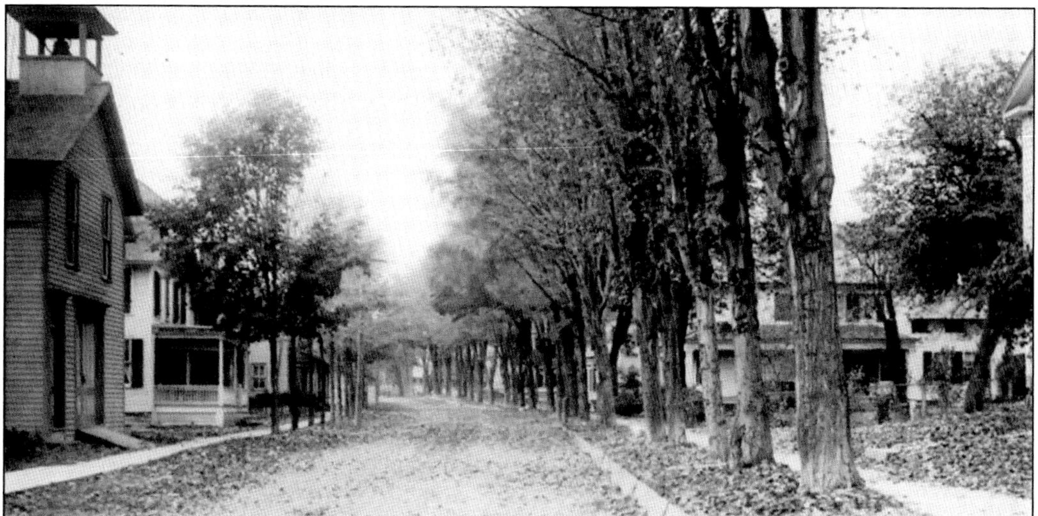

This pre-1907 postcard shows the old Oriskany Falls Engine Company No. 1 (left) on the south side of Main Street. The company was organized in 1871 with 33 members plus 10 members in the Douglass Hose Company, which was named after James A. Douglass, who donated this first engine house. The second floor of the building was used for a meeting room for the firemen and also for the village board. The basement had bars on the windows and served as the village lockup.

In 1833, members of a new Congregational Society organized and for $155, purchased land on which to build their stone church. The church was completed in 1845. Limestone from Putnam's Quarry was used in the construction of the structure. Known for its inexhaustible supply of limestone, the Falls quarry is now Hanson's, a British firm that succeeded Eastern Rock. In 1950, meager attendance resulted in the church's closure. Ownership was transferred to the village, and the building was used for storage. In 1979, the church was placed on the National Register of Historic Places.

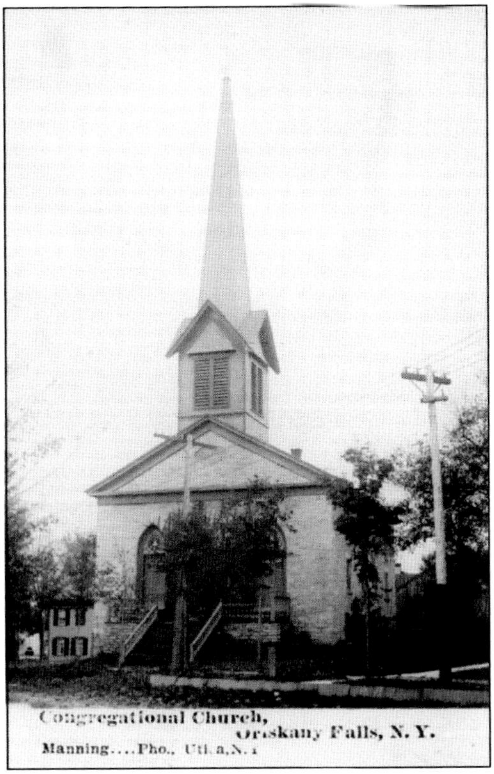

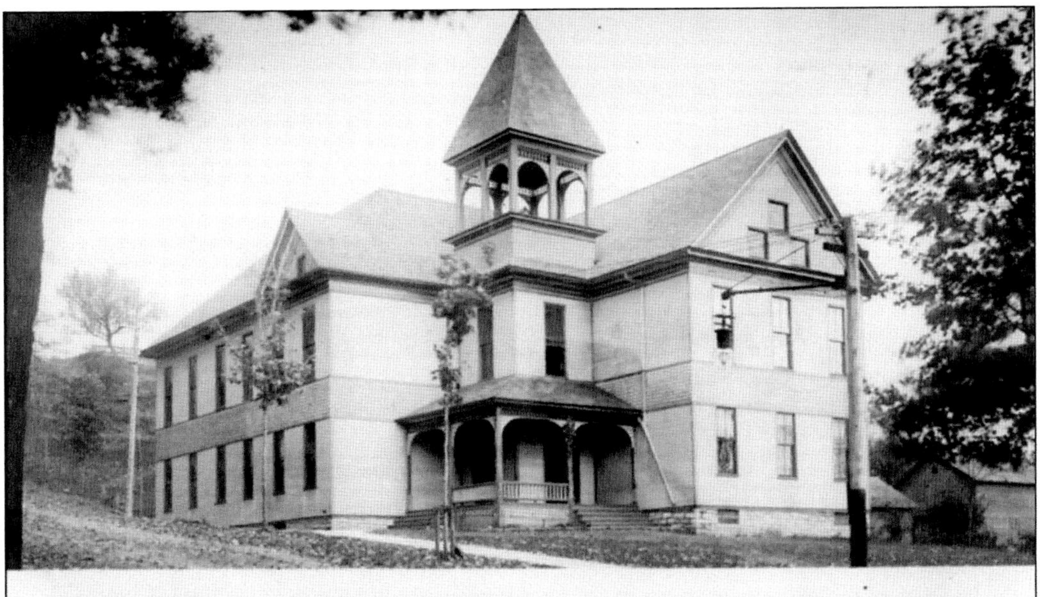

Located on College Road on a hill behind and north of Main Street, the Union Free School was built in 1892. The new school burned down soon after and was quickly rebuilt, graduating its first class in 1894. The school closed in 1983, and students then attended Waterville or Madison School. Sold and used for a time as an apartment complex, in 1998, it was taken over by the village. It is now privately owned and being refurbished for apartments.

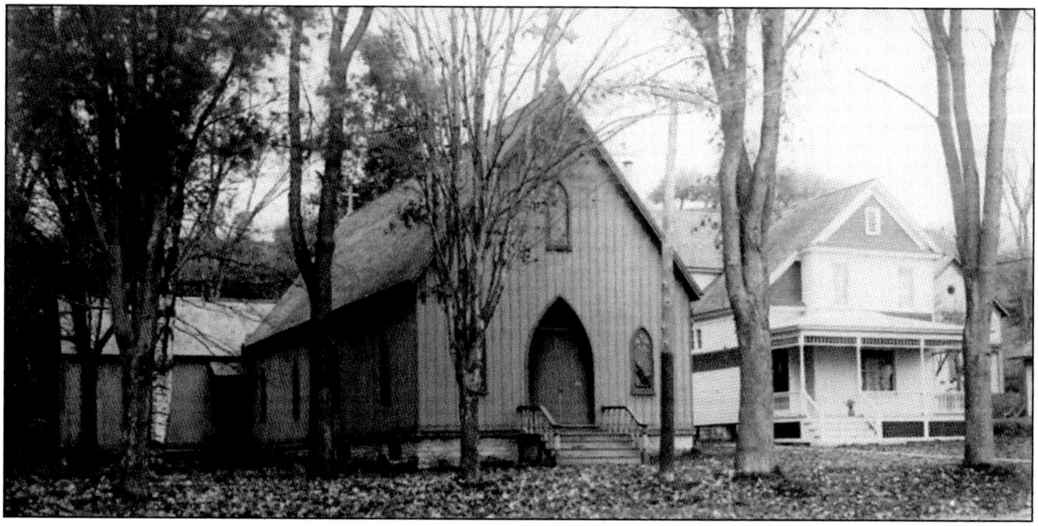

The Episcopal church on North Main Street is now home to the Limestone Ridge Historical Society. In the late 1860s, Rev. Russell Todd, an Episcopal pastor from the nearby Augusta Center church, formed a small group into a church in Oriskany Falls. In August 1871, a cornerstone was laid and a new church was built. Todd helped build the church, made church furniture, and married the church organist. Since this pre-1908 photograph, a fellowship hall was added, which is now used for an office and storage area for the historical society. (Courtesy of LRHS.)

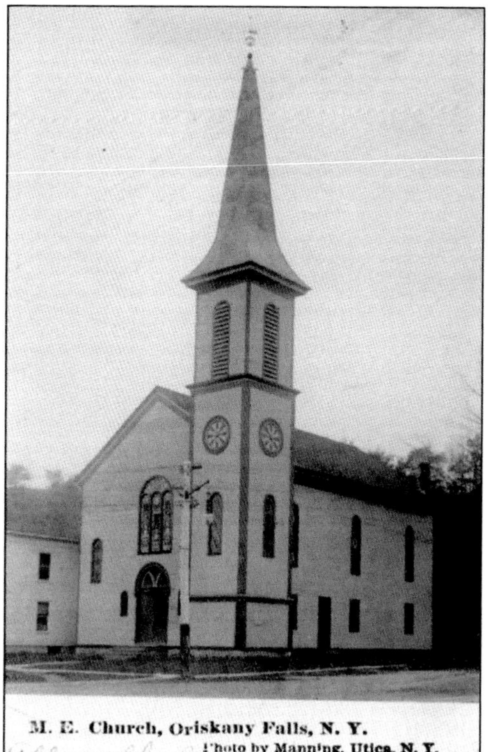

The Methodist church in Oriskany Falls originated in 1858. Services were held in the Stone Congregational Church, the schoolhouse, and various other places until 1872, when the Methodists purchased a lot on the corner of North Main Street and College Road and built their new church. Stained-glass windows were added in 1897, and in 1905, electric lights replaced the oil lamps. The Methodists celebrated their centennial in 1972. It remains an active church today. (Courtesy of LRHS.)

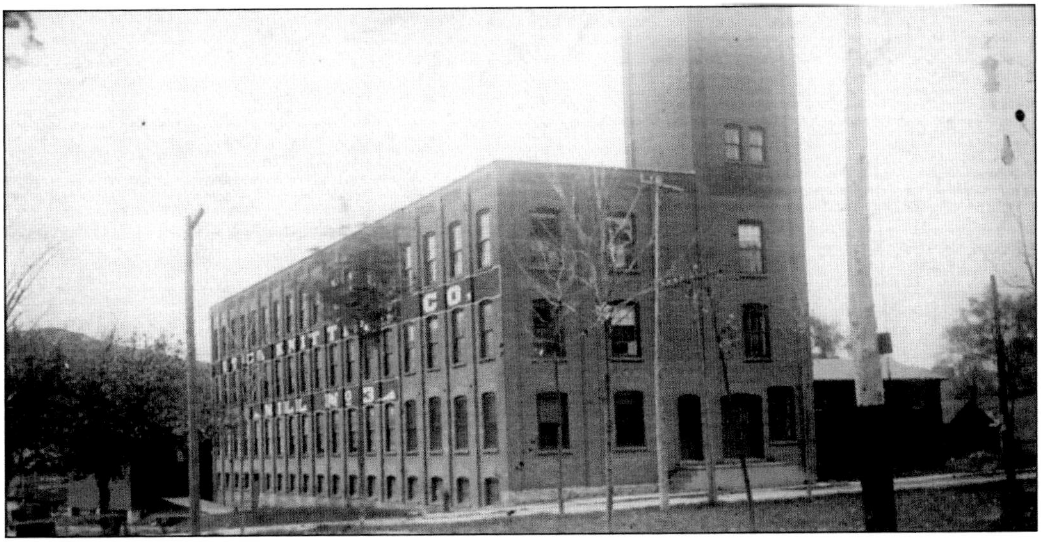

Located on the corner of South Main and Division Streets, the mill was constructed in 1897. The Oriskany Creek provided ample waterpower, and convenient railroad tracks made it an ideal location. Various businesses have operated from these factories, among them the Hatheway and Reynolds Cap Factory, established in 1876. The business eventually became an 11-building complex before selling out to a Syracuse macaroni manufacturer. The mill pictured was constructed in 1897 for the Utica Knitting Company. Closing in 1950, it was sold to Lily White Sales Company. In 1966, Chesebrough-Pond acquired the operation. Currently, the pharmaceutical firm Tyco Company is located here.

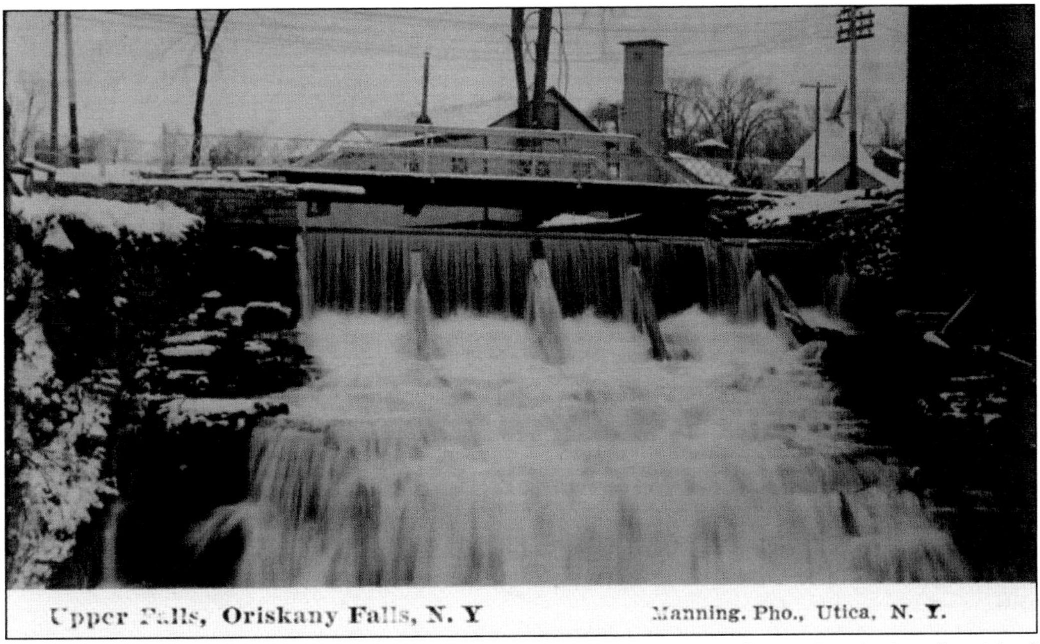

Just off Madison Street, on Broad Street, are the falls on the Oriskany Creek that furnished the waterpower for the numerous industries. On the north bank was a paper box factory with Farmer's Mills on the south. The creek turns sharply east at this point, then flows parallel to Broad Street, turns once again, and meanders north.

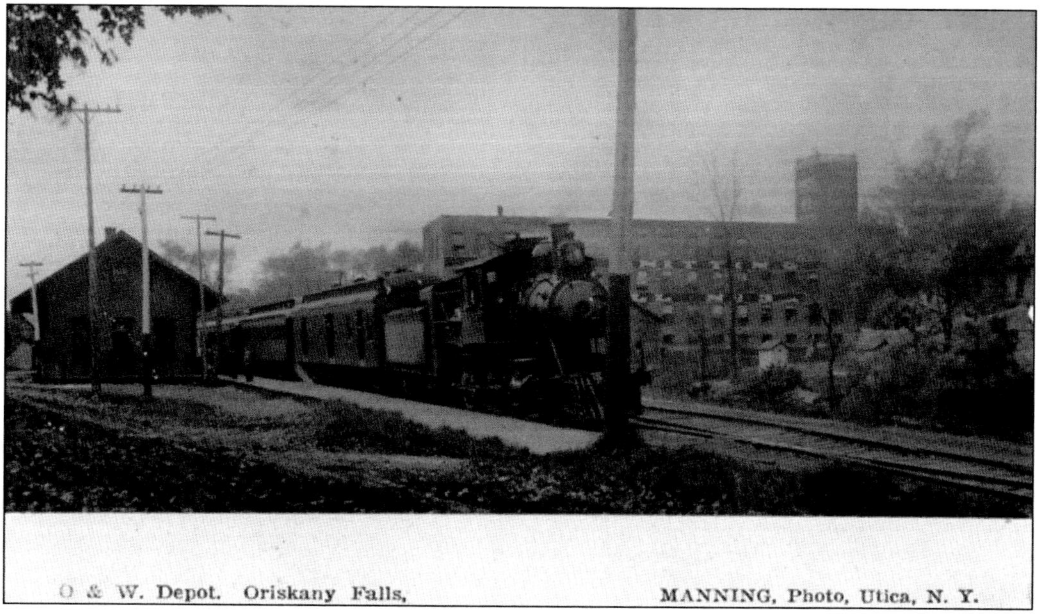

The Ontario and Western train depot at Oriskany Falls stood just across the tracks from the Utica Knitting Mill. Built in 1869 by the Utica, Clinton, and Binghamton Railroad, the depot, with its board-and-batten siding was typical of that period. The Ontario and Western Railroad replaced this depot with a larger one in 1911. When the new depot was operating, the old one was sold and moved across Madison Street to become a four-family apartment building. Later it became an antique store but is now deserted and forlorn.

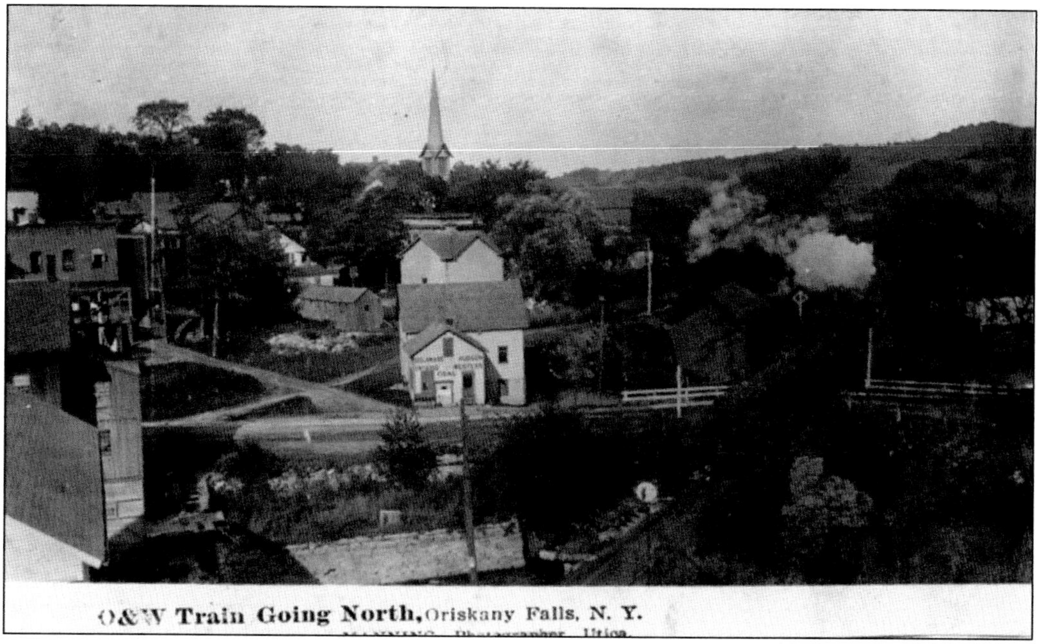

The steam billowing from an Ontario and Western northbound train, viewed from Liberty Hill, passes through the village. The train has just crossed a bridge over the falls. In the center is the Delaware, Hudson and Ontario and Western coal building. To the left of center, the steeple of the Congregational church can be seen. (Courtesy LRHS.)

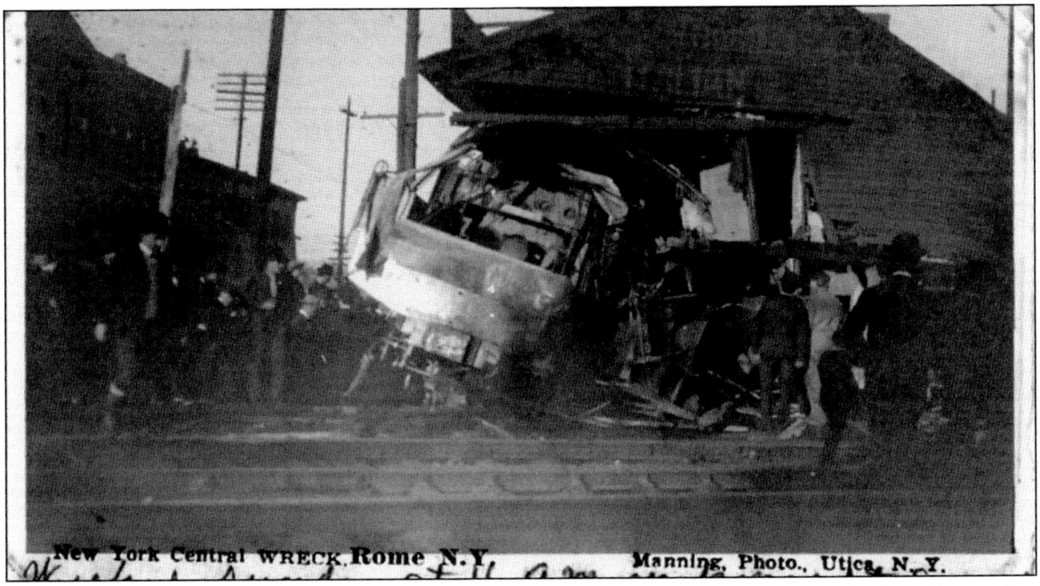

On November 6, 1906, the quiet of a Sunday morning in Rome was shattered when the engine of an eastbound New York Central freight train jumped the tracks and plunged headlong into Thomas Ferlo's saloon at 215 South James Street. Tragically the head brakeman and the engineer were killed. The Ferlo bakery and grocery store in the building were also heavily damaged. The engineer, Adelbert Brown of Little Falls, had been scalded by escaping steam and suffered a head injury resulting in his death. On July 7, 1908, another locomotive "visited" Ferlo's Restaurant, this time less tragically as there were no major injuries.

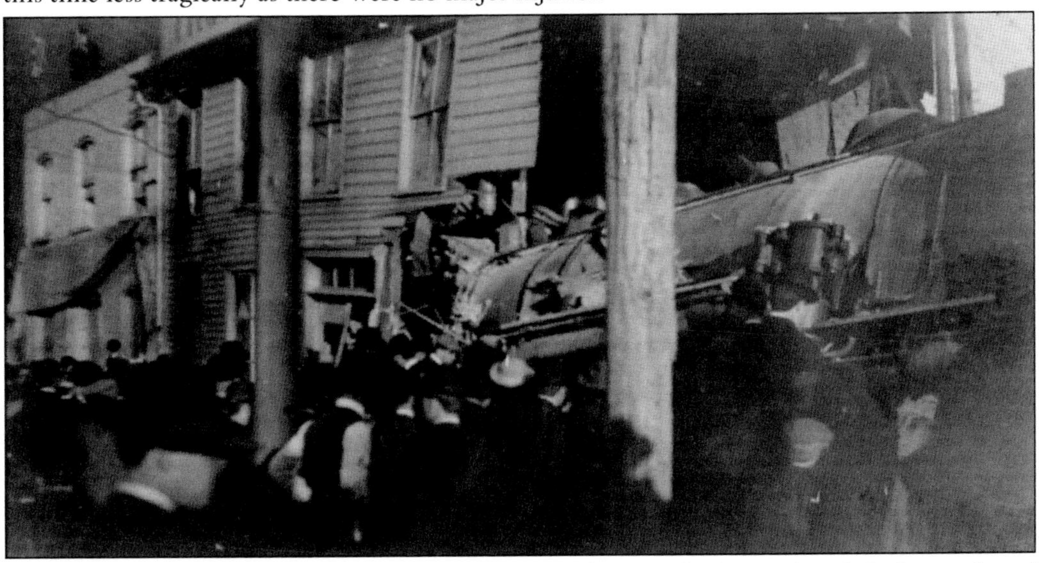

In the November 1906 wreck, three freight cars, along with the engine, left the track and wreckage was strewn over the South James Street crossing. A Rome police officer who witnessed the crash said he saw the engine rocking from side to side when it suddenly gave a lurch and the wheels on one side rose into the air two or three feet, and then fell back before crashing into the saloon. Head brakeman Robert Vandervoort of Albany was killed in the crash and had been with the railroad only a year. He had previously left Barnum and Bailey Circus, where he had been a bicycle stunt rider, because of the danger involved in its performance.

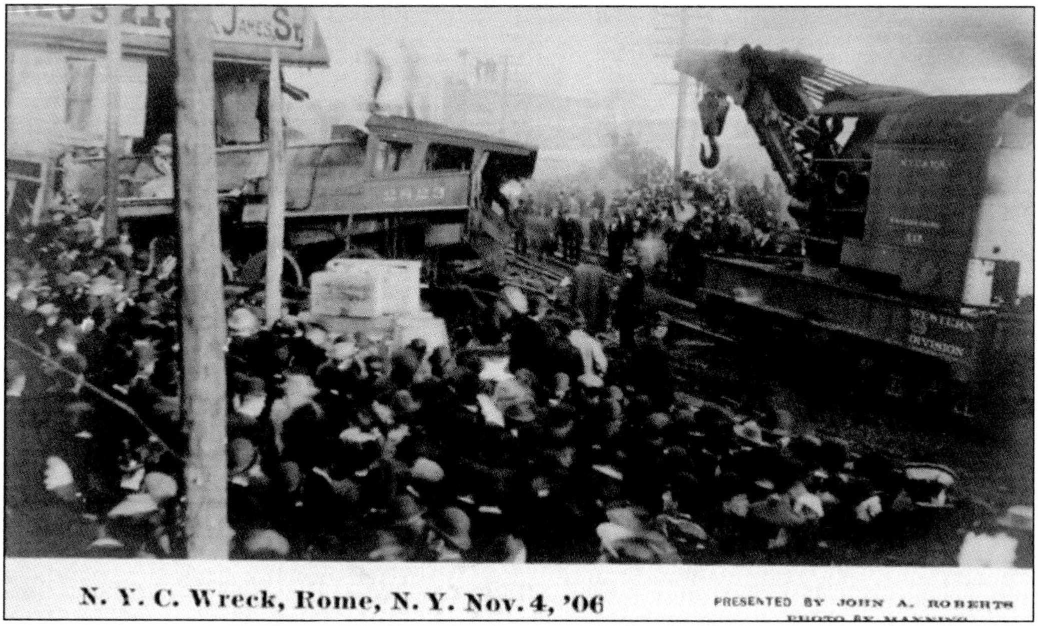

Throngs of people attired in their Sunday best viewed the wreckage of the New York Central train. As late as midnight there was still a crowd at the scene, a number remaining until the big locomotive was placed back on the track. Police were pressed to keep the spectators beyond the roped-off accident area so the crews could continue the cleanup. The cause of the wreck was thought to be that the new engine was "jacked up" too tight for the sharp curve.

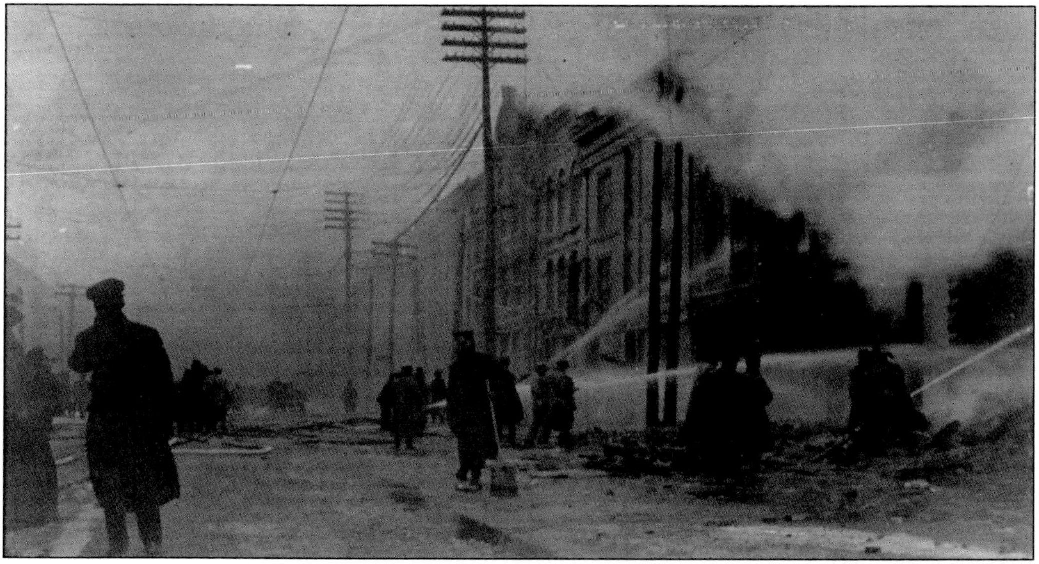

A disastrous fire struck Rome at noon on February 2, 1908, destroying three blocks and damaging several others. Originating in the F. E. Bacon and Company Department Store on the corner of Washington and Dominick Streets, it spread to two adjoining blocks. The total loss was estimated to be about $300,000. A call for aid brought Utica and Syracuse fire departments. Utica loaded trucks and equipment on two flat railroad cars, and firemen occupied a passenger coach. Arriving at 2:05 p.m., the firemen battled the blaze until 6:30 p.m., with snow and gale winds complicating their efforts.

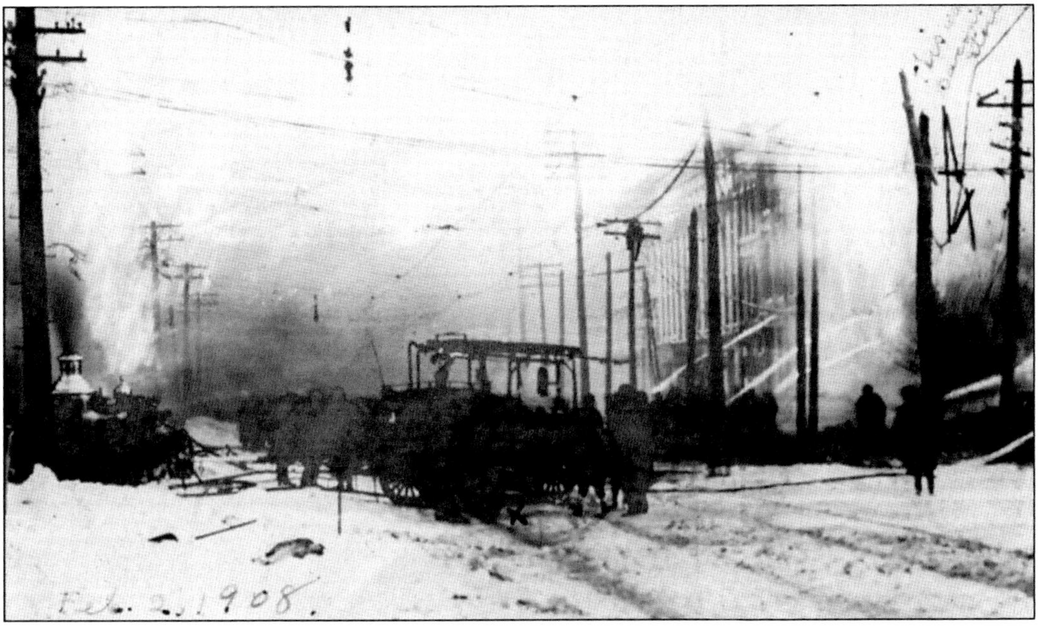

Firemen train hoses on the rapidly spreading fire. According to a *Utica Daily Press* article, flames broke out almost simultaneously from the front and the Washington Street side of the Ethridge Block and were spread by the wind half way across Dominick Street. At times, steam from the engines mingled with the snow, creating black clouds that concealed the buildings. A large crowd of spectators braved the cold and stormy day to view the conflagration.

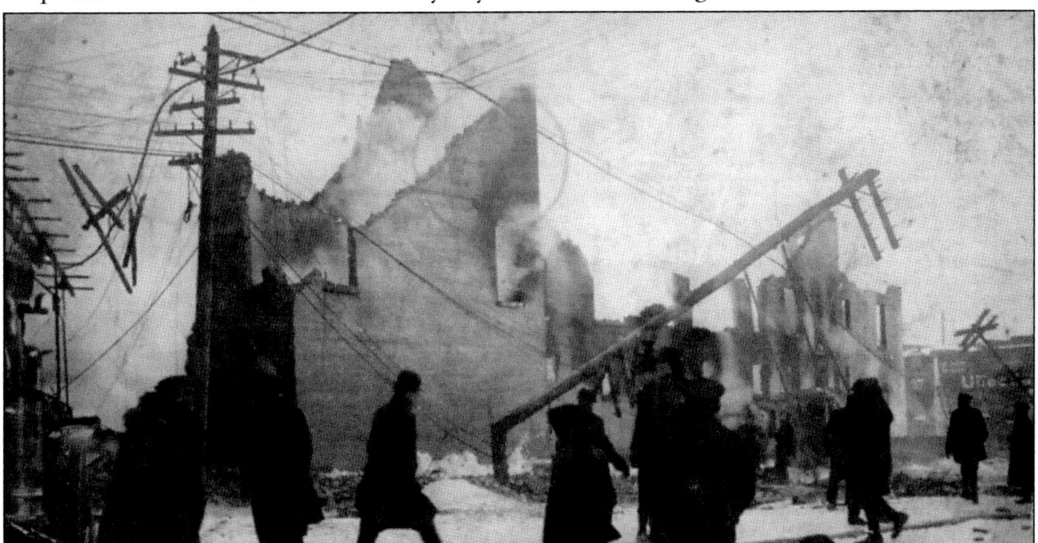

The flames, fanned by a high wind, gutted the buildings in an incredibly short time, leaving them almost completely destroyed. The big cables of the Bell Telephone Company were toppled by the falling walls. One man who volunteered his services was overcome by smoke. Firemen found him unconscious and thinking him dead, carried him to a nearby undertaking parlor. However, he was revived and was much surprised to find out where he was. Several firemen were injured during the fire by falling brick as the walls toppled over. The cause of the fire was never determined.

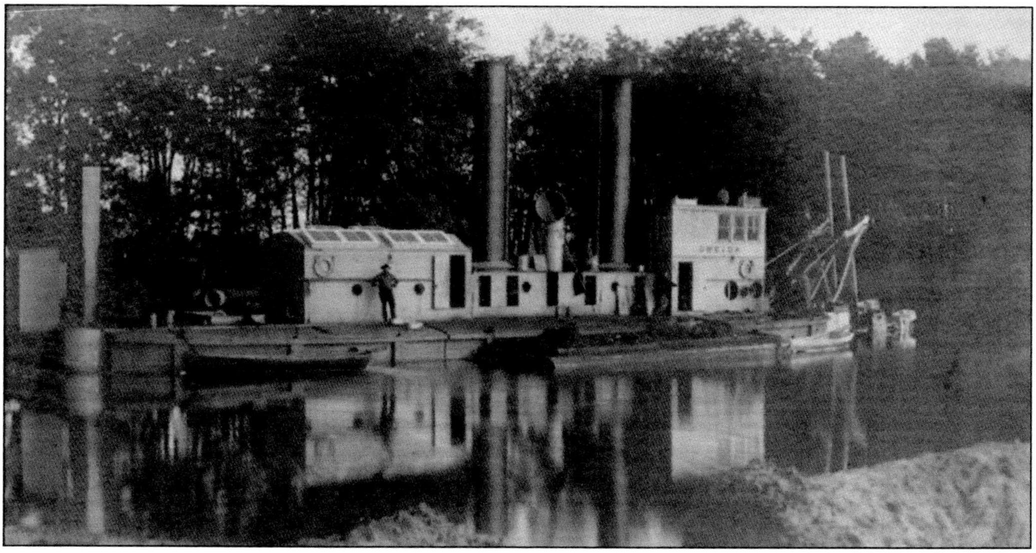

Fish Creek was the first settlement at the eastern end of Oneida Lake. The first Oneida Lake Canal connected the Erie Canal at Higginsville with Fish Creek. The canal dredger pictured here is dredging the canal east of Sylvan Beach by the hamlet of Fish Creek around 1910. A large crew was needed to operate the canal dredges, which were used to keep the channel deep enough for navigation. Hydraulic dredges operated like vacuum cleaners, sucking water and material from the bottom and running it through pipes before dumping it away from the waterway.

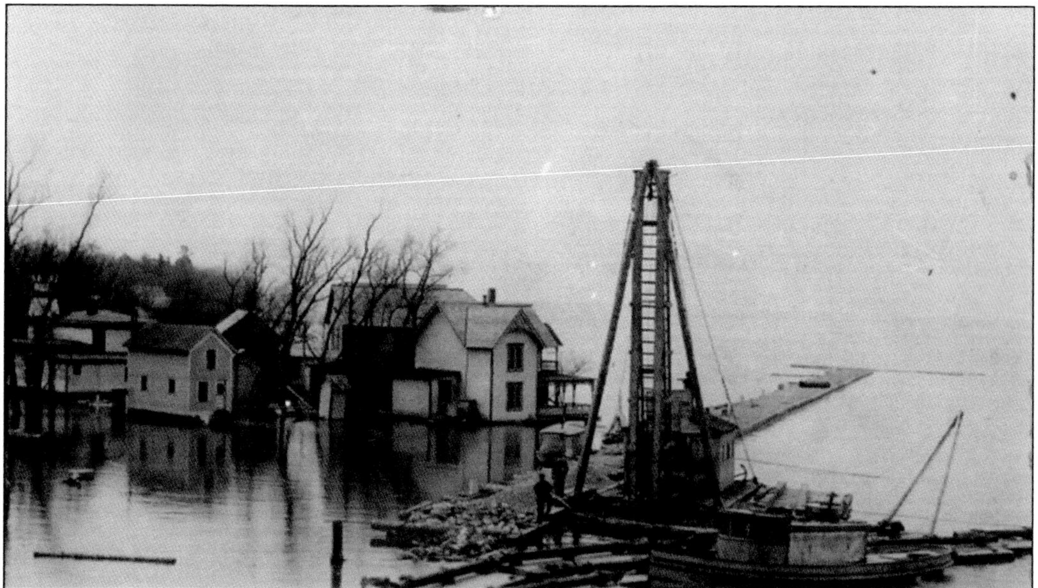

Scene on Barge Canal, Sylvan Beach, N. Y. MANNING, Photo, Utica, N. Y.

Shown here is the beginning of the construction of the Sylvan Beach pier. The dredge pictured was basically just "a big shovel mounted on a flat barge." Three long legs (called spuds), two on the front and one in back, kept the vessel steady while operating. These legs are lowered into the canal bottom, allowing the dredge to move about. Lacking typical propulsion, the dredge is towed into position by a tug boat.

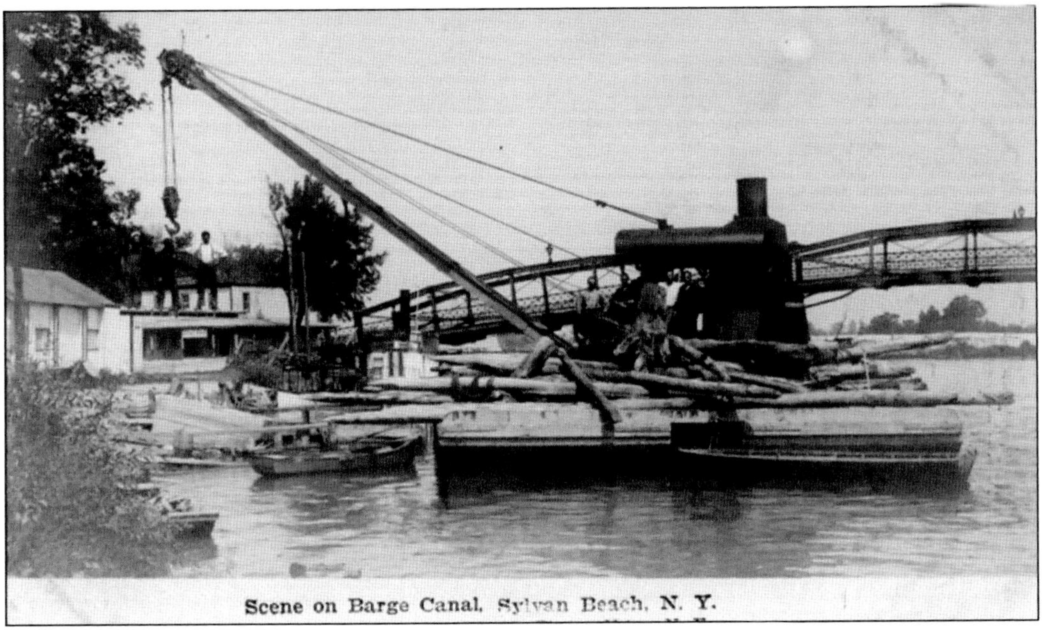

The bridge in the background was built in 1886. The Barge Canal project was begun at Sylvan Beach in 1907. The original Erie Canal, begun in 1817, was completed in 1825. It was enlarged to a seven-foot draft in 1862. The first Barge Canal system, started in 1905, was enlarged to accommodate larger vessels and opened in 1918. The Erie section of the canal runs from Albany on the Hudson River to Buffalo on the Niagara River.

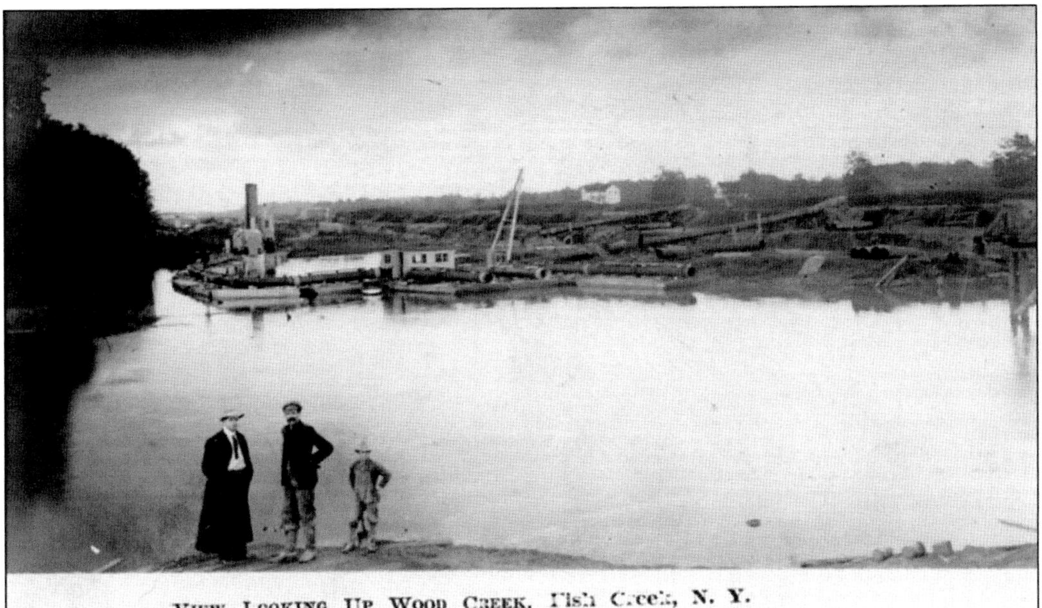

Sightseers stand at the mouth of Wood Creek just west of the Cove Road bridge across the creek from a dredge parking area. Not everyone was pleased with the dredges in the canal. They often churned up mud, sending it to the lake and distributing it on the beach, discouraging bathers. It also negatively affected productive fishing, sometimes for several seasons. (Courtesy of OCHS.)

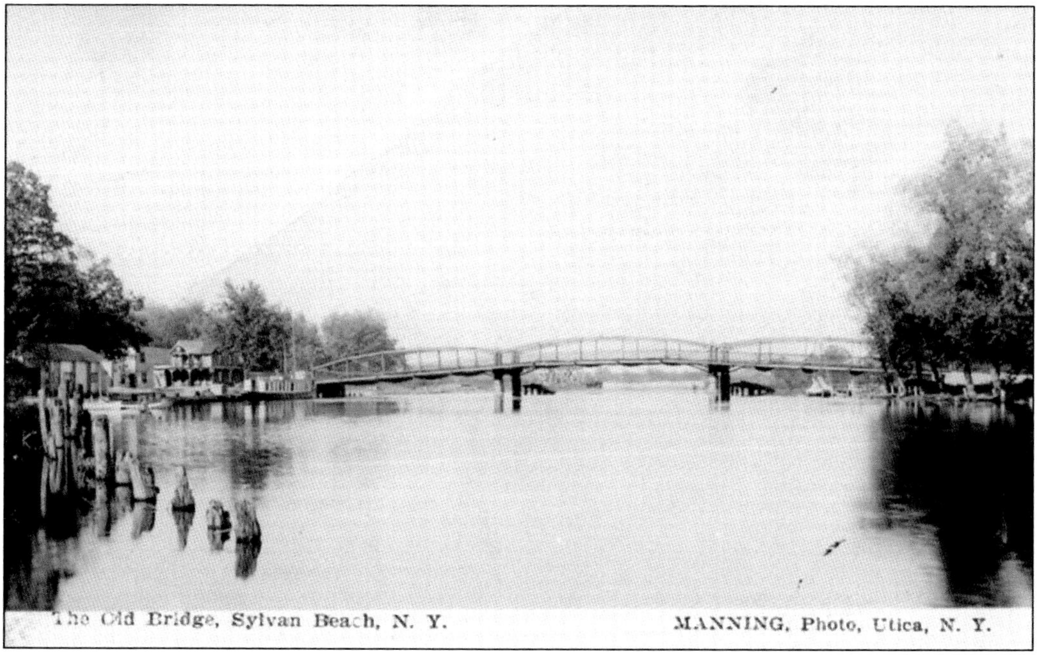

The first bridge built over Wood River-Fish Creek at Sylvan Beach on Oneida Lake was later replaced. This bridge made for easier access to the other side, previously provided by privately operated ferryboats. Oneida Lake in central New York is 20 miles long and an average of four miles wide.

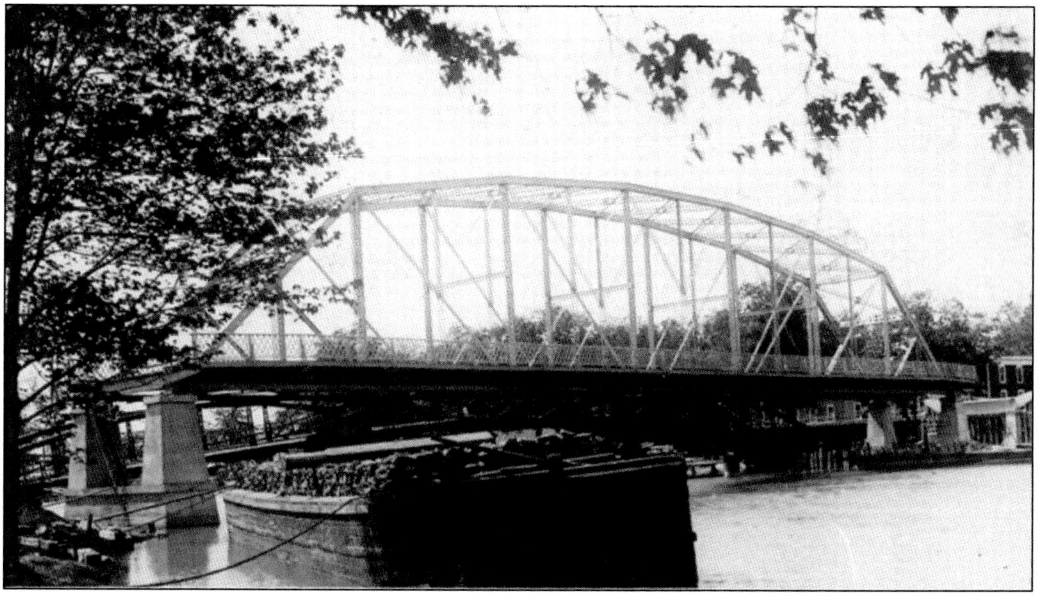

This new bridge replaced the old and it, too, met its demise and is now just a highway over the creek. Completed in 1908, the new bridge was slightly further east of the old bridge and provided a convenient route between Verona Beach to the south (now a state park) and Sylvan Beach. A standing-room-only crowd witnessed the dedication of the new bridge on Oct. 28, 1908. The village has many summer cottages along its eastern shore, numerous restaurants, and offers fishing, swimming, and boating. It is still host to thousands of summer visitors.

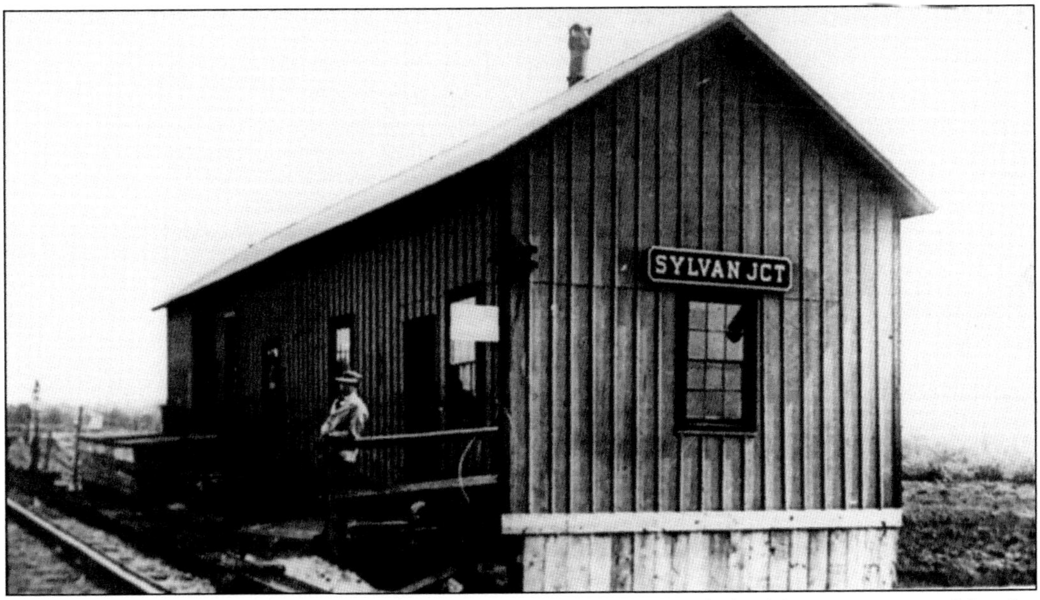

Sylvan Junction is located in the hamlet of Fish Creek. A simple building constructed by the Ontario and Western Railroad and the Canastota Northern Railroad, the depot was completed in 1887. Located south of the Wood River Bridge, it served as a station for the Ontario and Western Railroad and the Elmira, Cortland and Northern Railroad. The station is as it looked in 1907 when Harmie Roberts (on the porch) was the agent.

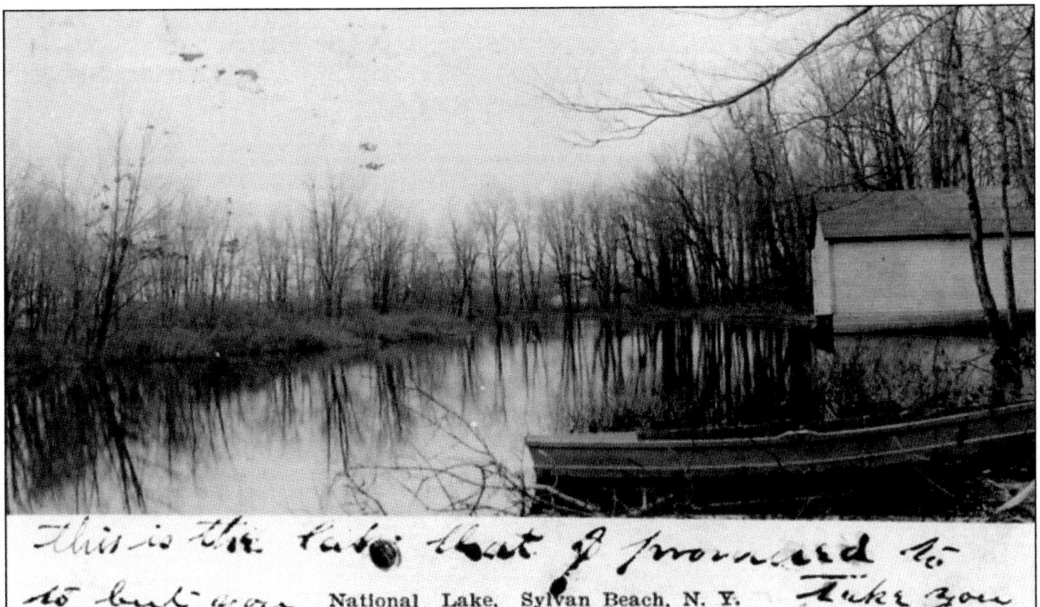

National Lake is located at the east end of Akehurst Avenue at Sylvan Beach. This was an old ox-bow of the Wood River, now the site of a marina and private residences. An ox-bow is a crescent-shaped lake formed in an abandoned meander loop that has become separated by a change in the stream's course.

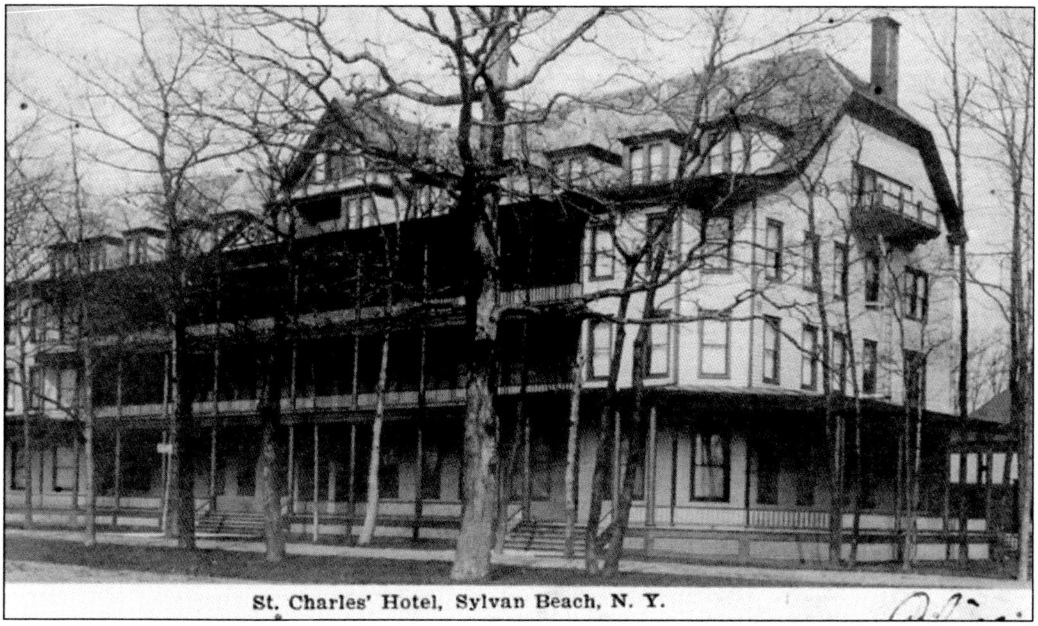

On the lakefront was one of the beach's more luxurious hotels, the four-story St. Charles Hotel, built in 1899 by Louis Chesebrough, maker of Vaseline products. A high-class hotel, the St. Charles Hotel had room for 150 guests with weekly rates of $14 and up. The popular hotel was destroyed by fire on September 17, 1914, and was never rebuilt. The Silver Sands Restaurant was later on this site, but it is now being developed by a local businessman.

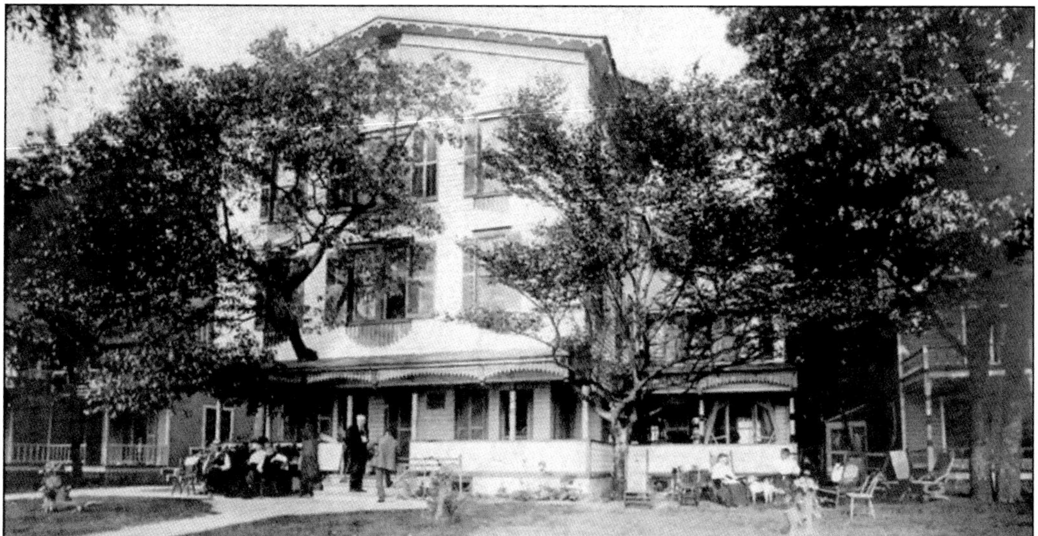

The Sanitarium on Oneida Lake at Sylvan Beach was founded by Dr. Martin Cavana whose "gold cure" offered remedy for various addictions, Cavana took a paternal interest in community affairs. Arriving in 1891 as the area was just beginning to realize its potential as a resort, he was a model citizen, working tirelessly on behalf of the village. He brought in new businesses and expanded the midway amusement area. Cavana was also instrumental in getting the Ontario and Western Railroad to build a depot in Sylvan Beach.

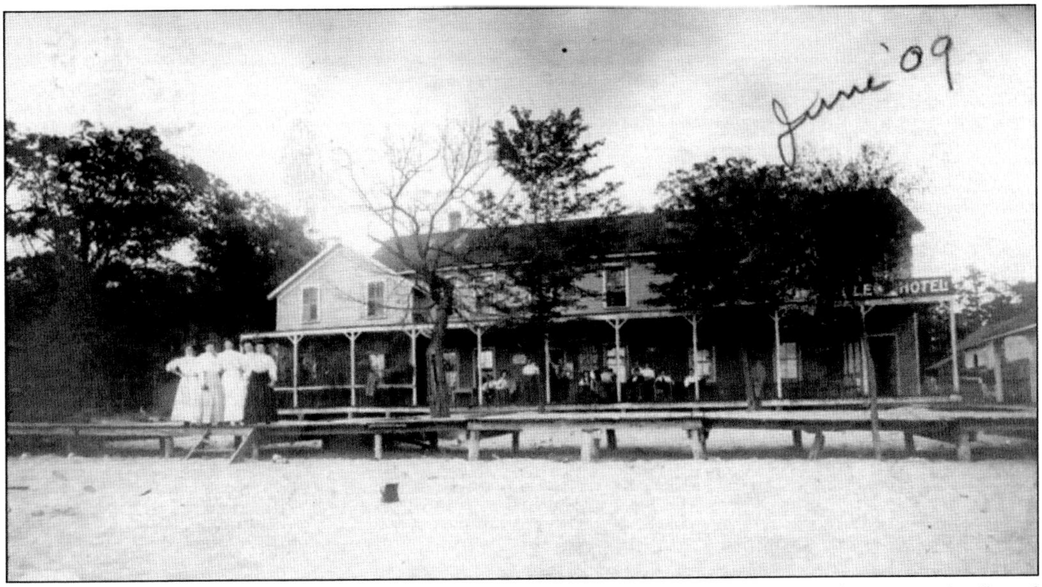

J. Frank Miller's Eagle Hotel was located just a short walk from the Ontario and Western Railroad Station. The hotel had its own steamboat landing and a dancing pavilion. In the 1920s and 1930s, the beach declined in popularity as people acquired their own automobiles, and the Eagle Hotel fell on hard times. One resident recalled that the foundation had deteriorated to such a state that "one could hear the wind whistle through it." In the 1950s and 1960s, DiCastro's, a bar and restaurant, occupied the site. The old Eagle Hotel was later torn down, and Pfohl's Beach House Bar now occupies the site.

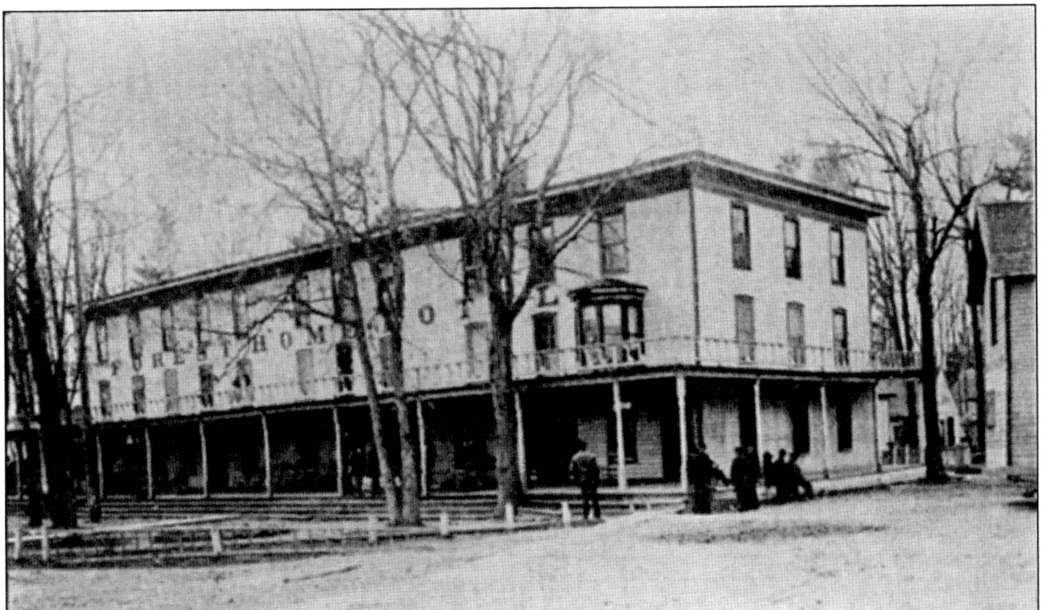

Lyman Spencer's Forest Home, built in 1879, was the first resort hotel at Sylvan Beach. Suffering the fate of many early structures, fire destroyed this landmark. The hotel had a large veranda that wrapped around its front. Amenities offered were a restaurant, boathouse, dock, and bathhouse, all adjacent to five miles of sandy beach.

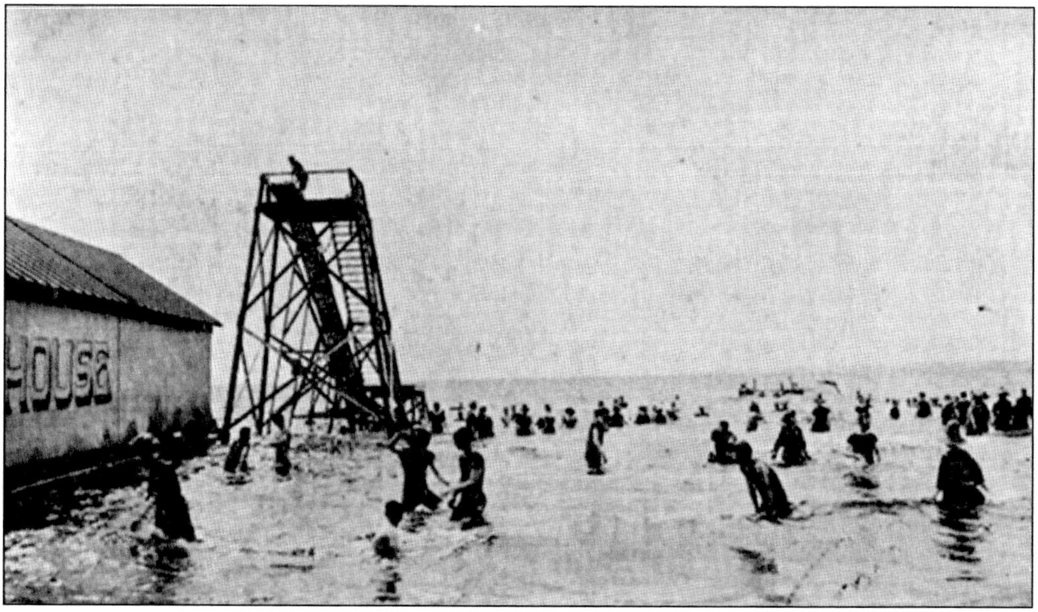

The bathhouse juts into Oneida Lake from the sandy beach. The toboggan slide attracted bathers seeking a thrill. The midway area farther down the beach provided entertainment to patrons with "rollie coasters" and carousels. Dr. Martin Cavana imported trapeze artists and acrobats to entertain tourists. Through Cavana's efforts, Carnival Park became a popular attraction and was touted as Upstate New York's Coney Island.

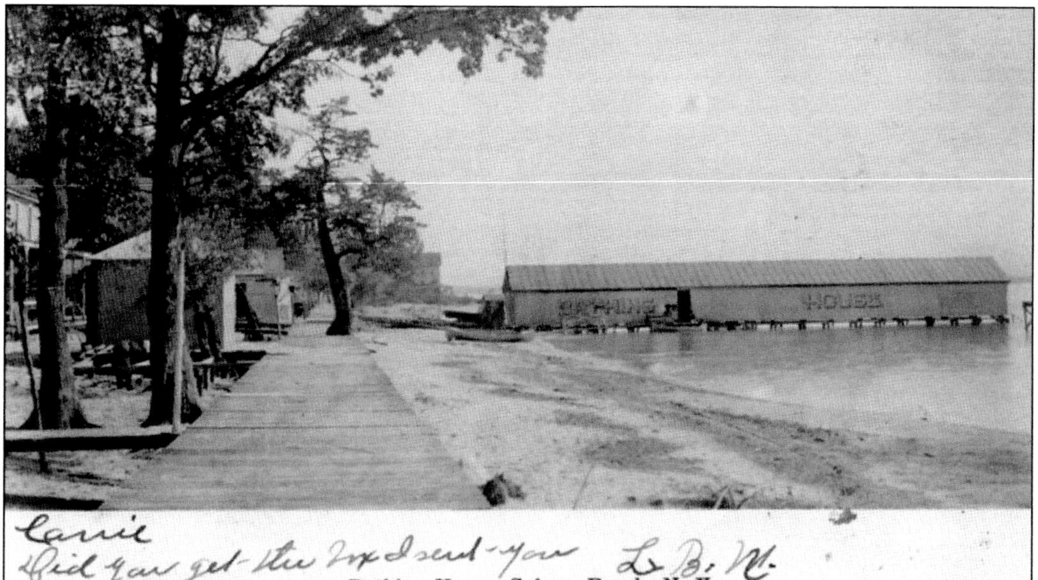

This tranquil scene of the boardwalk and bathhouse is a sharp contrast to one newspaper columnist's portrayal of Sylvan Beach. In the *Clinton Courier* on July 9, 1890, the writer expressed his view: "Sunday excursion trains are announced for Sylvan Beach. People who profess to regard the Sabbath as a day of holy rest should avoid visiting places for recreation, even on a week day, where beer and whisky are at flood tide night and day and where Sunday is especially devoted to bacchanalian revelry."

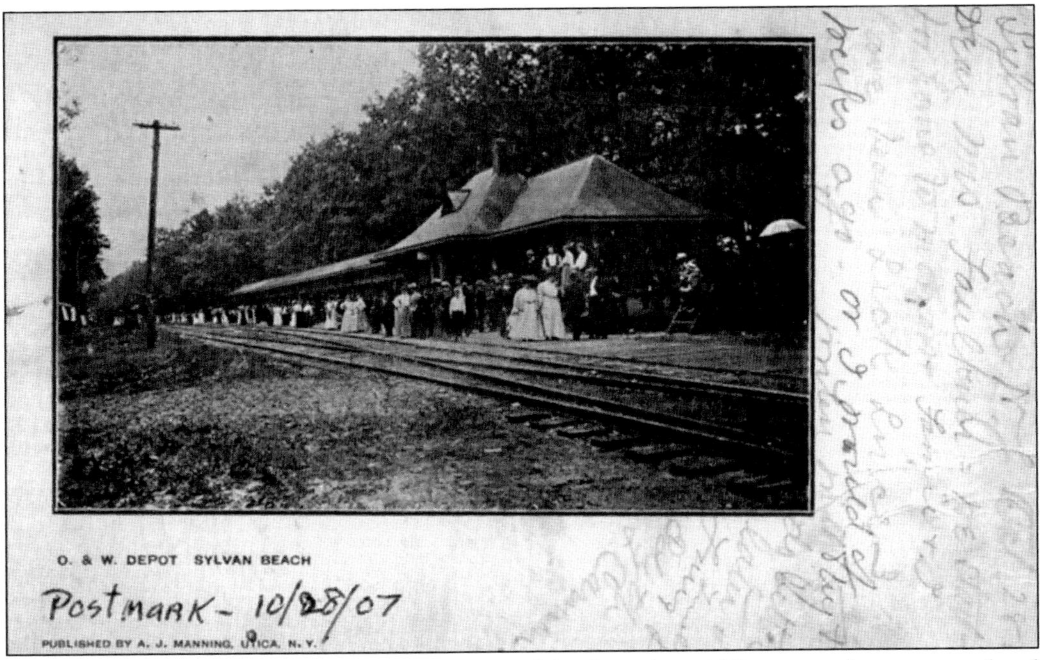

Built on the site of an earlier depot, construction of the Ontario and Western station was completed in 1892. A long, covered platform, shown here with throngs of people, led to the grove, a popular picnic area. Increasing numbers of tourists from all over the state took advantage of the easy train access to the beach. The annual Hop Growers picnic of 1892 required 130 Ontario and Western Railroad coaches and 48 cars from the Elmira, Cortland and Northern line. In the 1920s and 1930s, business declined as automobiles gained in popularity. Today Eddie's Restaurant is located where the depot once stood.

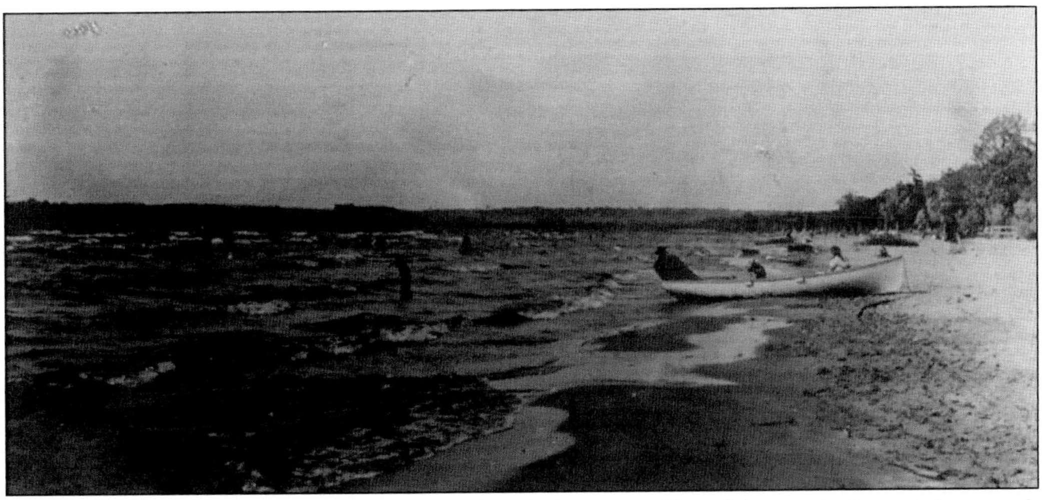

Passengers survey the lake, safely ensconced in their canoe. The whitecaps indicate it is a rough day on the lake, and likely not a good day for canoeing. In Jack Henke's book, *Tales of Oneida Lake*, he writes, "The lake often exhibits an untamed spirit and, when driven by strong winds, creates conditions that kill." The canoeists are wise to stay ashore. There are many tales of people who have had to be rescued from sudden storms that arise on the lake.

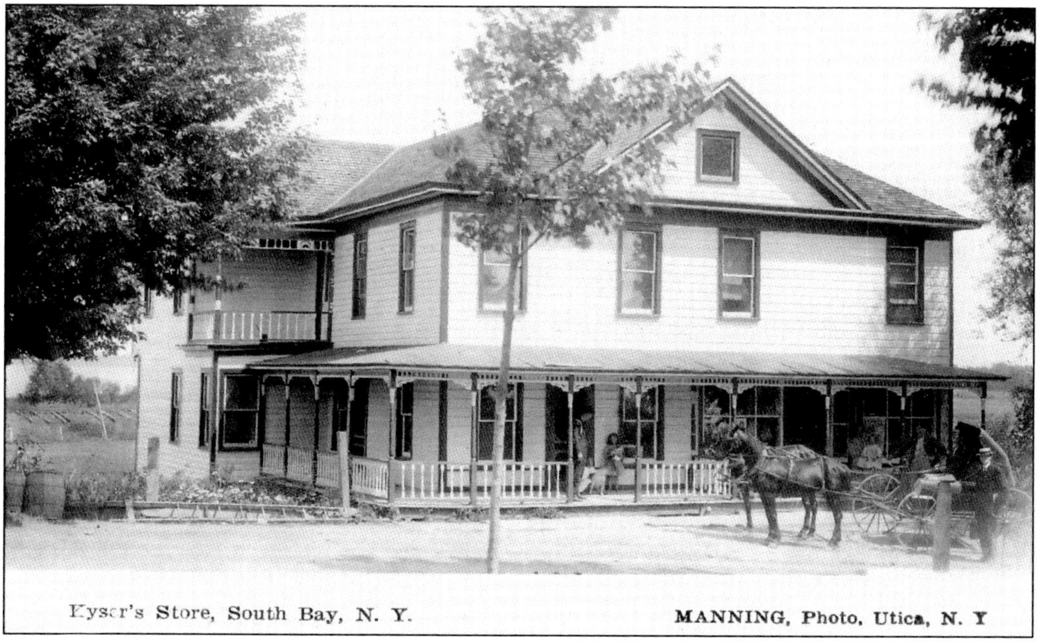

Jake Kyser was the owner of Kyser's Store, located just west of the junction of routes 13 and 31. He also operated the nearby Kyser Hotel. Kyser was known as the most accomplished fish pirate (one who sets illegal nets and sells the fish) on the east end of Oneida Lake. New York State officials wearied of trying to catch him and eventually made him a game warden. The former store was taken down when the road was straightened, but the hotel still stands. (Courtesy Tom Gates.)

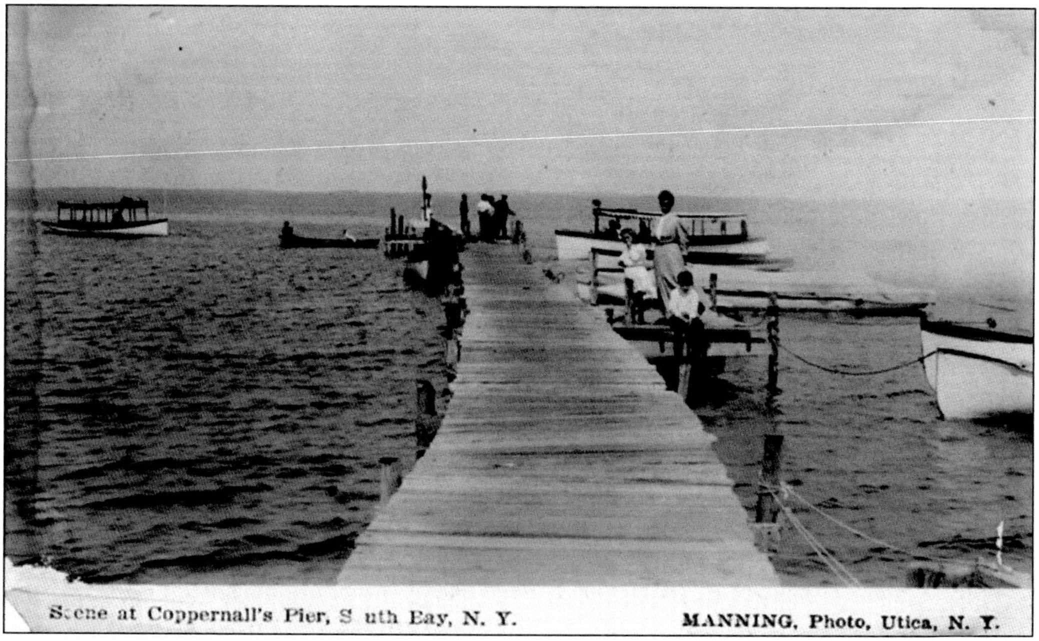

This steamboat landing on Oneida Lake was near Kyser's store and hotel. Steamboats picked up passengers to tour the lake and to transport them to the amusement area and other attractions along the shores of the lake. The Syracuse and South Bay Electric and the Oneida Lake Transportation Company provided both land and water routes to the beach.

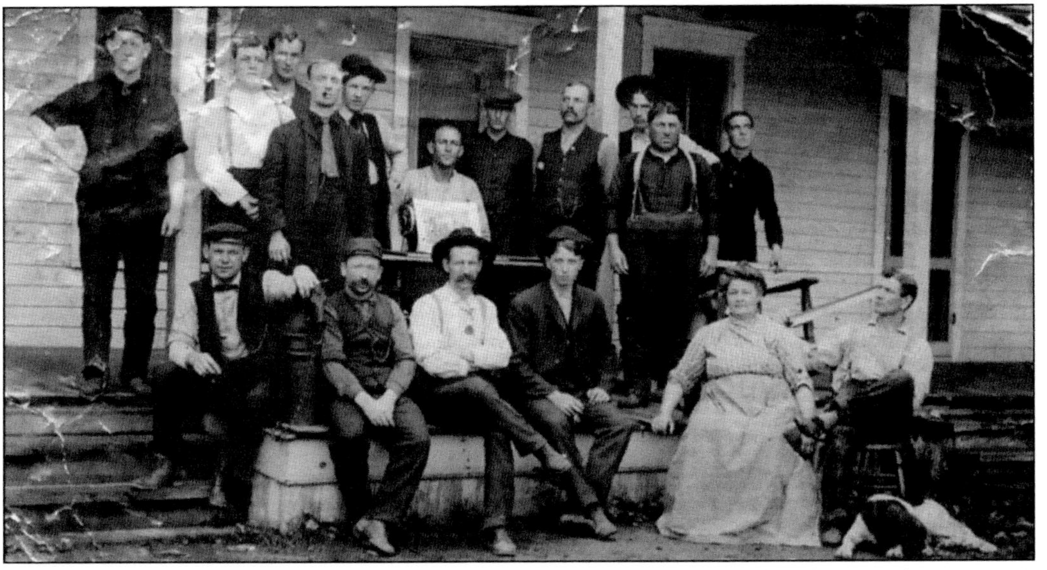

Workers for the railroad are pictured on the porch of a North Bay boardinghouse. The woman is likely the operator of the establishment. Pictured from left to right are (first row) Jesse Harding, Mike Hodge, Fred Thorpe, Leon Wood, unidentified woman (proprietor?), unidentified, and the boardinghouse pet dog; (second row) Bert Hagerty, unidentified, unidentified, unidentified, Leo Feeley (with hat), unidentified, unidentified, Matt Breed (with mustache), unidentified, "Gyp" Gillespie (with suspenders), and Tom Adams.

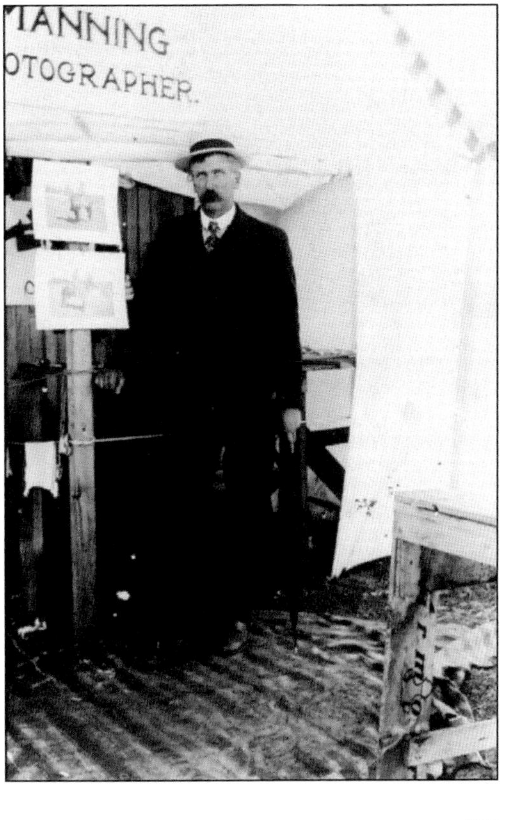

Where this real-photo postcard was taken is a mystery. The gentleman is identified as Peter Wellerhahn on the back of the card. The tent arrangement would indicate Manning had set up at a location other than his studio. There are also postcards taken at Pine Camp (see the last chapter), where Manning is set up with tents. Packing the necessary heavy camera equipment for taking photographs outside the studio presented a challenge.

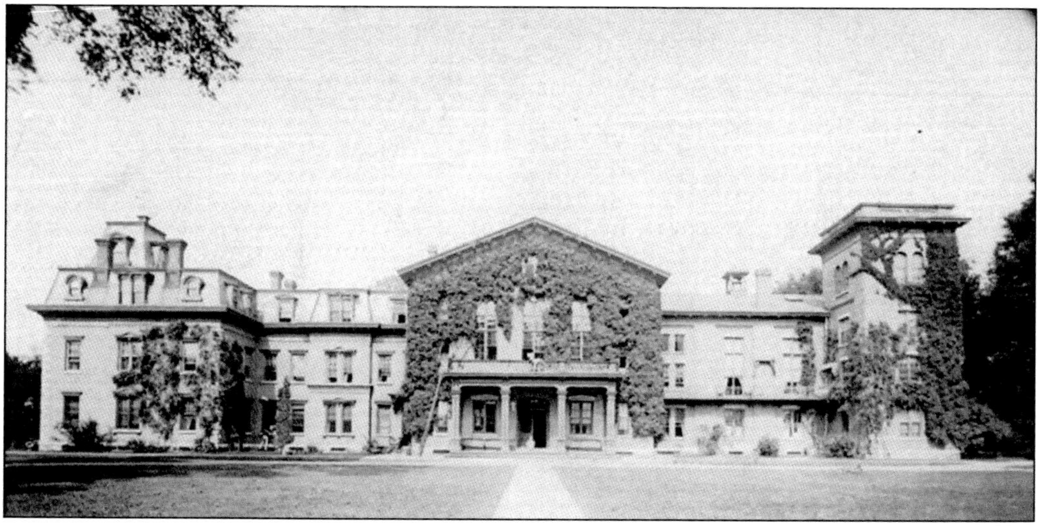

This spacious mansion house was a far cry from the primitive log huts that housed the early members of the Oneida Community. The Oneida Community were followers of John Humphrey Noyes, who adopted perfectionist beliefs (man could attain a state of perfect love between himself and God). Objections to the group's way of life and system of "complex marriage" (men and women were free from the confines of monogamy and conventional family life) resulted in vocal opposition from their Putney, Vermont, neighbors, causing the group to relocate to Kenwood-Sherrill, on the border of Oneida and Madison Counties, where they endured for over 30 years.

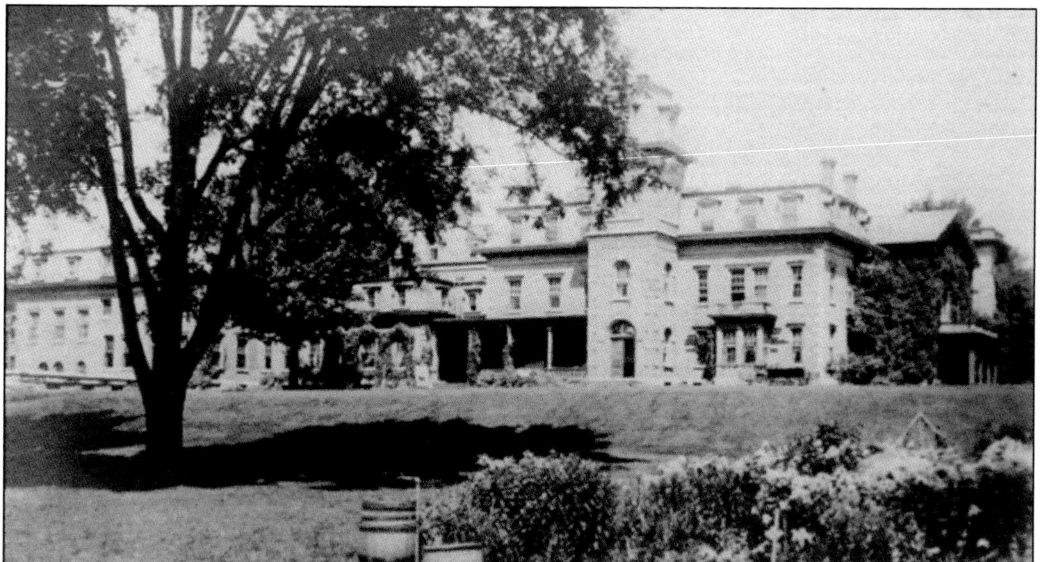

John Humphrey Noyes believed that the Second Coming of Christ had already occurred in AD 70, and believers were living in a state of grace free from the onus of sin. The perfectionists adopted a communal style of living where they lived as a family, sharing their property and labors without traditional marriage. By 1849, the group had built their first house, a simple frame building unlike the later mansion house built in 1860 with its brick towers, numerous sitting rooms, and large meeting hall. Today it is owned by Oneida Community Mansion House, a not-for-profit corporation, and is open for tours.

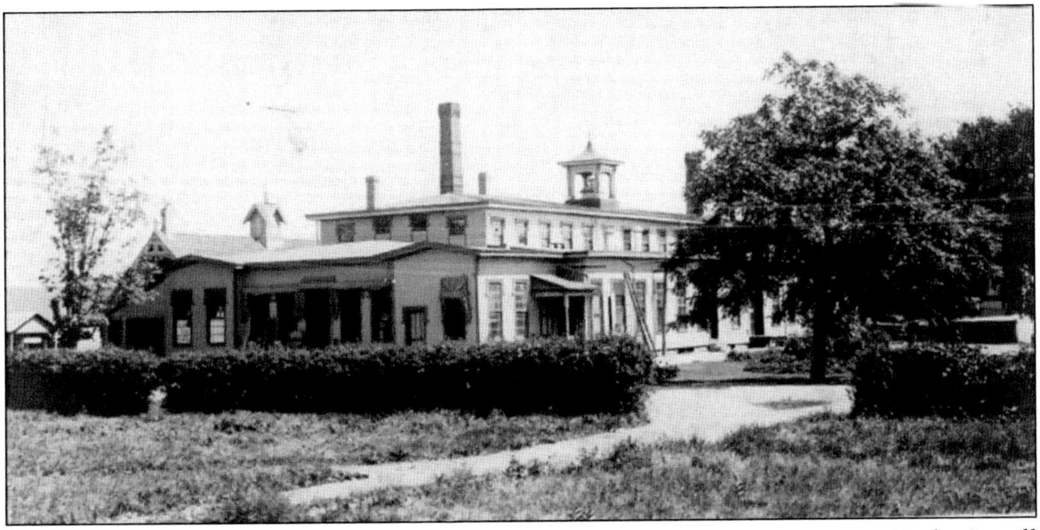

An early Oneida Community industry was the making of Newhouse game traps. Under Sewell Newhouse's guidance, the shop grew, and by 1860, traps were being shipped worldwide. Sales rose to $100,000 yearly. Other early Oneida products were silk thread and canned fruits and vegetables. In 1868, the fruit business was abandoned, but in later years it was brought back by popular demand, and ceased again in 1915. The Oneida Community Administration Office was later built on the site. In 1877, the community embarked on the manufacture of silverware.

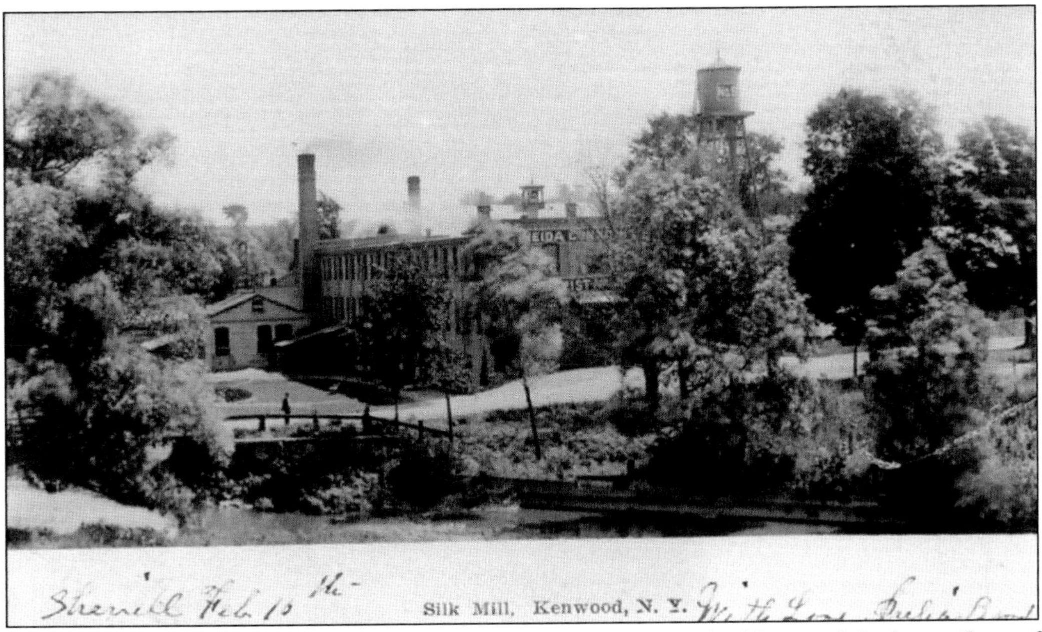

The Silk Department occupied the upper floor of the main trap building and the lower floor of the north wing. The raw silk was spun by machinery, then taken to the dye house located in Kenwood, just east of the present sales office. From there it went to the spooling room where it was put on spools and packed in boxes. Between 60 and 80 workers, mostly women, were employed in the silk mill. Every day thousands of dollars of silk spools were taken by horse and wagon to the express office in Oneida to be shipped.

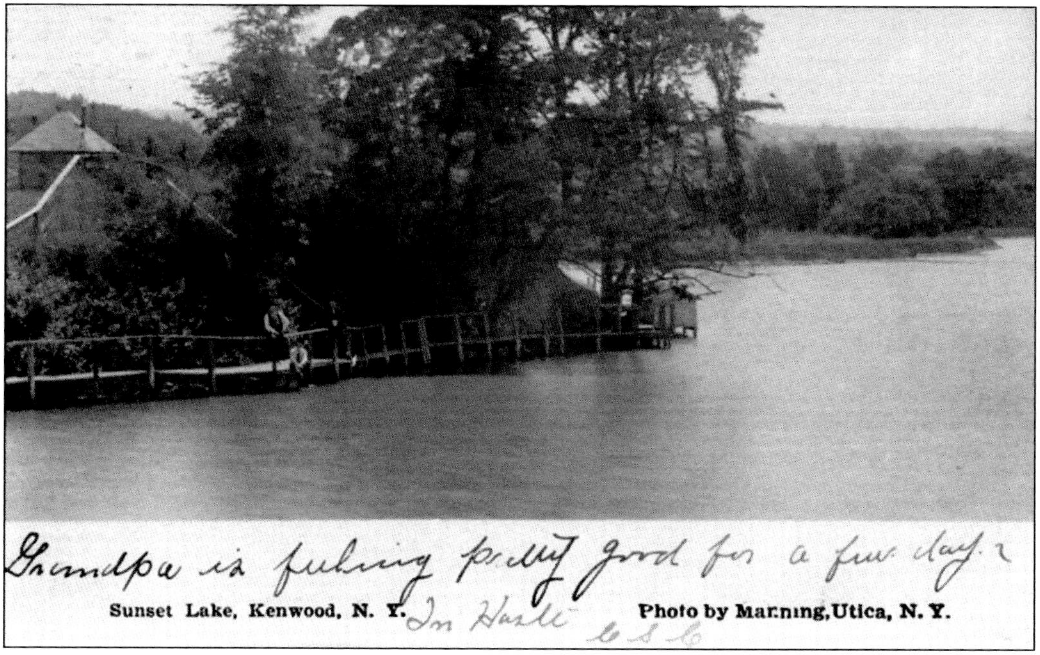

Sunset Lake, once owned by the Oneida Community, provided Sherrill residents with boating, swimming, and fishing in the summer. Many Sherrill youngsters became proficient swimmers here. No longer suitable for recreation except for anglers, its borders now have a thriving crop of algae, and it is a popular rest stop for geese heading south.

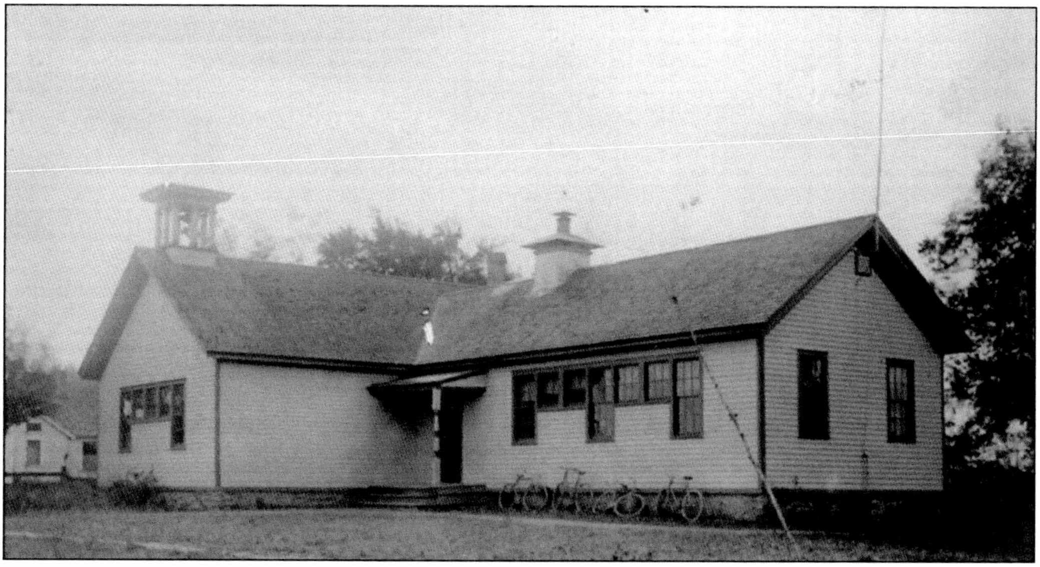

This Sherrill school building still stands on East Hamilton Avenue, opposite the southern end of School Street. When the school closed, the property was sold to the Methodist church and was converted into a church. Later it became Vanderlan's plumbing business, followed by Dr. Theodore Prowda's medical office before being converted to a private residence. A second story has been added to the wing at left. A new Vernon, Verona, Sherrill Central School was erected in 1955 in Verona to serve those communities. Grades kindergarten through 6 are taught at Kenwood Park Elementary School in Sherrill.

Six

City of Oneida in Madison County

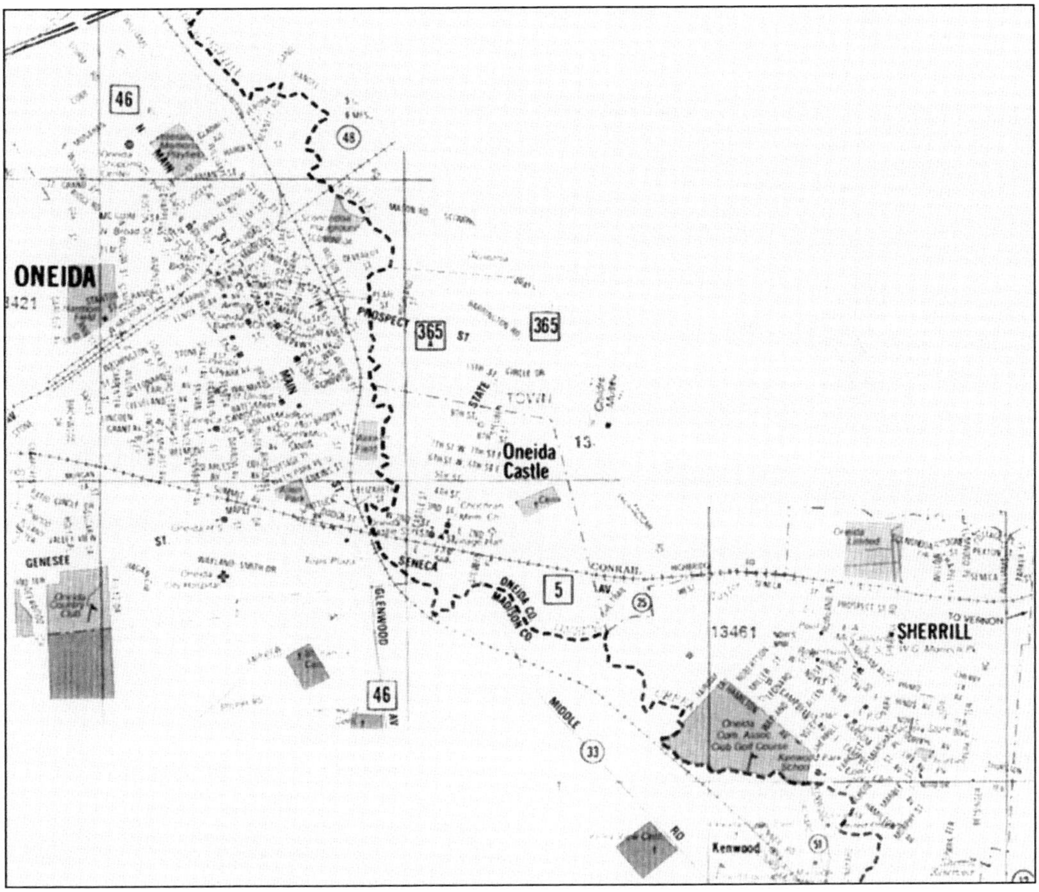

The city of Oneida is shown in this 1995 map.

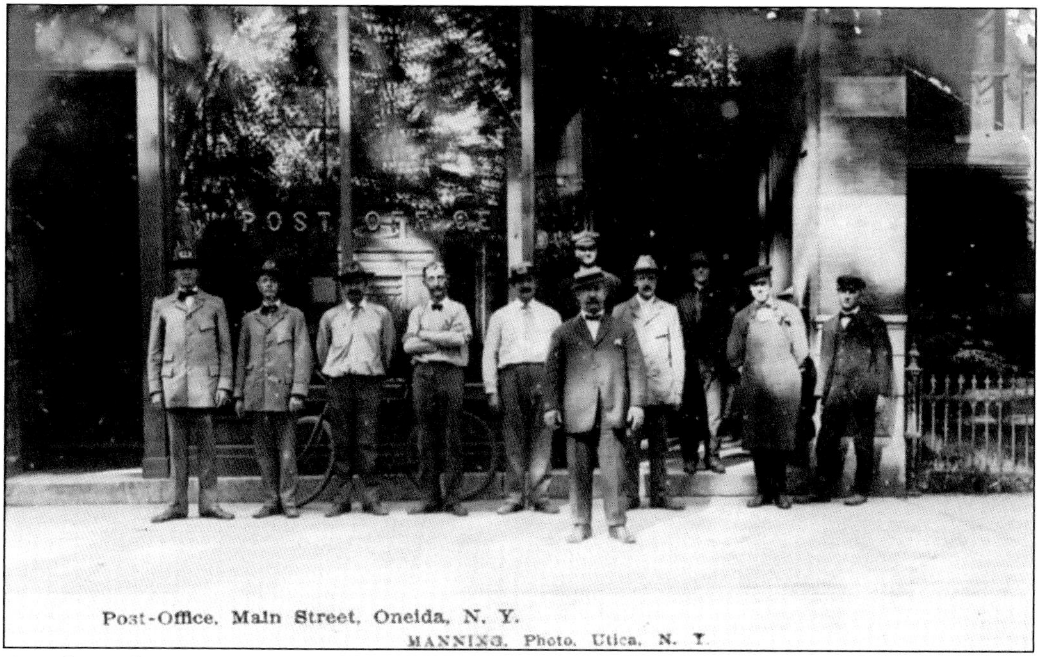

Oneida mailmen pose outside the Main Street post office in 1908. Among those pictured are postmaster John Munz (foreground), Frank Felts, U. S. Johnston, Otis Young, Fred Dean, Pete Bird, and a Mr. Wixon. The post office later relocated to the Torrey Building on Central Avenue, now Farrier Avenue. Jay Farrier was postmaster in 1907 and served until 1915. In 1921, he was again appointed postmaster and served for many more years. The building was later the site of a Woolworth's five-and-dime store.

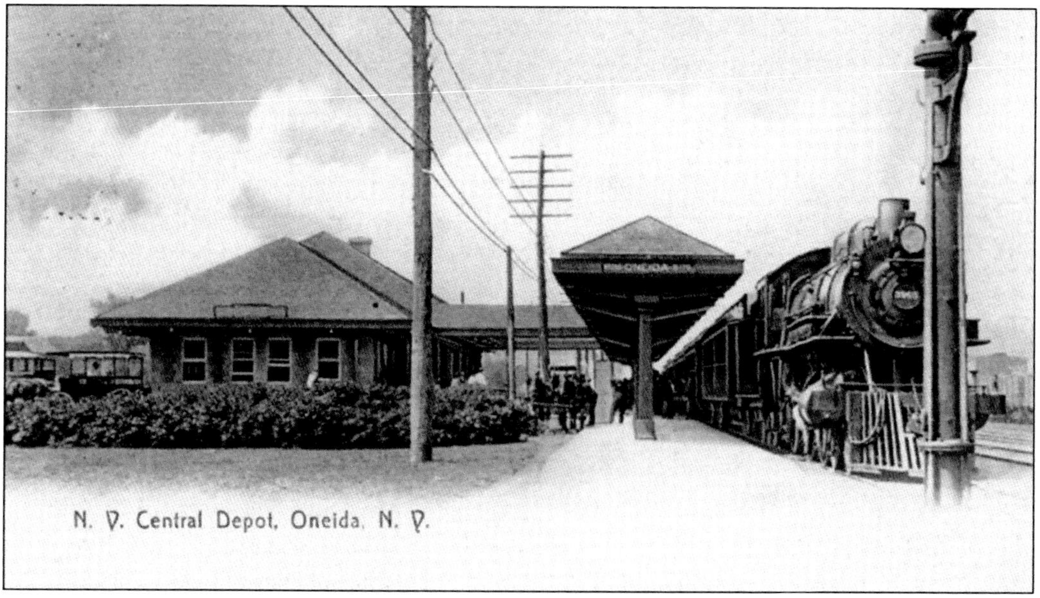

The New York Central Railroad Depot at 230 Farrier Avenue opened in 1903, replacing an earlier station at the foot of Broad Street. This depot saw men leave for two world wars and welcomed several campaigning presidents. The station closed in 1962 and was demolished in 1973 to be replaced by Oneida Towers, an apartment complex.

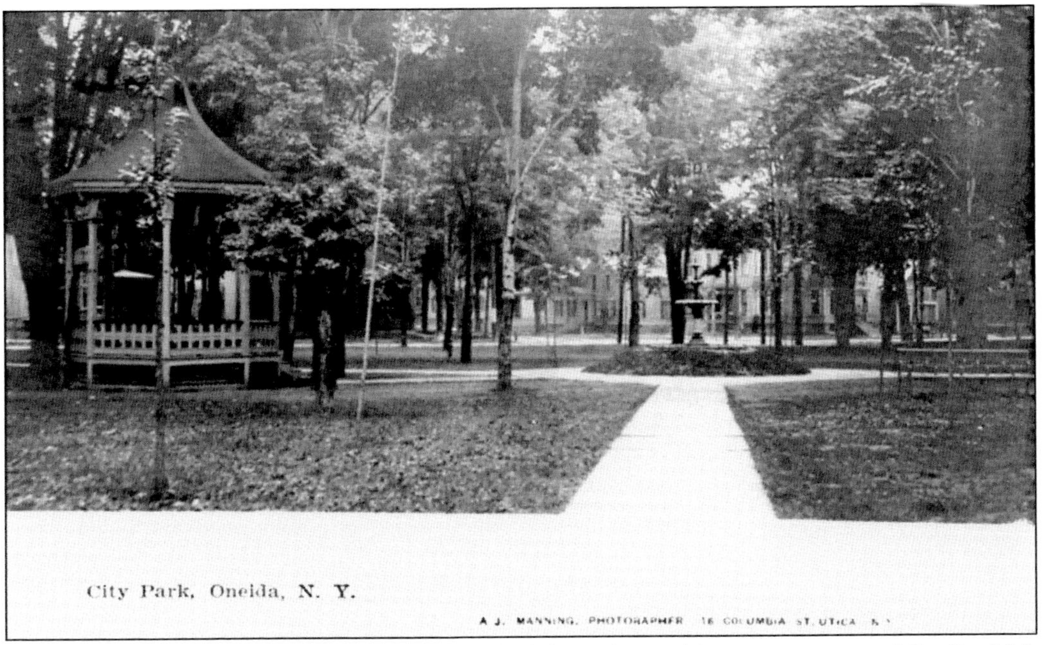

Higinbotham Park, bordered by Farrier, Vanderbilt, and Broad Streets, was named for Oneida's founder. The land was a gift of the founding family, as was the home that is now the Madison County Historical Society. The park is the scene of band concerts in the summer and Christmas celebrations in the winter. It provides a place for children to play and weary adults to rest.

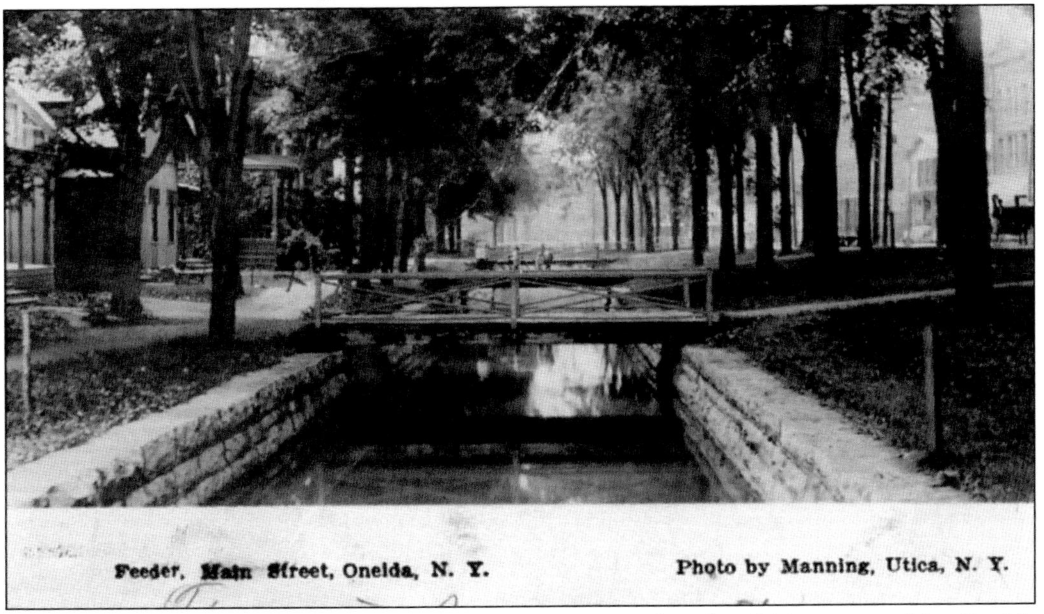

This feeder through Main Street in Oneida was constructed in the 1830s as part of the Oneida Lake Canal project. It connected Oneida Creek in Oneida Castle with the Erie Canal in Durhamville. The feeder was needed to supply the canal with water in order to supply the locks on the Oneida Lake portion of the canal. After the Barge Canal System opened, the unneeded feeder was gradually filled in, as it had become a dumping place for rubbish. Before the feeder's closing, local children enjoyed sailing boats there in summer and ice skating in the winter.

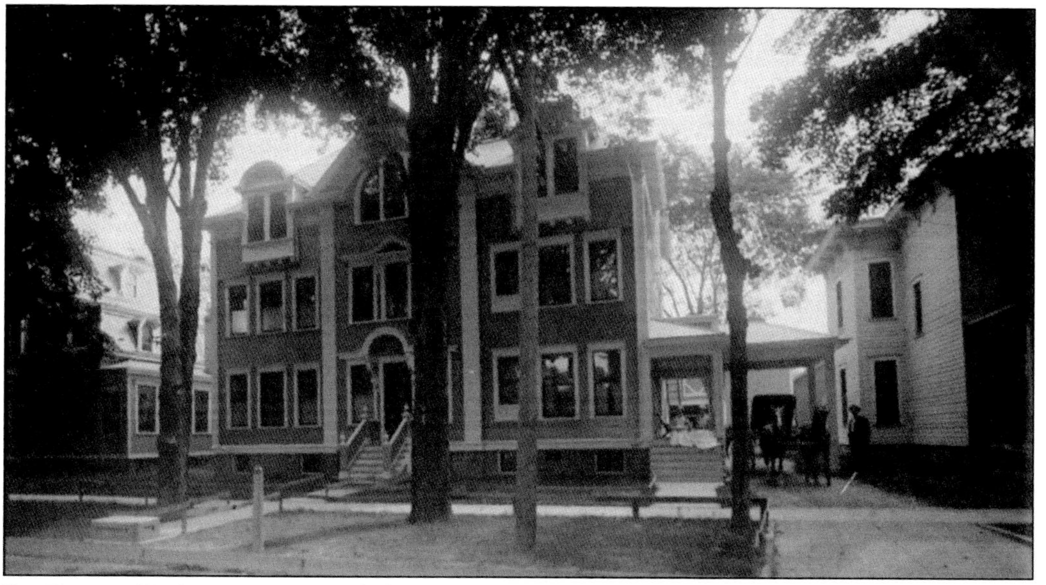

Dr. Eugene H. Carpenter opened the Broad Street Hospital in 1907. By 1914, it had expanded to 50 beds and a nurses training school was added. The doctor then turned the hospital over to a non-profit corporation. After the new City Hospital was built directly behind this one, the old hospital was razed and became a lawn for the new facility. Oneida now has a modern hospital on Route 5.

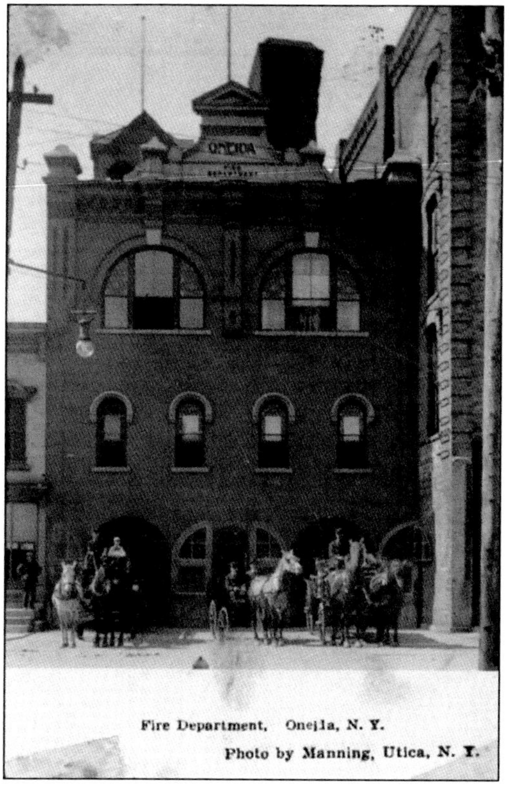

The first volunteer fire company in Oneida was organized in 1849. The first horse-drawn rig was purchased in 1860. The volunteer fire company went from a bucket brigade to a hand pumper to a horse-drawn engine. The Central Fire Station at 122 Vanderbilt Avenue was in use from 1867 until 1968. A paid fire department was established in 1895 and became completely motorized in 1920. The building pictured here still exists.

Seven

Herkimer County

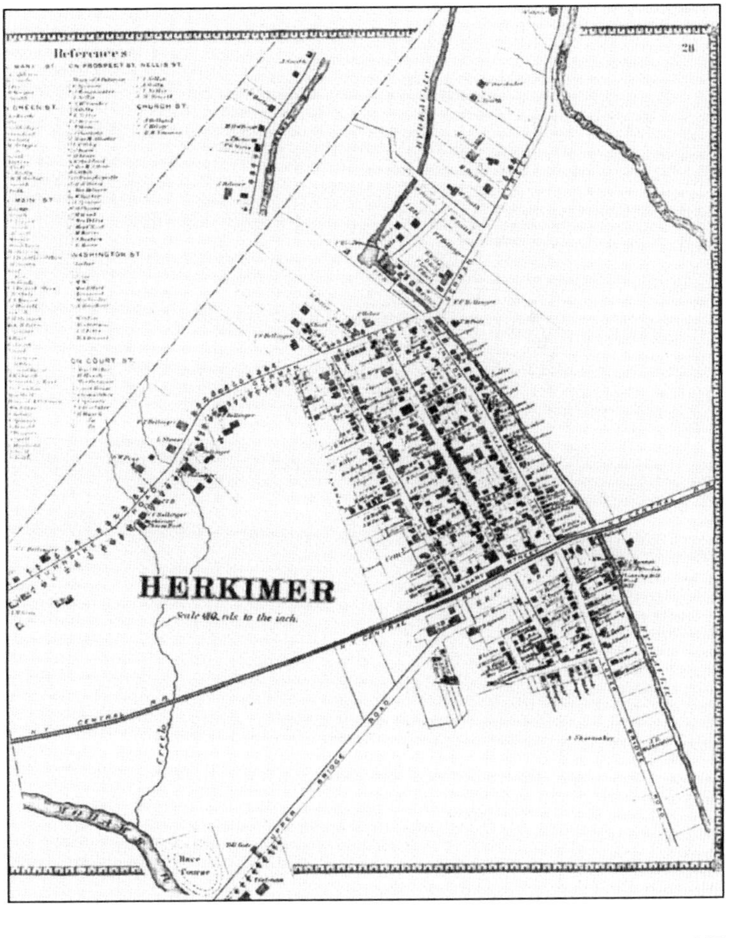

This village of Herkimer is shown in this 1868 map.

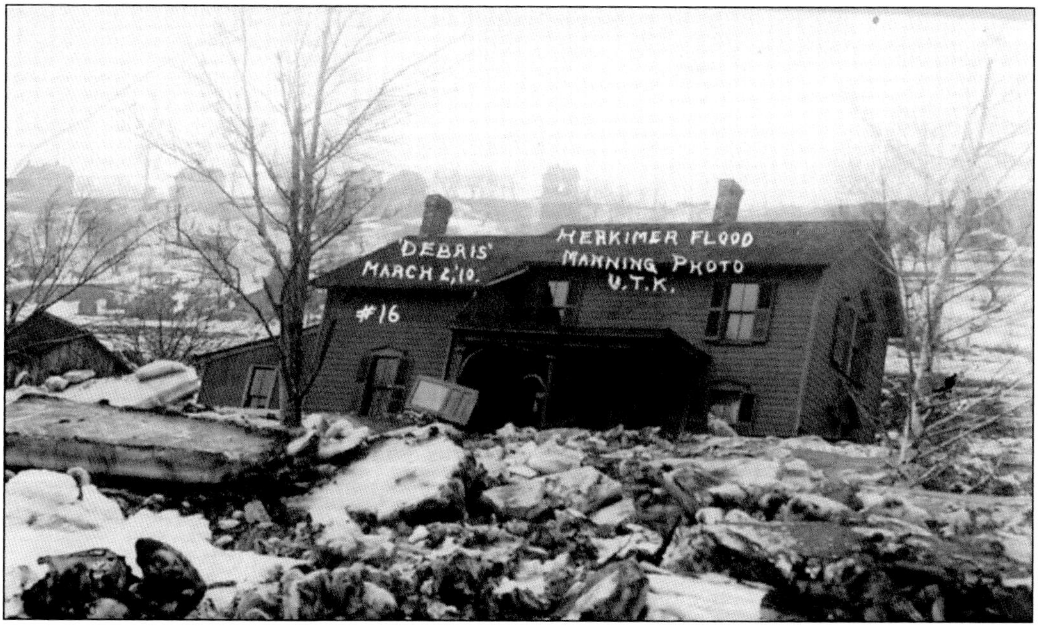

A devastating flood on February 28, 1910, affected large areas of Herkimer. Looking like a scene from *The Wizard of Oz,* this house was lifted from its foundation and partly overturned. Sightseers began to visit the leaning house. Its fame spread, and it was soon inundated by the curious. The enterprising owner began to charge 10¢ admission and used the proceeds to reduce losses sustained by his tenants who were displaced by the flood.

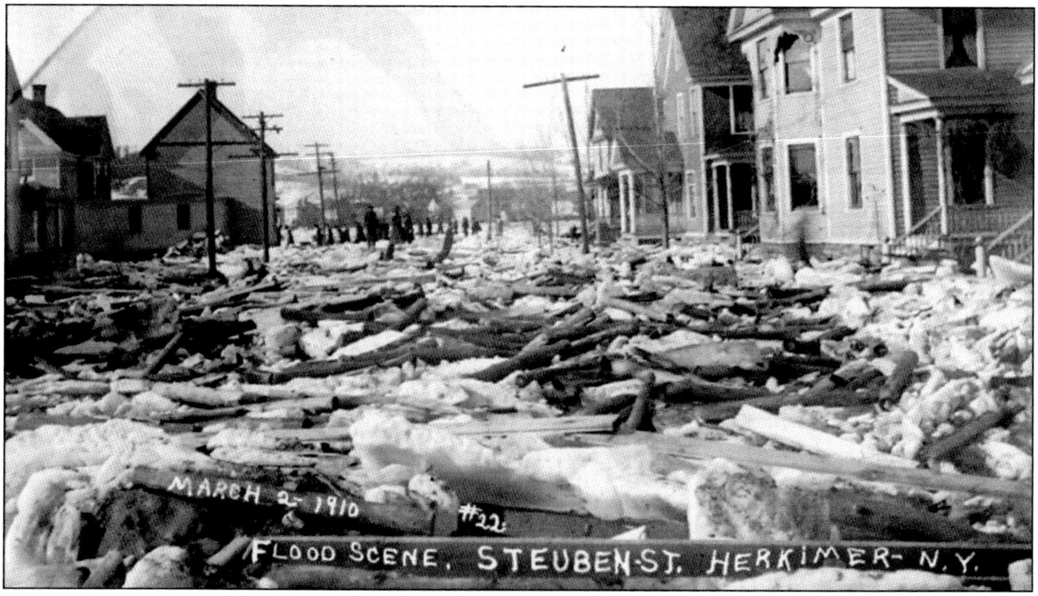

Acres of broken ice choked streets and halted traffic. An exceptionally cold winter with copious snowfalls, and a thickly frozen West Canada Creek were a prelude to what followed. In late February, a brief warm spell with rain showers resulted in the turbulent flood. On some streets the water was three feet deep. Spectators gathered to watch the dynamiting of an ice jam near where the Mohawk River and the West Canada Creek met, resulting in one fatality. A man was struck in the head by a large piece of ice following a blast.

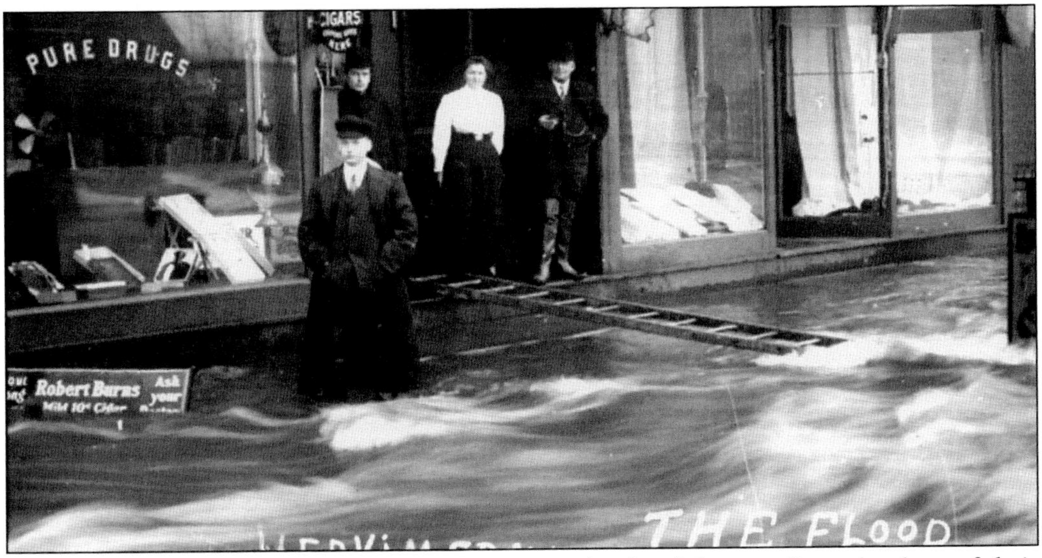

Mr. and Mrs. Delahunt, the store owners, survey the flood damage from the door of their drugstore. On back of this card is written: "Mr. & Mrs. Delahunt in 1910 then keeping drug store in Herkimer, NY—S. Washington Street. Also son Joseph now priest. Also Mr. Filahaven drug clerk." Many businesses were affected by the disaster. The flood caused a loss of power, and water was contaminated, making it unfit to drink. Horrocks Desk Company's machinery, generators, and a large quantity of stock were submerged. The Munger Department Store employees moved some of the stock to safety.

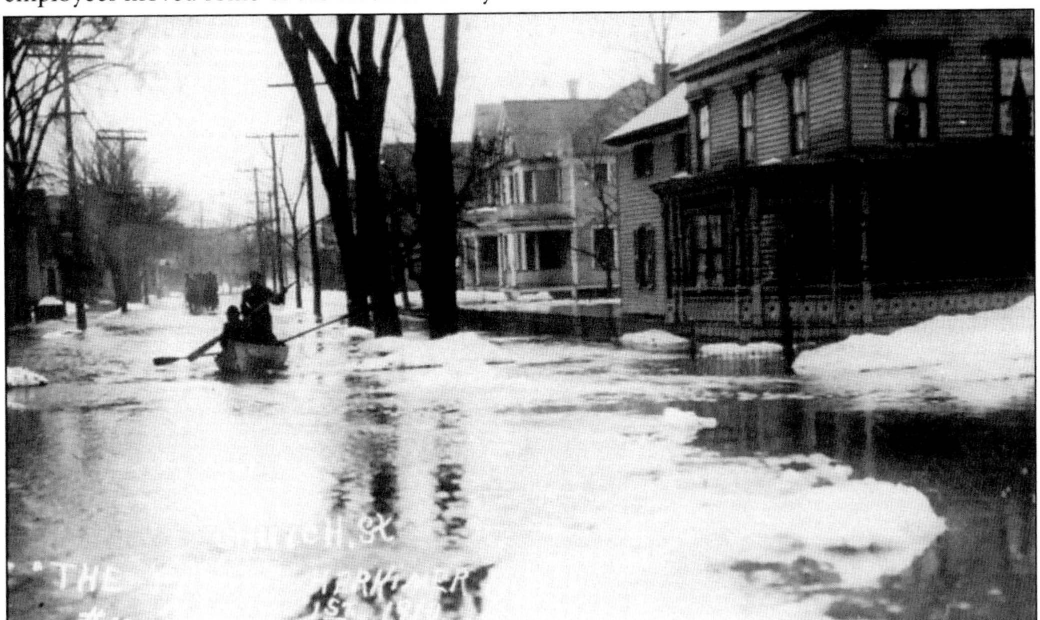

Many streets were blanketed with water. Resourceful citizens propel a boat down the street as the flood turned it into a swift stream. In some places, the water reached to the top of street mailboxes, turned lawns into ponds, and in some areas created lakes. The volunteer fire department, assisted by firemen and boats from Little Falls, Rome, Ilion, and Mohawk provided manpower and equipment.

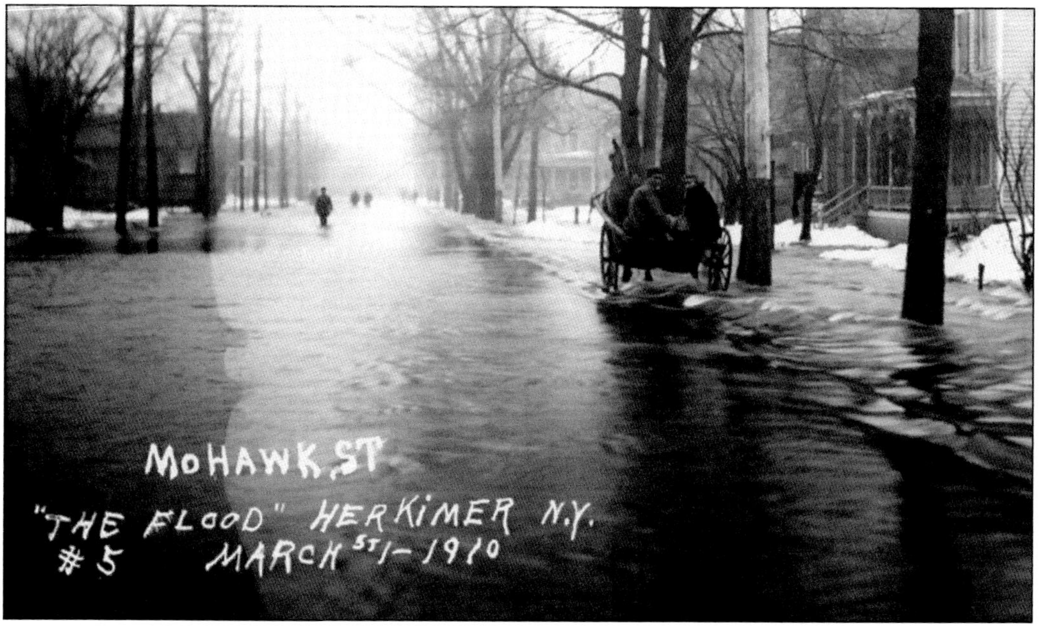

Both men and beasts were pressed into service to help in flood relief efforts. Horses were considered unsung heroes. One horse drowned while engaged in a rescue mission. A Herkimer resident characterized the village as "a saturated sponge which nature was taking its time about squeezing." The flood, which began on Monday, February 28, 1910, attracted 20,000 to 30,000 sightseers the following Sunday.

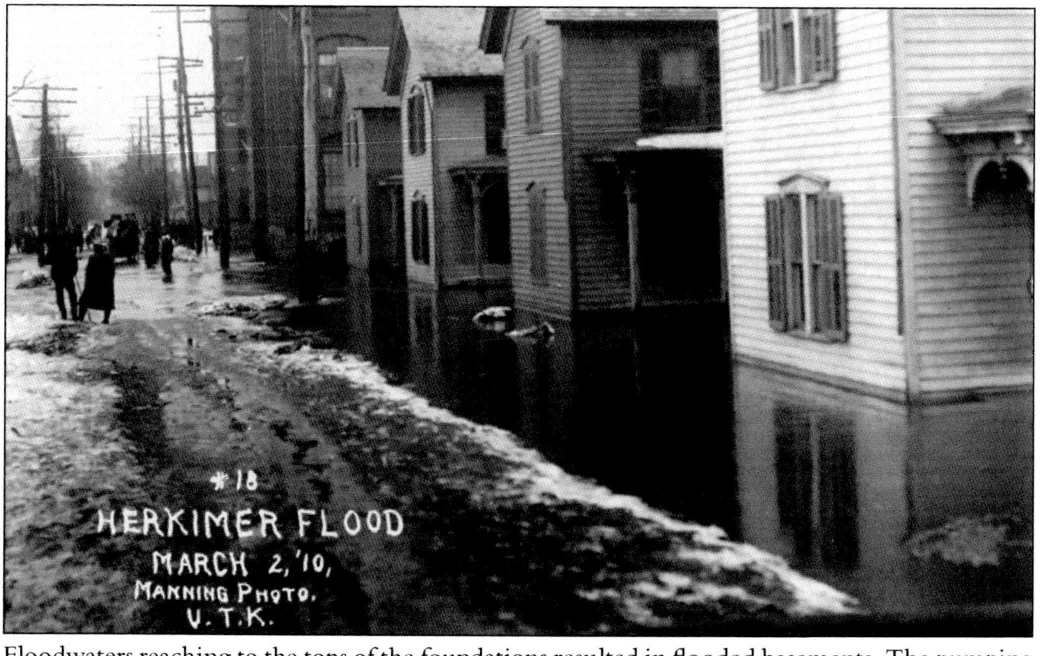

Floodwaters reaching to the tops of the foundations resulted in flooded basements. The pumping of cellars was ongoing. The message on this postcard reports on the situation: "Arrived in Herkimer safe this morning. You ought to see some parts of this town now. I guess you would think there had been a flood. These houses are across the street from Aunt Add's."

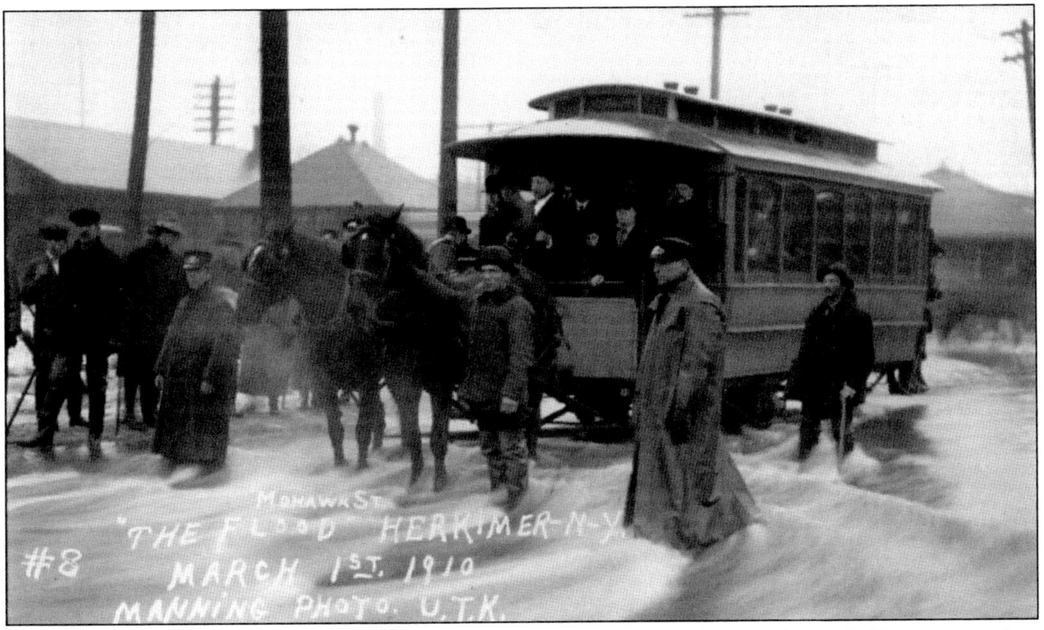

The flood submerged both the New York Central Railroad and trolley tracks, and all transportation ceased to operate. When the trolley car motors failed, the cars were drawn by teams of horses. Passengers were forded to and from the trolley on the backs of men hired for the purpose.

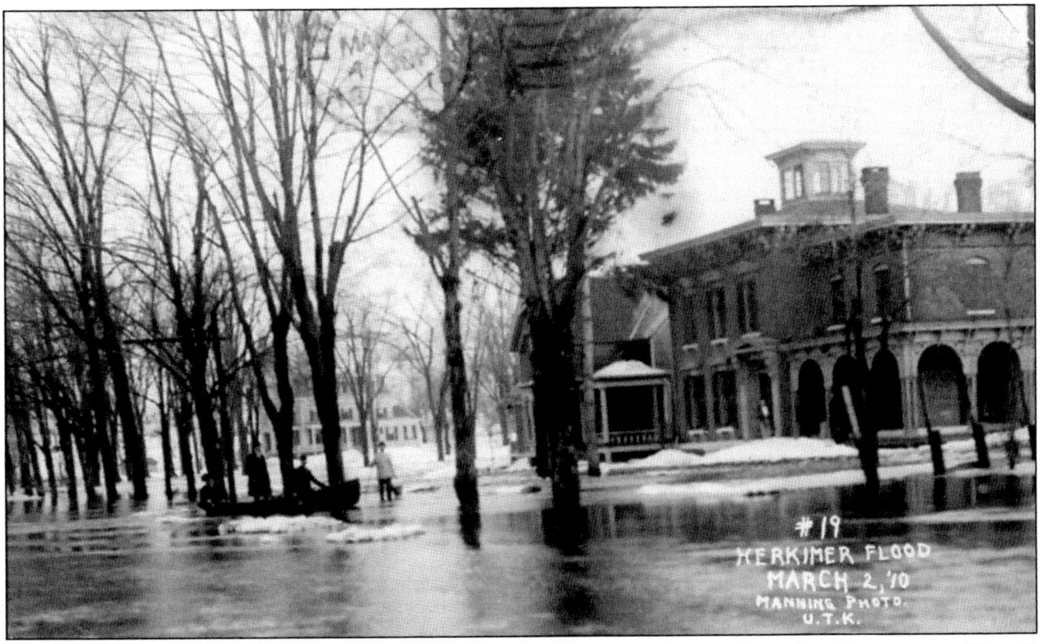

A Herkimer resident sent a postcard to her mother in nearby Little Falls. She wrote, "I will send you this card so you can see how we looked during the flood. It is getting so it looks quite natural again. Will thinks there is about a foot of water in the cellar yet."

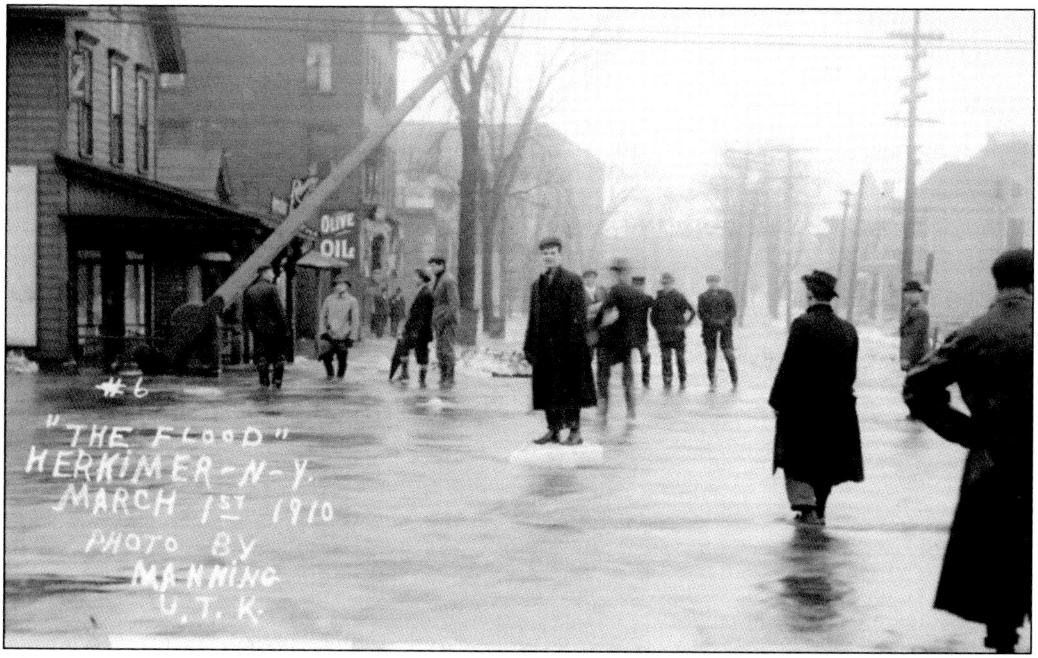

The railroad crossing gate stands useless in downtown Herkimer. The tracks are totally submerged by the flood of February 28, 1910. In the center, one gentleman surveys the scene from atop a block of ice. By Thursday, four days after the onset of the flood, the immediate crisis was over and the cleanup work had begun.

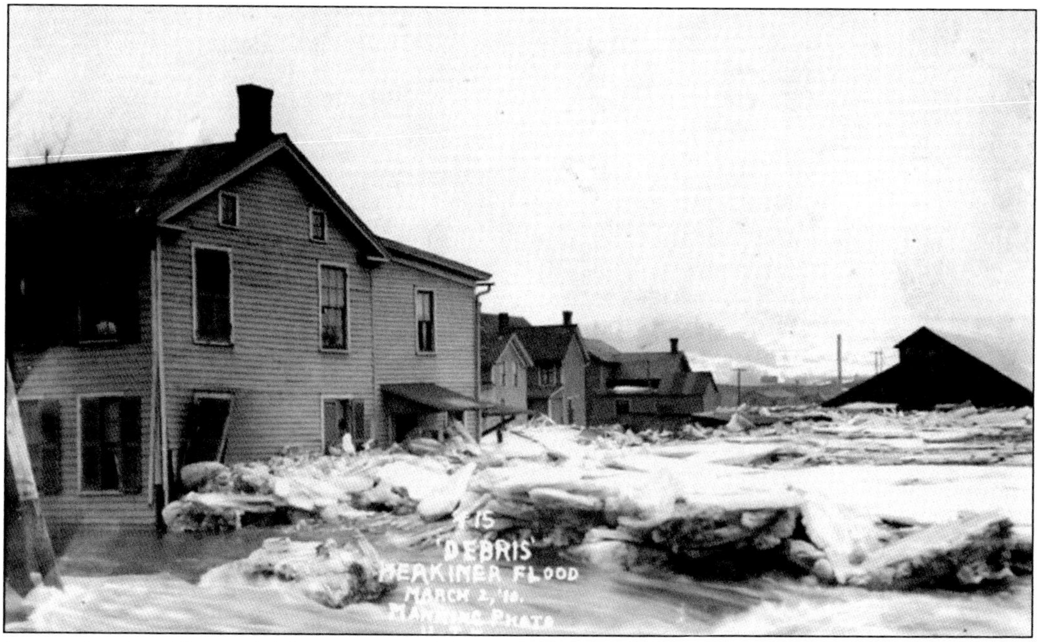

Large chunks of ice and debris surround these homes. Many sections of the village were under three feet of water. Officials used dynamite to break up the ice, and chunks slowly began to flow toward the river. Officials in 1910 estimated damage from the flood to be several hundred thousand dollars.

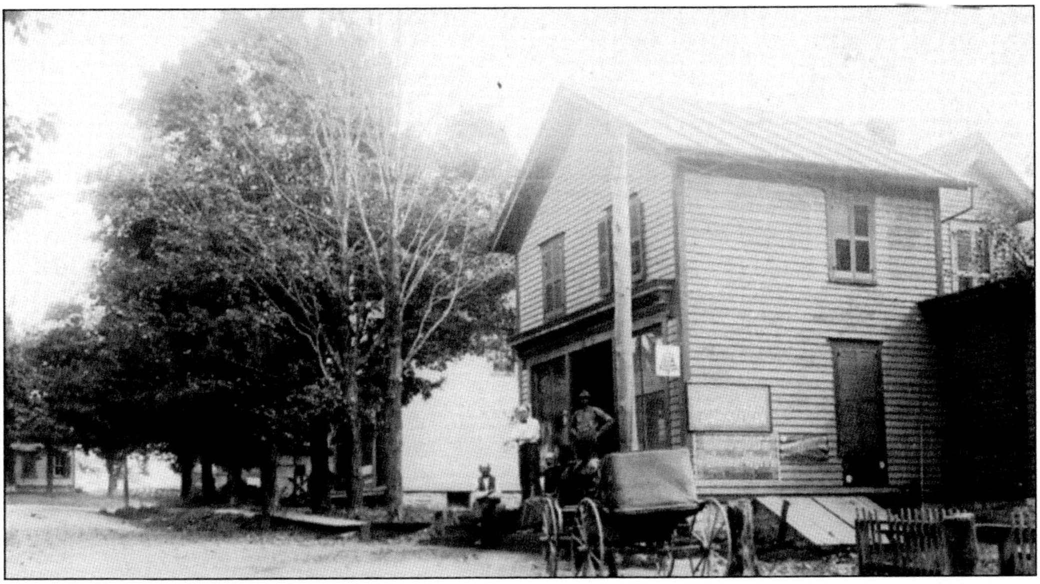

This country store and post office stood on McKoons Road, just behind today's Mr. Shake's Ice Cream Stand on Route 28. No longer a country store, it has undergone several reincarnations. When the store closed in the 1950s, the home became a residence, and today it is Aunt Martha's Bed and Breakfast. South Columbia in Herkimer County was settled by George Lighthalls after the Revolutionary War. Northwest of the village was once a Native American camping ground. Many old Native American trails became highways for white settlers. Portions of these trails later became State Route 28.

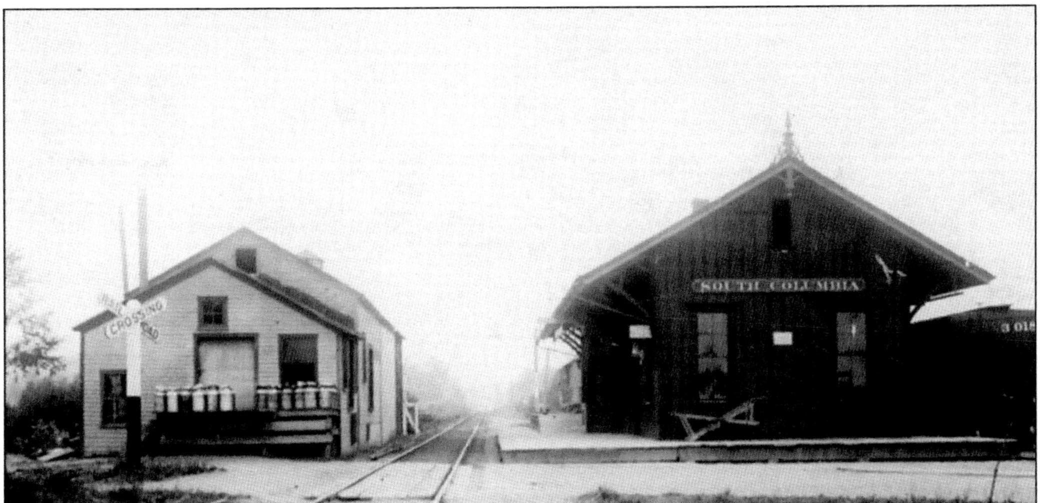

The Utica, Chenango and Susquehanna Railroad, in 1869, opened a station in South Columbia. In 1870, the railroad was leased to the Delaware, Lackawanna and Western Railroad for 99 years. The once-grand railroad depot has been converted to a private residence near its former site. The still-existing building at left was a creamery. South Columbia was also the birthplace of Ellen H. Clapsaddle on January 8, 1865. She was a talented artist who created thousands of holiday postcards for International Art Publishing and the Wolf Publishing Company. Today those postcards are valuable collectors' items.

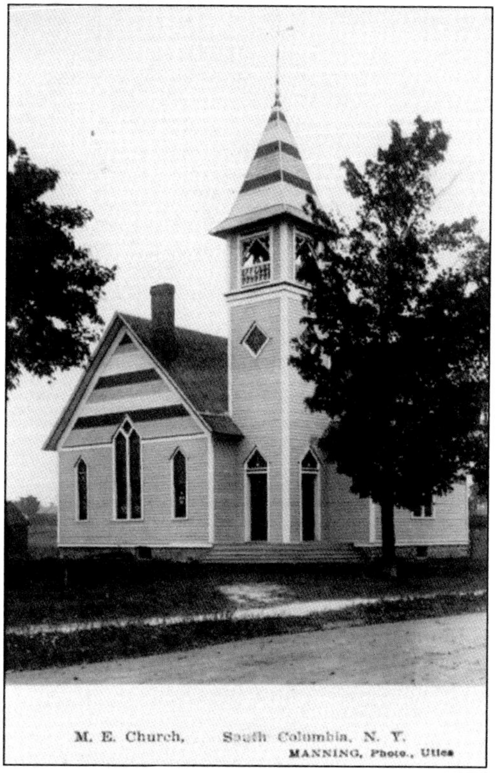

A 1956 newspaper article stated that the South Columbia Methodist Church had fallen into disrepair and only meetings would be held there periodically by visiting clergymen. In 1957, the church was razed, and the membership transferred to the First Methodist Church in Richfield Springs on Route 20. The Methodist church's circular rose window, not visible in this *c.* 1907 postcard, was removed and inserted in the front wall above the main entrance of the Richfield Springs church. The Trinity Reformed Church now occupies the brick building. The property where the South Columbia church stood is a nearly vacant lot, inhabited only by a vintage sky-blue trailer.

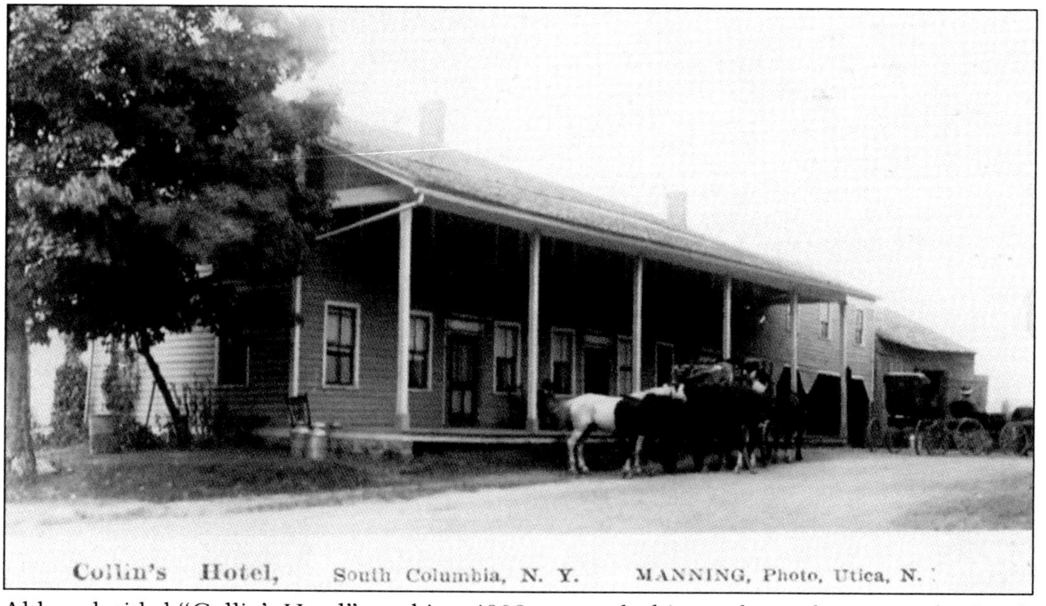

Although titled "Collin's Hotel" on this *c.* 1908 postcard, this was better known as the South Columbia Inn. The inn was erected in 1808 by Simeon Hammond. Owned in 1956 by Matheas Mueller, the inn still was held together by its original wooden pegs and handwrought nails. Contents of the old hotel were sold at auction in 1961. Once on the corner of McKoons Road and Route 28, it has been replaced with a white house surrounded by a picket fence. The old inn was removed due to the straightening and relocation of the highway.

Eight

Pine Camp in Jefferson County

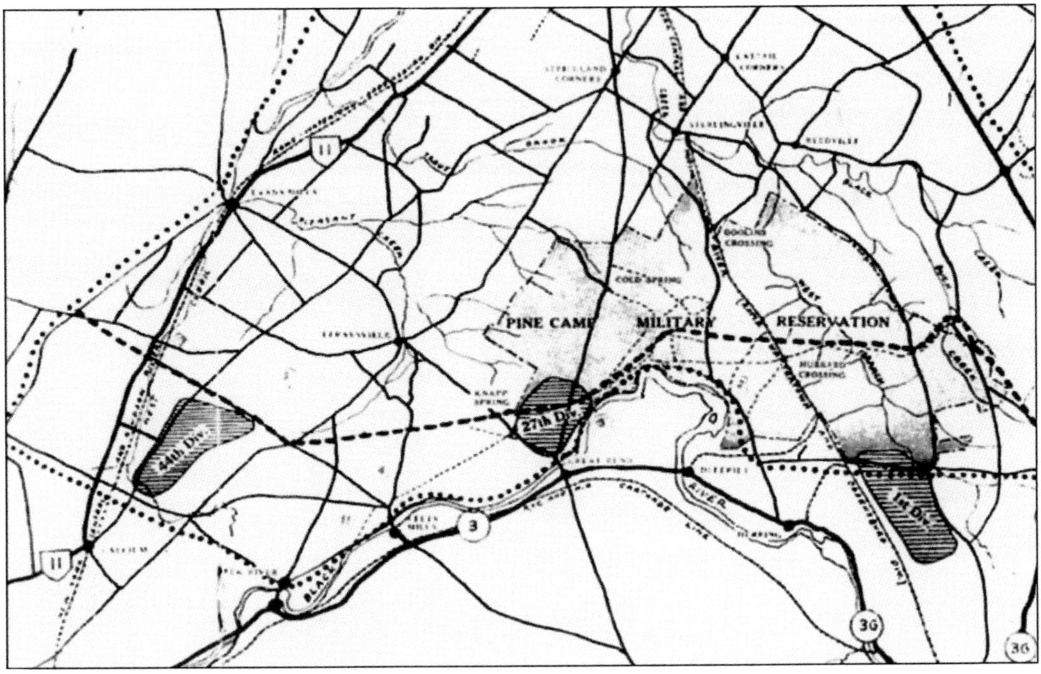

This is a map of Pine Camp.

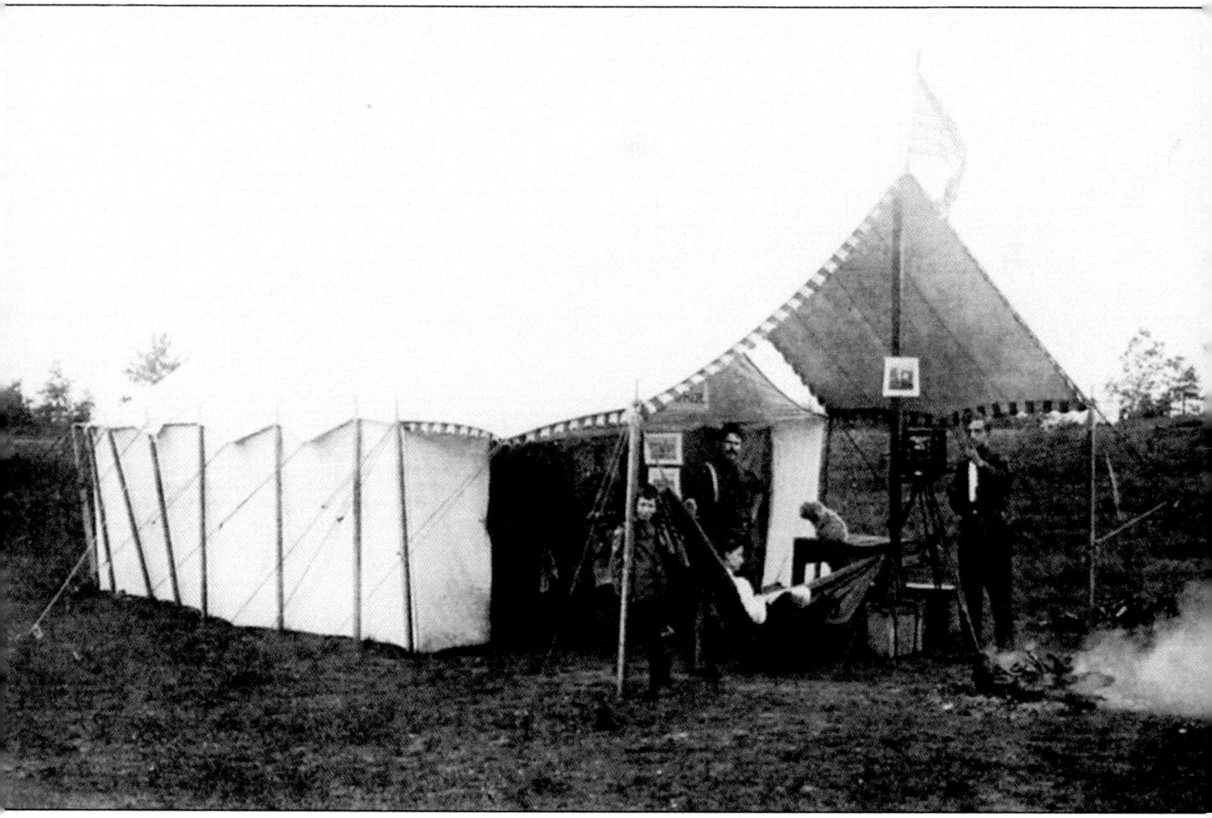

Early-20th-century photographers traveled many miles on primitive roads, and at times in primitive vehicles, to capture people and scenes of the times. Although some traveled by train, a few had early automobiles. These Allen J. Manning real-photo postcards in this chapter were taken between 1908 and 1910. It is likely that Manning took the New York Central train from the Utica Station to Pine Camp with all his photographic equipment and his tent. Pine Camp (known as Fort Drum today) near Watertown in Jefferson County is approximately 70 miles north of Utica. On the back of this postcard is written "Mannings, Utica, NY., Photographers tent, Pine Camp, N. Y. ca. 1908-10." Pictured is the Manning family, Wallace at left; his mother, Emma, seated; and his father, Allen, standing by her. Also pictured sitting on the table is the little white dog referred to on the postcard of Wheelman's Fountain (page 15). On this card was a message written by E. E. Manning (Emma), she related they had bought Wallace a little white dog that "he was wild about." The cameraman may be Allen's partner, Earl D. Williamson, whose name appears on the back of the Genesee bridge postcard on the bottom of page 58. Real-photo postcards transport people back in time and help them realize what it was like in the early days of the 1900s and the efforts these traveling cameramen made to record the history of the times. It also helps one appreciate the ease of travel today. (Courtesy Tom Gates.)

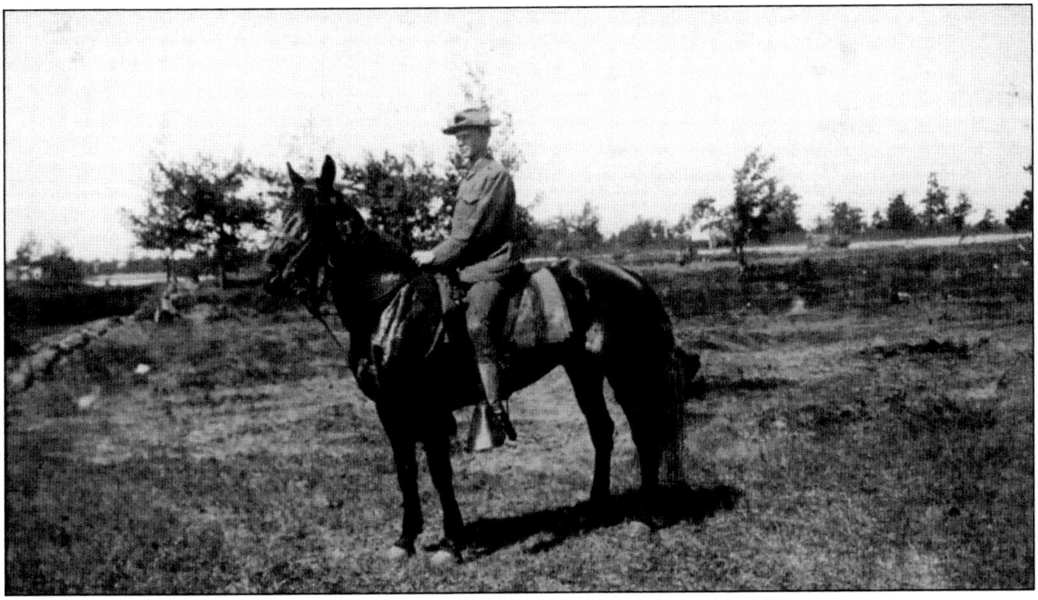

A cavalry officer astride his horse surveys the scene at Pine Camp. A temporary encampment at Camp Hughes, a short distance from Pine Camp, was moved to the new site in 1907. Camp Hughes was named to honor New York governor Charles Hughes. In 1909, Congress appropriated $75,000 to provide for the purchase of 11,000 acres of land known as Pine Plains for a permanent military camp. This land became Pine Camp.

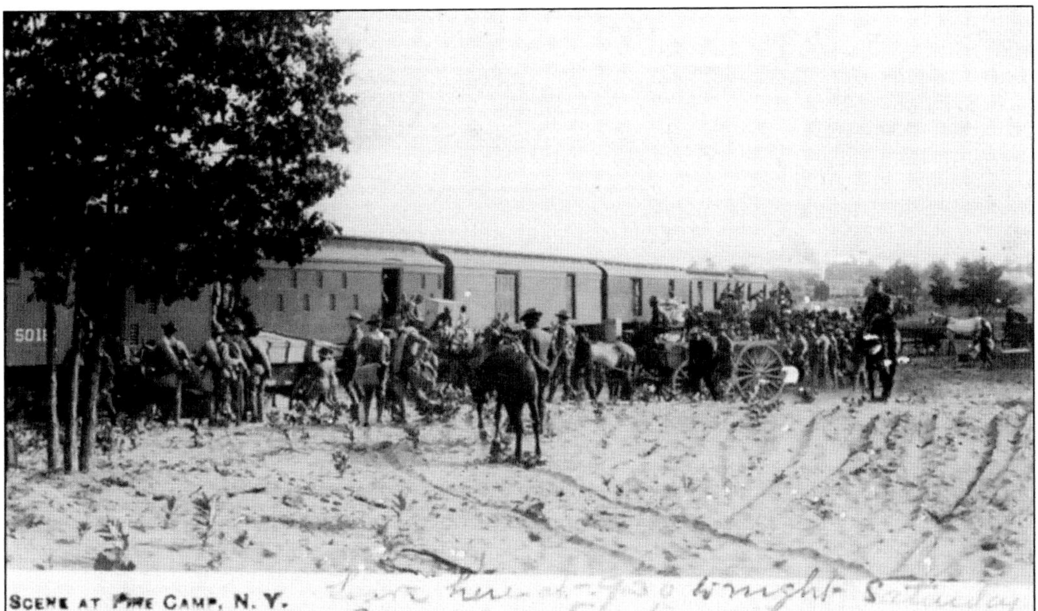

Waiting to board the train at Pine Camp, the soldiers and horses appear to be a cavalry unit. A military training site since 1908, the camp began with about 11,000 acres prior to World War I. In 1907, the New York Guard used the camp on the Black River for summer maneuvers. In 1908, Brig. Gen. Frederick Dent Grant, son of general and president Ulysses S. Grant, was sent to Pine Camp to train troops.

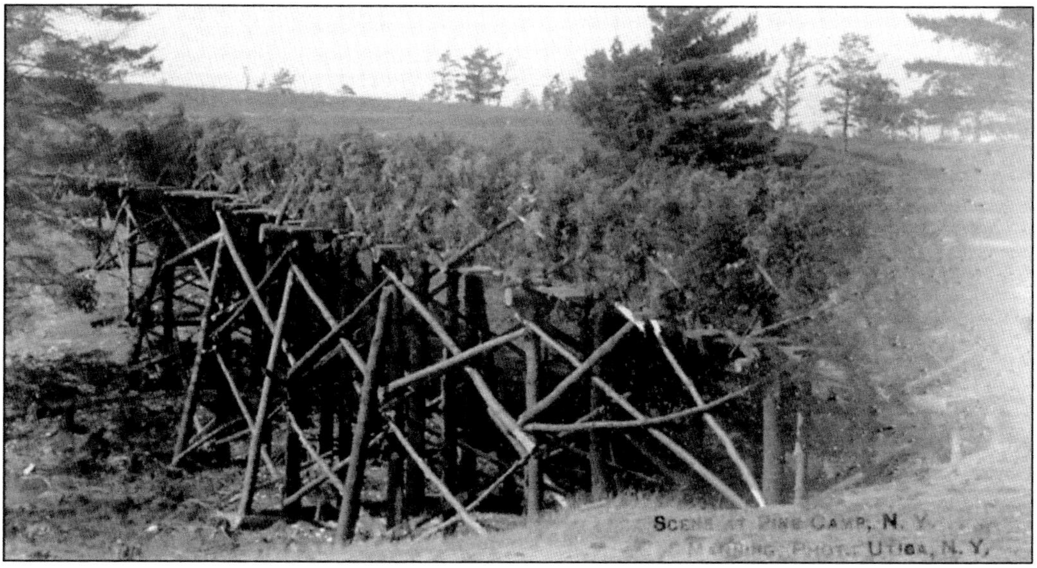

Camouflaged palisades provided a wooden barricade, making use of the abundant pine branches available in the area. The United States Signal Corps constructed a signal tower from the tall pines, leaving branches to use for climbing to the platform at the top. In 1951, Pine Camp became Camp Drum and in 1974 was designated Fort Drum. In 1984, it became home to the 10th Light Infantry Division, later changed to the 10th Mountain Division. Many in this division have served in the most recent Iraq conflict. During World War II, prisoners of war were interred here.

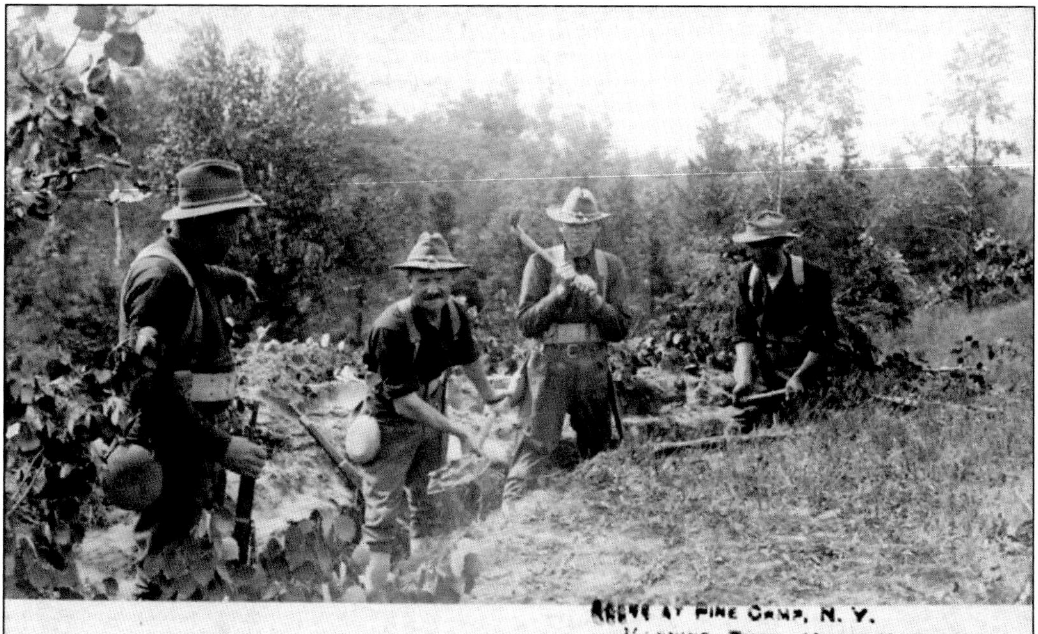

Hard at work digging a trench with pick and shovel, these soldiers pause to observe the photographer. National Guard troops still train at the former Pine Camp. A major expansion at the time of World War II added 75,000 acres to the facility. About 800 buildings were constructed, including barracks, mess halls, warehouses, officers' quarters, recreational facilities, and a hospital. Today the fort encompasses 107,265 acres.

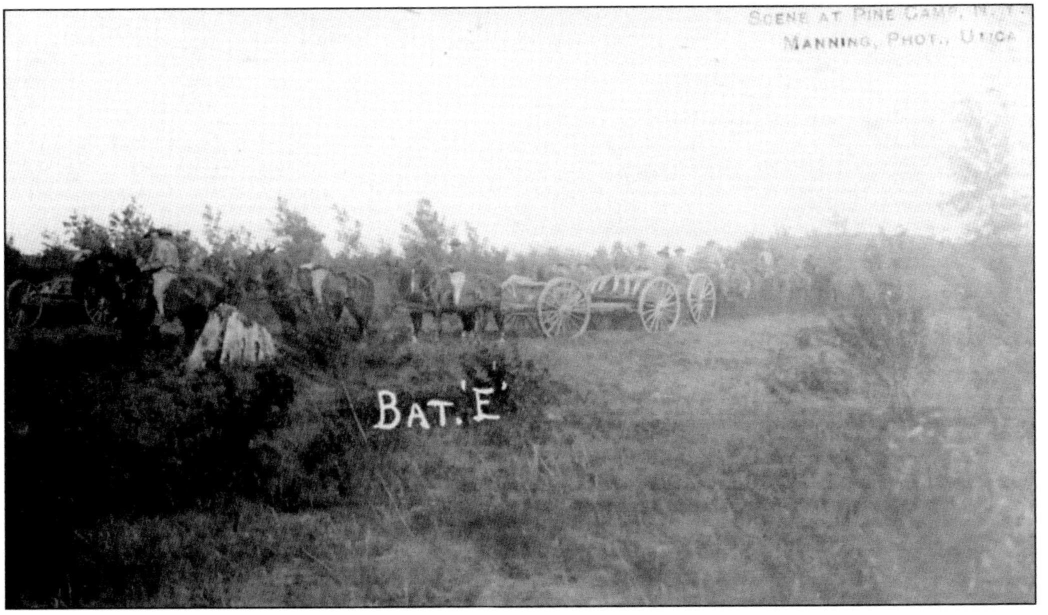

Battery E wagons transport the troops as they prepare to partake in field maneuvers and training. A Pine Camp souvenir booklet outlines their daily routine. First call was at 5:15 a.m., and reveille (under arms) was at 5:25 a.m. After mess (breakfast) at 5:45 a.m., drills, except on Sundays, were conducted at 6:50 a.m. Mess (dinner) was at midday followed by more drill. Retreat after mess (supper) was at 6:30 p.m., and their day was done with taps at 10:00 p.m.

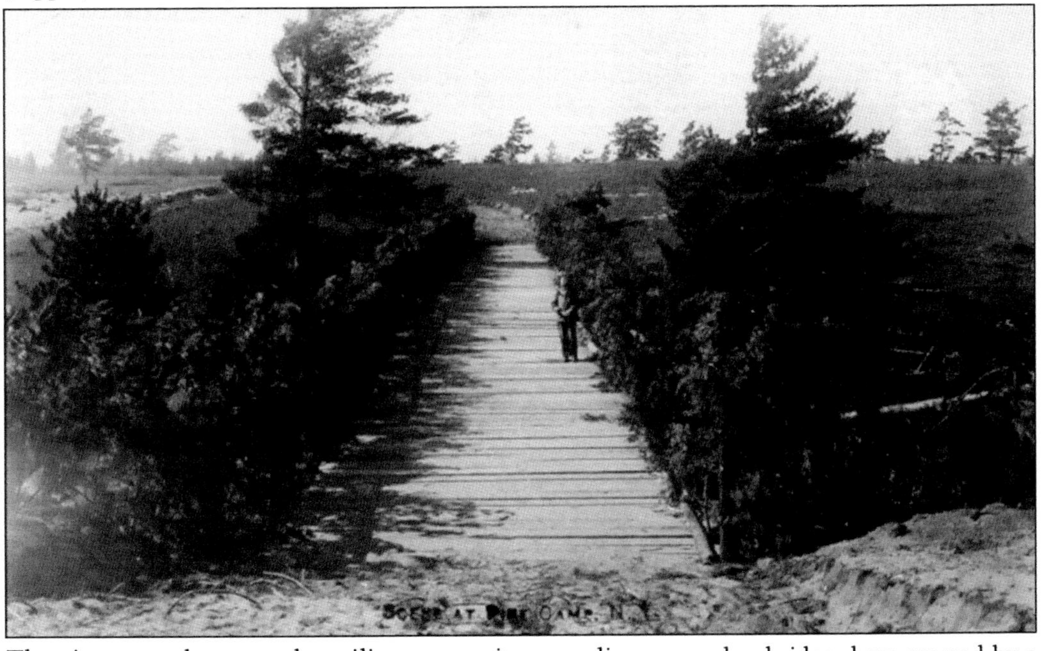

The pine trees that gave the military camp its name line a wooden bridge, here crossed by a young boy, perhaps daydreaming of being a soldier at Pine Camp one day. The bridge may have been constructed by the 1st Battalion of Engineers, Companies B and C, 10th Cavalry, from Fort Ethan Allen in Vermont, who were assigned to Pine Camp in 1910. The 22nd Regiment of Engineers from New York City also served there that year from August 1 to August 10.

Bibliography

Clarke, Dr. T. Wood. *Utica, for a Century and a Half,* Utica, NY: Widtman Press, 1952.

Cookinham, Laura Day. *The Romantic History of Old New Hartford,* New Hartford Historical Society, 1997.

Durant, Samuel, ed. *1878 History of Oneida County,* Everts and Farris, 1878.

Henke, Jack, *Oneida Lake, "The Only Happiness": Place Names and History,* Utica, NY: North Country Books, 1989.

———*Sylvan Beach: A History,* Utica, NY: North Country Books, 1975.

The History of Oneida County. Oneida County publisher, 1977.

Holland Patent Bicentennial Committee. *The Holland Patent, More Than a Village, 1797-1997.* Steffen Publishing Company, Holland Patent, 1997.

Hurd, Edith. *Life in No Man's Land,* New Hartford Historical Society, 1975.

Jones, Pomroy. *Annals and Recollections of Oneida County,* self-published, 1851.

Langone, Louis. *Railroad Days: Memories of the Delaware Lackawanna and Western Railroad and Erie-Lackawanna Railway Company,* Waterville, NY: Hickory Hill Books, 2006.

McFee, Michele. *A Long Haul, The Story of the New York State Barge Canal,* Purple Mountain Press, 1998.

New Century Atlas of Oneida County, 1907. Philadelphia: Century Map Company, 1907.

Owens, Stanley R. *Bicentennial History of Bridgewater, New York,* 1976.

Parker, Robert Allerton. *A Yankee saint; John Humphrey Noyes and the Oneida community,* New York: G. P. Putnam's Sons, 1935.

Rogers, Henry C. *History of the Town of Paris and the Valley of the Sauquoit,* Utica, NY: White and Floyd, 1881.

Scenes from Oneida's Past. Oneida Valley National Bank.

Souvenir of Pine Camp and Watertown, NY. Comins and Cornack publisher, 1910.

Taibi, John. *Rails Along the Oriskany: a History of the New York, Ontario and Western Railway's Utica Division and Rome Branch,* Fleischmanns, NY: Purple Mountain Press, 2003.

——— and A. Bruce Tracy, *When the Railroad Went to the Beach,* Depot Square Publishing, 1999.

Town of Richfield Springs booklet, a collection of local history articles, published by *Richfield Springs Mercury,* 1961.

Wager, Daniel E., ed. *Our County and Its People,* Boston History Company, 1896.

Walsh, John J. *Vignettes of Old Utica,* Utica Public Library, 1982.

Westmoreland Bicentennial Committee. *Westmoreland, 200 Years 1776-1976.*

White, Donald F., compiled and edited. *Exploring 200 years of Oneida County History,* published by Oneida County Historical Society, 1998.